ketebe.co.uk

Original Title: *Islam Između Istoka i Zapada*
English Title: *Islam: Between East and West*

Revised Edition in English, November 2025

Published by Ketebe Publishing
UK | Türkiye

ISBN: 978-625-5888-81-5

Translated by Azra Blekić Aydoğan
Copy Editing by Sarah Saey

Editor: Ömer Faruk Yeni
Cover design by Yasin Çetin
Interior design by Nilgün Sönmez

Printed in Türkiye

For permissions or inquiries:
books@ketebe.com

Islam: Between East and West

ALIJA IZETBEGOVIĆ

KETEBE

Alija Izetbegović

He was born on 8 August 1925 in the town of Bosanski Šamac, Bosnia and Herzegovina. At the age of two, he moved with his family to Sarajevo, where he would spend the rest of his life. He graduated from high school in 1944. During his youth, he showed interest in Islamic activities and the problems of Muslims. In 1946, on the grounds of being a member of the organisation Mladi Muslimani (the youth branch of the El-Hidaje organisation), he was sentenced to three years in prison.

After his release, he first enrolled in the Faculty of Agriculture. He then left this programme and transferred to the Faculty of Law. During this period, he devoted himself to intellectual work and in 1970 published The Islamic Declaration. Ten years later, he completed Islam Between East and West. In 1983, due to his ideas, he was once again sentenced to fourteen years in prison, of which he spent five years incarcerated.

During the dissolution of Yugoslavia, he founded the political party Stranka demokratske akcije (SDA – Party of Democratic Action) and was elected as its president. Following the collapse of the communist regime, in the first elections held in June 1990, he was elected the President of the Republic of Bosnia and Herzegovina. During the war of independence against Serbian and Croatian forces, he assumed the role of Commander-in-Chief. In 1995, he signed the Dayton Agreement, which ended the war. In the 1996 elections, he was elected to the tripartite Presidency. In 2000, citing health problems, he resigned from the presidency.

Three years later, on 19 October 2003, he passed away in Sarajevo. He was buried at the Kovači cemetery, alongside the martyrs with whom he had fought for independence.

His books published in Bosnian include:

- Problemi islamskog preporoda – Islamska deklaracija (The Problems of the Islamic Revival – The Islamic Declaration)
- Islam između Istoka i Zapada (Islam Between East and West)
- Moj bijeg u slobodu – Bilješke iz zatvora 1983–1988 (My Escape to Freedom – Prison Notes 1983–1988)
- Sjećanja – Autobiografski zapis (Memoirs – An Autobiographical Record)
- Bosna je velika tajna – Intervju 1989–1995 (Bosnia is a Great Secret – Interviews 1989–1995)
- Doba znanja i strpljenja – Intervju 1996–2003 (The Age of Knowledge and Patience – Interviews 1996–2003)
- Robovi biti nećemo – Govori 1990–1995 (We Shall Not Be Slaves – Speeches 1990–1995)
- Dani hladnog i gorkog mira – Govori 1996–2003 (Days of Cold and Bitter Peace – Post-War Speeches 1996–2003)
- Na razmeđu svjetova – Izjave, obraćanja, poruke, pisma 1990–2003 (At the Crossroads of Worlds – Statements, Addresses, Messages, Letters 1990–2003)
- Dostojanstvo ljudskog izbora (The Dignity of Human Choice)

CONTENTS

FOREWORD

EBRAHIM MOOSA

Mirza Family Professor of Islamic Thought &
Muslim Societies, University of Notre Dame, USA

It is a privilege to pen the foreword to the new translation of *Islam: Between East and West*. Its author, Alija Izetbegović (1925–2003), was for much of his life a Muslim political activist and, in the final act of his remarkable life, the President of the Presidency of the Republic of Bosnia and Herzegovina. Philosopher, activist, and statesman, Izetbegović united the life of the mind with the demands of political responsibility, seeking the most principled and practical outcomes in an age of extraordinary conflict, war, and division in Eastern Europe and the Balkans.

The Bosnian conflict of the late twentieth century became a touchstone for pan-Islamic consciousness and for the moral integrity of a significant Muslim community in Europe. It echoes, in its moral gravity, the continuing ordeal of the Palestinian people in the first quarter of the twenty-first century, both confronting the same specter of genocide while some parts of the world hesitated to name, let alone prevent, the horror of such crimes.

For President Izetbegović, the question of religion and morality lay at the heart of his lifelong intellectual and political project. In this book-length meditative essay, *Islam: Between East and West*, he wrestled with the nature of moral life—its origins, limits, and transcendent aims. For him, morality, like art and religion, belonged to the same "genealogical branch" that "springs from the act of creation." Morality could not be grounded in progress or in harmony with nature, for such reductionism betrayed the mystery at its core. The essence of piety and morality, in his view, was akin to that of art: inscrutable. As a philosopher, Izetbegović understood that this inscrutability was not alien to orthodox Islamic thought, which admits the limits of human comprehension before divine wisdom. There is, in his treatment of moral law, a resonance with the Kantian sense of duty—an ethical imperative that commands obedience, not because it is expedient, but because it is right.

Islam: Between East and West is, at once, a meditation on the human condition and a philosophical reflection on the meaning of Islam. Written from within the crossroads of civilisations, it contends that modern humanity is torn between two one-sided worldviews: the spiritual idealism of Christianity and the materialistic humanism of modern atheism. Each, in its own way, has alienated the human being from himself—Christianity by denying the body, and materialism by denying the soul.

Against this tragic division, Izetbegović proposes Islam as a synthesis that overcomes dualism. Islam, in his view, is not merely one religion among others but the *principle of harmony* between spirit and matter, faith and reason, religion and society. In its essence, it mirrors the unity of the human being—body and soul, temporal and eternal. The vision he advances is not that of a compromise but of an organic unity in which the secular and the sacred, the rational and the revealed, find their proper balance.

In the closing pages of this work, Izetbegović returns to the central demand of Islam—submission to God. Yet he treats submission not as passive resignation but as the active drama of human destiny. "Human destiny," for him, is neither a fixed historical fate nor a biological outcome, but the ceaseless struggle to reconcile our dual origin: the clay of the earth and the breath of heaven. To be human is to live at the meeting point of these two worlds.

In articulating this vision, Izetbegović draws upon a lineage of philosophical reflection that transcends cultural boundaries. He finds kinship with the American essayist and poet Ralph Waldo Emerson (1803–1882) and the Spanish philosopher José Ortega y Gasset (1883–1955). For both, destiny is not a predetermined path but the emergence of human greatness under the weight of tragedy. For all heroic peoples, Izetbegović observes, destiny produces the capacity to face the tragic and the dramatic, and they shun the sunny optimism that leads to futility. These are the thoughts of a man whose will was forged in the crucible of life-and-death struggle, and whose philosophical reflections bear the stamp of that experience.

Morality, for Izetbegović, is inseparable from freedom and goodness. He embodied this conviction not only in thought but in action. His life was a testament to his belief that moral freedom and realism, far from being opposites, must coexist. In him, the philosopher and the statesman were one.

The book opens with a fragment from a poem by the Indian poet-philosopher Muhammad Iqbal (1877–1938), who speaks of the sun breaking free from "the shackles of East and West," possibly the inspiration of the title. The resonance between Iqbal and Izetbegović is unmistakable. Both sought to awaken the Muslim spirit from passivity and imitation. Iqbal wrote that the task facing modern Muslims was "immense," requiring them to "rethink the whole system of Islam without completely breaking with the past... The only course open to us is to approach modern knowledge with a respectful but independent attitude and to appreciate the teachings of Islam in the light of that knowledge, even though we may be led to differ from those who have gone before us" (Iqbal, 1960).

Like all great poets, Iqbal's light is born of agonism. While he calls for Muslim intellectual renewal, he also warns against the seductions of Western modernity:

> "I fear this cry for modernism
> Is only a ruse to make the East imitate the West."
> (Iqbal, 1983)

It is as though Izetbegović sought to carry Iqbal's vision to its next horizon. When Iqbal died in Lahore in 1938, Izetbegović was a boy of thirteen in Bosnia. Yet both, in their different worlds, were animated by the same yearning—to secure for Islam and Muslims a place within modernity that neither capitulated to the philosophy of the West nor isolated itself from the rest of the world. They shared a conviction that renewal (*tajdīd*) could only arise from a distinctive moral and spiritual selfhood, not from mimicry.

For both thinkers, life was not about making simplistic choices in the play of destiny but about living within its tensions with integrity. Many people, Izetbegović recognised, struggle to distinguish between the secular and the sacred, treating them as irreconcilable realms. To such confusion, Iqbal offers a profound corrective: "An act is temporal or profane," he wrote, "if it is done in a spirit of detachment from the infinite complexity of life behind it; it is spiritual if it is inspired by that complexity" (Iqbal, 1960).

This insight finds its perfect echo in Izetbegović's own words: "Islam is not only a religion or a way of life but primarily the principle of the organisation of the universe." Just as humans are "a unity of spirit and body," so too "Islam is a unity of religion and social order." For him, the sacred is not what stands apart from life but what *informs* it, giving the world coherence and meaning.

In an age when humanity once again feels the fracture between the technological and the moral, between the spiritual and the political, Izetbegović's message resounds with renewed urgency. His life and thought remind us that the synthesis of religion and social order is not an abstract ideal but a lived reality. He embodied it—in prison and in presidency, in solitude and in statecraft.

In *Islam: Between East and West,* Izetbegović speaks not only as a philosopher of Islam but as a witness to the possibilities of a reconciled human order. The unity he describes—of faith and reason, religion and civilisation, morality and power—remains one of the most pressing challenges of our age. Few have expressed it with such clarity; fewer still have lived it with such courage.

References

Iqbal, Muhammad 1960. The Reconstruction of Religious Thought in Islam, Lahore, Shaikh Muhammad Ashraf.

Iqbal, Muhammad Sir 1983. The Rod of Moses: Versified English Translation of Iqbal's Ẕarb-i Kalīm, Lahore, Iqbal Academy Pakistan.

“Though it is from the East that the sun rises
—bold and bright, unveiled—
it only burns with inward fire
once freed from the shackles of East and West.
Drunk with splendor, it rises from its East
to master all horizons.
Its nature is innocent of both East and West,
yet in origin, true, it is an Easterner.”

— Javid-nama, Muhammad Iqbal
(1877–1938)

INTRODUCTION

1.

The modern world is marked by a sharp ideological conflict that has persisted for years, with no end in sight. We are all drawn into this conflict, one way or another, either as participants or as victims. What is the place of Islam in this enormous confrontation? Does it play any role in shaping today's world? This book aims to provide at least a partial answer to that question. There are only three integral worldviews, and no more than these: the religious, the materialistic, and the Islamic.[1]

They correspond to three fundamental possibilities that we have been taught to refer to as consciousness, being, and humanity—or they may be projections of these. The vast and colourful mosaic of most diverse ideologies, philosophies, and systems of thought from the dawn of time to the present can ultimately be reduced to these three foundational worldviews. The first perspective begins with the exclusive or primary existence of spirit; the second with the exclusive or primary existence of matter; and the third with the simultaneous ex-

1 The term 'religion' in this book is used in the meaning it has in Europe. Accordingly, there cannot be an equal sign between Islam and religion, from the stance of this book. Islam is more than a religion.

istence of spirit and matter. If only matter existed, materialism would be the only consequential philosophy, rendering religion completely unnecessary. Conversely, if spirit exists, then human beings also exist, and life would be meaningless without some form of religion or morality. Islam represents one principle of the unity of spirit and matter, with human life as its highest form.

Human life is consistent with itself when it fulfils the human concept while simultaneously acknowledging and even affirming all the zoological preconditions of existence. Most human failures ultimately stem from either a religious rejection of biological life or a materialistic negation of humanity. Some people invoke nature, mesmerised by its order and security, and declare it the only reality. Others begin with humanity, and while gazing at the starry sky within their souls, they discover a new sense of purpose worth living for. We, the third group, emphasise the unique position of humans in the world. While the soul is eternal, human existence is limited by time, and within that time lies a mission that cannot be neglected (Qur'an 28:77). Elders have traditionally stated that there are two substances: spirit and matter. These terms imply two primordial beginnings, two worlds, and two orders of existence that are fundamentally different in origin and nature; they are not derived from each other, nor can they be reduced to one another. Even the most insightful spiritual and intellectual leaders have struggled to reconcile this differentiation, despite their varied approaches. We can envision these two worlds as either successive—different in time (the present and the future)—or as simultaneous, distinct in nature and meaning but not in time. The latter perspective aligns more closely with the essence of the matter.

Dualism is the most familiar human experience, but it is not the highest philosophical standpoint. In fact, all the great schools of philosophy are rooted in monism. While humans live, feel, and perceive the world in a dualistic manner, monism underlies the essence of every philosophy and school of thought. Philosophy itself does not accommodate dualism; however, this fact does not mean so much, because life, being superior to thought, may not be judged by it in the hierarchy of existence.

In truth, simply by being human, we inhabit two distinct realities. We may deny or refuse to acknowledge these two worlds, but we cannot escape them. Life does not conform to our understanding of it. Thus, the question is not whether we will live two lives simultaneously—since living otherwise is impossible—but rather whether we will do so voluntarily and with an understanding of the ultimate meaning behind it. This is the profound essence of Islam. Every life is dual; it became technically impossible for man to live one life, from the moment he ceased to be plant or animal, from the time of Qalu Bala. Since the moral puzzle was set in heaven, and since humanity was 'thrown' into this world or 'thrown into social reality', a person may contemplate or believe in a single life, but in practice, they live two lives.

We have no rational proof of the existence of another world beyond the physical, sensory one, yet we sense that producing and consuming is not the entirety of human existence. A scientist or thinker dedicated to uncovering the truth will not find this higher existence solely through thought; rather, it is revealed in the very act of seeking truth and transcending a purely animalistic life. When we fight for others or for ideals such as truth, justice, and goodness, we negate the confines of a finite existence. Those who sacrifice their lives, freedom, or peace in loyalty to a moral law exemplify the infinite nature of life and its higher purpose. These sacrifices illuminate the darkness like flashes of lightning on a stormy night, briefly revealing distant horizons. Though we may still wander in darkness, those fleeting glimpses are neither lies nor mirages: they represent profound truths that endure.

Even our most honest answers to the question of where we belong often do not reflect our actual beliefs. Each of us constructs a personal image of the world, typically inconsistent and held together by our lack of critical examination. We label this image as religion or atheism, though it often bears little resemblance to those concepts. Religious individuals who attempt to validate their faith through science, and atheists who advocate for sacrifice in the name of 'higher goals' or admire the works of Michelangelo and Rodin, fall into this category. How many would find themselves utterly confused when confronted with the reality they have imagined? Both materialism and strict religion owe their apparent mass followings primarily to the fact that most people do not grasp their true meanings.

2.

These two enduring lines of thought in human history can be easily outlined. They run parallel and simultaneous to one another, showing little progress over time. Their contours were already evident in ancient Greece with thinkers like Epicurus (or Aristotle) and Plato. Aristotle's famous maxim that 'pleasure and pain are great initiators of human life' (a sentiment echoed nearly untouched two millennia later in Holbach's work) finds an almost immediate counterpoint in Plato's assertion that an unjust man is unhappy, and even more so if he remains unpunished—an idea at the core of every genuine ethical framework. Despite their stark opposition, these two lines of thought continue to influence modern philosophy. We can trace clear Epicurean ideas through Lucretius, Bacon, Hobbes, Gassendi, Helvetius, and Holbach, eventually reaching thinkers like Spencer and Marx, and even Russell in our century. Likewise, Plato's ideas are carried forward by all of the Christian thinkers and further developed by figures such as Al-Ghazali, Malebranche, Leibniz, Fichte, Cudworth,

Schelling, Hegel, Kant, and more recently, Bergson and Whitehead. Upon reconstructing these philosophical systems consistently, we may find the results surprising, yielding an image that might be unexpected for many.

In the realm of practical human goals, these two polar opposites of thought can symbolise progress and humanism. Religion does not inherently drive progress, nor does science inherently promote humanism. At best, these may be side effects, as there is no such thing as pure religion or pure science. In reality, no religion exists without some degree of scientific influence, and no science is devoid of certain religious aspirations. This complexity creates a mixture where the true origins of phenomena or trends become unclear. The overwhelming majority of people tend to conflate these concepts, applying their own preferences and biases without understanding the critical distinctions.

In analysing these opposing stances, our aim is to present them in their 'pure forms', beginning with their most extreme, logically consistent, yet often practically absurd conclusions. It becomes evident that these two frameworks are internally coherent systems that begin to reinforce each other at certain points. This interplay can sometimes be illustrated, as when a gap in a mosaic can be filled by a completely opposing argument. For instance, when materialism asserts that historical events are driven by objective forces independent of individuals, the antithesis necessarily posits that extraordinary personalities, or 'heroes', shape history. Indeed, it does not take a long search to find a heroic explanation of history (e.g. Carlyle). Some argue that 'history has no mind of its own' (Marx), while others contend that it is indeed crafted by geniuses.

In the same way that Christian personalism had to confront historical materialism in the aforementioned example, by the same necessary logic, creation must oppose evolution, ideals must challenge personal gain, freedom must counter uniformity, and the individual must stand against society, and so on. The religious demand to 'destroy desires' finds its counterpart in the civilisational imperative to 'create more and more desires'. At the end of this introduction, the reader will encounter a comprehensive attempt to classify ideas according to this pattern. Although incomplete and merely a summary, this classification aims to illustrate that religion and materialism are the two fundamental worldviews that cannot be further reduced or subsumed into one another—much like the 'two seas that do not overtake one another' (Qur'an, 55:19-20).

This 'anatomy of ideas' may not sit well with those who are content with the current state of confusion, but proper differentiation is the essential starting point for any meaningful discussion. Seeking rational arguments to prove the truth of either worldview is a futile endeavour, as each represents a self-contained logical system. No logic exists above them that can arbitrate between them. In both theory and practice, the only thing greater than these worldviews is life itself. To live—and more than that, to live righteously and fully—surpasses every religion and every form of socialism. Christianity seeks and offers salvation, but only of an inner nature; socialism seeks and offers only external salvation. Confronted by these two parallel worlds in an unsolvable logical conflict, a person may feel compelled to accept aspects of both, finding a new centre of gravity between them. Together, they divide and share half of the whole truth about life and human destiny.

3.

There are certain fundamental facts that everyone accepts in life, regardless of their official philosophy. Whether taught by common sense or learned through personal defeats, these facts include family, material security, the pursuit of happiness, sympathy for justice and truth, health, education, work, aspiring to freedom, interest, force, responsibility, and so on. When we compare these facts, we notice that they cluster at varying distances around a central axis, forming a realistic, though perhaps inconsistent and heterogeneous system. This system bears a resemblance to the basic principles of Islam.

The differences between the comparative teachings may seem foundational and insurmountable—at least in theory. In practice, however, despite deep-seated antagonism, there is an ongoing process of mutual borrowing of ideas. Many things once vehemently criticised are now being justified and integrated, while other principles remain mere theoretical constructs.

For instance, Marxism attacked the institutions of family and state, yet in practice retained them. Similarly, every consistent religion, in its ideal form, has rejected concerns for worldly affairs, but as a practical ideology for real people, it has adopted slogans of social justice and become a force in the fight for a better life. Marxism, despite its principles, had to acknowledge a certain level of freedom, and religion, contrary to its philosophy, accepted the practical utility of force. And so on. It has become evident that it is often impossible to stay within the bounds of common sense while remaining loyal to a single, consistent philosophy.

The question here is not whether Christianity or materialism—two opposing ideologies—can overcome the difficulties they encounter because they are inherently unsuitable for life or incompatible with human nature. Rather, the question is whether they can do so while remaining true to their principles without stepping outside their respective frameworks. Often, the way out is found through impermissible borrowing from the other side. For instance, Christianity, now institutionalised as the Catholic Church, addresses issues like work, property, hierarchy, education, science, marriage, law, and social justice. Meanwhile, materialism, which has evolved into socialism as a political system, begins to discuss topics such as morality, humanism, upbringing, art, creation, justice, responsibility, freedom, and other spiritual matters that fall outside the realm of materialism.

Instead of pure, uncompromising doctrines, we are presented with diluted versions for 'general use'—a form of religion or materialism for the masses—which are anything but consistent representations of these ideologies. Both religion and materialism are being distorted, deviating from their original teachings, almost as if by some physical law. This is because, in both cases, an ideology that reflects only one aspect of life is being applied to life as a whole. As a result, while one may identify as a materialist or Christian in theory, whether in radical or moderate forms, much is left out in practice. In reality, no one lives as a fully consistent materialist or Christian.

Modern utopias found in countries like China, (North) Korea, and Vietnam, which consider themselves the most consistent expressions of Marxist teachings, are actually remarkable examples of compromise and inconsistency. Rather than allowing a new social model to emerge from evolving economic relations, these regimes have co-opted traditional moral values—especially humility and respect for elders—and integrated them into their systems.[2] As a result, these two key tenets of local religions now stand alongside the principles of radical Marxism at the foundation of these societies. The architects of these systems may be reluctant to acknowledge this fact, but the conclusion is undeniable, and the reality remains regardless of whether we admit it. In some socialist countries that profess loyalty to Marxism, moral incentives (rather than material rewards) are offered for labour.

This phenomenon warrants analysis, beginning with the question of whether these moral incentives are part of a

2 Humility is welcome in a society with very low living standards and respect for elders smoothly turned into untouchable respect for authority.

materialistic framework or if they are borrowed from elsewhere. One thing is immediately clear: no form of moral incentive can be explained within a consistent materialist philosophy. The same applies to the use of humanistic slogans—such as justice, equality, freedom, and inalienable human and civil rights—concepts whose authentic source lies in religion. While everyone has the right to live according to their own beliefs, including the right to deviate from their own ideological principles, it is crucial for anyone seeking to understand the world—whether an observer, an analyst, or otherwise—to know the true origin and meaning of the ideas that shape and drive the modern world.

The greatest danger in this inquiry lies in accepting 'obvious facts' and 'universally accepted' notions without scrutiny. The sun does not revolve around the Earth, despite how obvious it might seem; the reverse is true. A whale is not a fish, despite what most people may believe. Similarly, materialism and freedom are fundamentally incompatible, no matter how often they are paired together in slogans. Despite the confusion, exacerbated by the disconnect between what people think, say, and do, the nature of things remains unchanged. Ideas influence the world not through their temporary or superficial meaning but through their original, true purpose and essence.

4.

We have now reached a definition of Islam as presented and supported by this book. Keeping this fundamental relationship in mind, we can describe Islam as an attempt to first understand and accept, and then to transcend, the primary dualism of the world. The term 'Islamic' is used here not only to describe the set of rules and institutions typically associated with Islam but, more importantly, to refer to the underlying principle or idea at their core. It reflects a deeper analogy (qiyas) that emphasises an inherent harmony in the very core, in the idea, and in the principle. The adjective 'Islamic' is employed more as a method than as a fixed solution, representing a synthesis of opposing and contradictory principles.

The foundational principle of Islam echoes the pattern that Nature used in creating life and its many forms. It seems that the same inspiration that unified the freedom of the spirit with the determinism of nature in life also unified purification and prayer in the form of Islamic prayer. A strong intuition could reconstruct the entirety of Islam just from its prayer, and similarly, the universal duality of the world from Islam itself.[3] Europe has never fully succeeded in finding and maintaining a middle path in this regard, with England being a notable exception, as we will discuss later. This is why it is nearly impossible to express the essence of Islam using European terminology.

Islamic terms like *salah*, *zakat*, *khalifa*, *jamaat* and *wudu* are not simply equivalent to prayer, taxes, ruler, community, or ablution. The definition that views Islam as a synthesis of religion and materialism, positioned midway between Christianity and socialism, is overly simplistic and can only be accepted with reservations. It captures one aspect of Islam, but only in an approximate way. Islam is not merely an arithmetic median between these two ideologies, nor is it their average. Terms like salah, zakat, and wudu cannot be further reduced, as they express deeply personal, indivisible experiences—certainties that require a single word for their verbal expression, a single image, yet still convey a dual state of being. The parallel with human nature is clear: a human being is both the measure and explanation of these terms.[4]

---

3 Defining Islam as a principle has essential value to its future development. It has been stated countless times, rightfully so, that Islam and the Islamic world became rigid and reserved. This situation is without doubt in connection with the vision of Islam as a finished and once-and-forever defined teaching.

4 One sentence in the Qur'an seems to be speaking directly about this: 'So set your face toward the religion, inclining to truth, the natural disposition (fitrah) upon which Allah has created mankind' (Qur'an, 30:30).

It is well known that the Qur'an can seem unsystematic and even contradictory to the casual reader or analyst. However, the Qur'an is not literature; it is life itself. The complexity disappears when we stop viewing it as a theoretical framework and instead see it as a guide for living. The only authentic commentary on the Qur'an is life itself, and as we know, that life was embodied by the Prophet Muhammad (pbuh). What may seem elusive and contradictory in Islamic teachings is perfectly expressed through his life as a complete, natural harmony—a highly effective unity of love and power, the sublime and the practical, the divine and the human.

When it was transformed into the life of a nation, this potent combination of religion and politics unleashed an immense amount of high-level energy. At a certain point, the formula of Islam aligned perfectly with the formula of life itself. Islam's middle position is evident in its need to defend itself from two opposing criticisms: from the side of pure religion, which views it as too natural, materialistic, and worldly, and from the side of science, which criticises it for containing religious, mystical, and unscientific elements. Yet, there is only one Islam, though, just like a human, it has both a soul and a body. Its appearance to the observer depends entirely on their standpoint: a materialist will always see Islam as purely religious and mystical (a 'right-wing' tendency), while Christians will often view it as a social and political movement (a 'left-wing' tendency). The unique path of Islam can be traced through these differing perspectives, revealing its central position.

5.

This dual impression reappears when viewed from within. Again, two distinct perspectives emerge. No original Islamic institution belongs strictly to either pure religion or pure science (politics, economics, or worldly affairs). Mystics have always emphasised the religious side of Islam, while rationalists focus on the practical side. Yet both groups have struggled with Islam because it resists being neatly categorised into either framework. Strictly speaking, neither mystic nor rationalist is a Muslim. Let us take wudu, for example. A mystic will define it as religious purification with symbolic meaning; a rationalist will reduce it only to hygiene. Both of them are right, but each only partially. The inadequacy of a mystical explanation means that wudu may become a mere formality, a set of symbolic movements, which, following the same logic in other areas, will gradually reduce Islam to mere religion, eliminating, bit by bit, all the physical, intellectual, and social components. Rationalists, on the other hand, will move in the opposite direction and, by suppressing religion, will degrade Islam to political slogans gathering people, creating a new form of nationalism—Islamic nationalism—devoid of any religious and ethical content, empty and indistinguishable from other nationalisms in that regard. Being a Muslim, then, would carry no calling or duty, no moral or religious striving, and no relation to universal truth; the term would signify only affiliation to one group, distinct from others.

Meanwhile, Islam never aimed to be merely a nation. It aspired to be 'people who call to do good and prevent evil' (Qur'an, 3:190; 22:41, etc.), thus fulfilling a moral mission. Neglecting the political component – indulging in religious mysticism – causes us to lose historical footing and tacitly accept oppression and servitude. Conversely, neglecting the religious component of Islam means we cease to be any kind of force in the moral and broader human cultural sphere. Does it matter whether imperialism is called British, German, or Islamic if, in any case, it is reduced to mere domination over men and things?

For the future and practical human endeavours, Islam represents a call to create a person as a bearer of harmony between body and soul, and to build a society whose laws and socio-political institutions are designed to preserve that harmony, not disrupt it. Islam is, or should be, a constant pursuit of a state of inner and outer balance in the course of history. In any case, there is no demand more natural, yet so rarely explored or tested. This goal stands before Islam today, and it will be its specific historical task in the years to come.

6.

Based on the problems it defines, discusses, and seeks to address, this book ties itself to the most remarkable characteristic of the current historical state of affairs: the division of the world into two opposing camps with ideological conflict at its core. This conflict of ideas has projected itself into reality more clearly than ever before, taking on quite concrete and specific forms. This image gains new details and circumstances every day, with polarisation increasing to a painful, almost palpable clarity. Today, we have two worlds divided to their core – ideologically, emotionally, and politically. A giant historical experiment concerning the duality of man's world is unfolding before us.

Still, one part of the world is not enveloped by this polarisation, and the majority of that world consists of Muslim countries. Certainly, this phenomenon is no accident. Muslim nations sense that there is nothing to gain in the existing ideological conflict, so even if they do not formulate an active stance, they at least adopt a position of non-alignment. This process of Muslim countries gaining ideological and political independence will continue.[5] However, this non-engagement is not merely political. It is accompanied everywhere by an equally resolute demand to reject foreign models and

5 When this book was first prepared for printing, two major Muslim countries, Iran and Pakistan, cancelled their membership of the pro-Western Central Pact. Earlier, Indonesia, Sudan and Somalia thwarted the attempts of being dragged under the ideological domination of the Eastern Bloc.

influences—from both East and West. In fact, Islam is ideologically independent and non-aligned by its very definition. This is a natural and sound state of affairs.

Not only does Islam recognise the truth of socialism and Christianity, but it in fact insists upon them. For if socialism is a lie, then Islam cannot be complete truth either. To prove the veracity of Islam is to prove the veracity of socialism and Christianity—while acknowledging the imperfection of their truths. This is the special position of Islam in today's historical moment. Islam need not see its opportunity in the negation or destruction of either of these worlds. Its superiority lies in its capacity to recognise the elements of truth and justice within them. The global opposites, whose historical expression are the existing blocs of countries, can only be overcome by constructing a third world that incorporates the elements of justice these worlds now contain.

What is now clear is that the conflicting ideologies, in their extreme forms, cannot be imposed upon humanity and that they must strive towards synthesis—a middle ground—we seek to demonstrate how harmoniously Islam aligns with this natural flow of human thought, accepting it, encouraging it, and gradually becoming its most consistent and complete expression.

In today's polarised world, Islam—which has more than once served as a bridge between East and West—must become aware of its mission. Just as it mediated between ancient civilisations and Europe in the past, today, at a time of dramatic dilemmas and alternatives, Islam should once again assume its role as the 'intermediary nation' in a divided world. This is the meaning of the third way—the Islamic way.

7.

In the end, a few words about this book. It is divided into two parts. The first part discusses the matter of religion in the broadest sense of the word. The second part is devoted to Islam—more precisely, a specific aspect of it: its bipolarity.

Otherwise, this book is not theological—and its writer is not a theologian. In this regard, the book is more an attempt to 'translate' Islam into the language spoken and understood by today's generation. This circumstance might explain some of its errors and inaccuracies. After all, there is no such thing as a perfect translation.

THE CHART OF OPPOSITES

Introductory Remark

The three columns in this chart represent the religious, Islamic, and materialistic worldviews. The first takes spirit as its fundamental principle, the second takes the human being, and the third takes matter. All terms, ideas, or phenomena within a single column share a kind of internal coherence or vertical harmony. Moreover, each element in one column has its opposing counterpart in the corresponding column on the opposite side (a horizontal relationship).

These worldviews emerge as integrated wholes. For instance, belief in matter—as opposed to consciousness—as the primary substance of the universe (the materialist worldview) is almost always accompanied by a range of associated beliefs and opinions. A materialist will typically uphold the primacy of society over the individual, be inspired by Darwin, favour collective social upbringing over family-centred nurturing, and value progress over humanism. They will tend to view historical developments—and even individual behaviour—as governed by inexorable laws, untouched by human will or intention. In ethics and law, such a worldview favours social rights and state-guaranteed security over individual freedom and inalienable rights.

If we continued this analysis, we would discover a deep interrelation between evolutionist theories and the rejection of natural human rights, or between atheism and phenomena like Stalin's purges. In the same way, the column representing the religious worldview also displays consistent internal logic, even across ideas that may at first seem disconnected.

The chart, of course, is a simplification—too rigid to capture the full nuance of real-world thought. But given the complexity of the subject matter, this schematic approach is unavoidable.

Religion	Islam	Materialism
SPIRIT		MATTER
Consciousness	HUMAN	Being
Soul	HUMAN	Body
Subject	-	Object
Ding an Sich (Kant)	-	Phenomenon
L'etre en soi (Being in itself)	-	L'être pour soi (Being for itself)
Organic	-	Mechanic
Prayer	SALAH	Hygiene
Charity	ZAKAT	Tax (expropriation of expropriators)
Judgements of value - Ethics	-	Judgement of Logic - Mathematics
Critique of practical mind	-	Critique of pure mind
Consciousness - Ideal - Idea - Sin	-	Need - Interest - Fact - Damage
Meditation - Inspiration - Intuition		Observation - Intelligence - Experience

Holy secret	-	Problem
Drama - Moral issues - Metaphysics	-	Political economy - Social issues - Physics
Monastery - Temple - Art gallery	MOSQUE - SCHOOL	School - Laboratory - Factory
Morality	Law - Sharia	Force
Love - Non-resistance to evil	JUSTICE - JIHAD	Class fight (Force serving the interest)
Monk - Saint	SHAHID	Knight - Political fighter - Hero
Style	-	Function
Aesthetic shaping		Technical perfectioning
CREATION		EVOLUTION
Human was created by God		Human is a product of nature
Prologue in heaven. Humanisation of human		Live matter - Animal - Human - Übermensch
Michelangelo		Darwin
Moral drama. Fight for salvation		Fight for survival. Natural selection
Animism - personalism		reism - thingism (fr. chosisme)
Christian personism		Historical materialism
Heroic understanding of history		Materialistic understanding of history
'History is made by geniuses'		'History has no mind of its own'

Gradual development of Absolute spirit		Progress of means of production
Triumph of idea of liberty		Classless society
The Last Judgement		Entropy
People are moved by ideas (ideals)		People are moved by needs (interests)
Asceticism - Upbringing		Dressage - Education
Classical education		Technical education
Power over oneself		Power over nature
Destroy desires		Create more desires (needs)
Deeds are judged by intentions		Deeds are judged by consequences
Principle of guilt - punishment	PROTEC-TIVE PUN-ISHMENT	Principle of social protection - measure - purge
CULTURE		CIVILISATION
Humanism		Progress
Culture - Consensus-Individualisation		Mass culture - Manipulation - Uniformisation
DRAMA		UTOPIA
PERSONALITY	HUMAN	SOCIAL UNIT
Spiritual community	Jamaat	Social class
Civitas Dei	UMMAH - CALIPHATE	Civitas Solis
Liberte - Egalite - Fraternite	-	Class solidarity
Human dignity	-	Social security
Human rights	-	Social rights

American Bill of Rights (1776)	-	Soviet Declaration on rights of working and exploited people (1918)
Humiliated and injured ones - Dostoevsky	-	Exploited ones - Marx
Eastern sin. Chastity. Celibacy	MARRIAGE	Sexual freedom. 'Sexual revolution'
Marriage as a sacrament		Marriage as a contract
Religious cult of old age. Wisdom		Civilisational cult of youth. Biopotential
Home. Mother. Family upbringing		Kindergarten. Kindergarten teacher. Social upbringing
Three-generational family		Nursing home
Jesus	MUHAM-MAD (PBUH)	Moses
CHRISTIANITY	ISLAM	JUDAISM

PART ONE

DEBATING PREMISES

CHAPTER 1

EVOLUTION AND CREATION

DARWIN AND MICHELANGELO

The origin of humankind is the cornerstone of every worldview. Any consideration of the proper way for a person to live their life always leads back to the question of human origins. As with other inquiries, the answers provided by science and religion are contradictory here, too. Science views the emergence of humans as the result of a long process of evolution from lower life forms, where the boundaries between the zoological and the human are not sharply defined. This process involves a lengthy transitional period of humanoid apes or ape-like humans (ape-men). Regardless of what science identifies as the defining moment of separation—bipedal walking, toolmaking, or the acquisition of articulated speech—it always attributes this transition to external, material factors. These factors pertain either to the development of human physical constitution or the mastery of nature for personal benefit. Here, humanity is portrayed as a child of nature, nurtured within her lap, never fully detached from her. Religion and art, on the other hand, speak of the creation of humanity as an act of divine intervention—an event, not a process. This act is depicted as momentary, painful, and catastrophic. Religious visions of the creation of humankind, represented in various images across nearly all faiths, describe humanity as being cast into matter, as experiencing a 'fall' to Earth. They explore the contradictions between humanity and nature, framing the encounter with the natural world as one with a foreign and hostile force. The question of whether humanity is the result of an evolutionary process or a 'creation' thus becomes the question of whether humans are a part of the world or fundamentally distinct from it. To materialists, a human being is a 'perfect animal', a *homme machine* or a 'biological machine'. They argue that there is no qualitative difference between humans and animals, only a matter of degree. For them, there is no 'special human essence'.[6] Instead, there is only a 'tangible, historical, and social definition of humanity', and 'economic and social history is the only history that is concrete and that truly exists' says György Lukács, a Hungarian Marxist, in his 1948 essay *Existentialism or Marxism*.[7]

'A human is just one system, like any other in nature, subject to the inevitable and universal laws of nature', wrote Ivan Pavlov in *Experimental Psychology*. According to this view, one external, objective factor plays a central role in human evolution—labour. 'Humans are products of their external environment and their own labour' (Friedrich Engels). Thus, the emergence of humanity is presented as an external, biological process determined by external, material factors.

> The hand both causes and expedites the development of psychological life.... Its 'discovery', along with the 'discovery' of language, marks the end of zoological history and the beginning of human history. [8]

These clear and convincing attitudes seem very evident. However, what is less obvious is that they, in a certain sense, represent a clear negation of humanity.

Man is often reduced to his 'components', and it appears that he completely dissolves by the end of this process. First, there

---

6 As John B Watson says, there is 'no dividing line between man and brute.' John B. Watson, 'Psychology as the Behaviorist Views It', *Psychological Review*, vol. 20 (1913), pp. 158–177.

7 Lukács, György, *Existentialism or Marxism?*, trans. by M. Livingstone (London: Merlin Press, 1972).

8 H. Berr, in the introduction to Morgan's *Prehistoric Humanity*.

is Engels, who analyses social man and demonstrates how he is a product of social relations, or more precisely, the existing relations of production. Here, the man himself is nothing and creates nothing; on the contrary, he is merely the result of these given facts. Then Darwin takes this depersonalized man, reduced to a mere biological fact, and quite consistently shows how this creature that talks, walks upright, and crafts tools gradually evolved as a product of natural selection and the struggle for survival from his close animal relatives.

Biology completes this image of the process, showing how all forms of living beings are reduced to primordial life forms, which, in turn, are reduced to physics and chemistry—a mere interplay of molecular forces. Life, consciousness, and the human spirit, in this view, do not truly exist; they are merely especially complex forms of interaction between these impersonal forces. There is no such thing as an original or 'insoluble' human essence.

Now, if we turn our thoughts from this slightly bleak yet clear and comprehensive scheme to the interior of the Sistine Chapel, and stand before Michelangelo's famous frescoes covering its ceiling, letting our gaze wander from *The Expulsion from Paradise* to *The Creation of Adam* to *The Last Judgement* above the altar, we are compelled to ask ourselves: What do these images—considered perhaps the most exciting works of art of all time—mean? Do they contain any truth about these profound subjects we are discussing? If they do, what is that truth? Put even more precisely, in what way do these images convey truth?

Greek tragedies, Dante's visions of heaven and hell, the spiritual songs of Black people, Shakespeare's dramas, Faust's *Prologue in Heaven*, Malaysian masks, ancient Japanese frescoes, or even the paintings of some modern artists—I mention these examples without any particular order, for art, in this respect, serves as a unified and consistent testimony—cannot be related in any way to the Darwinian conception of humanity. Nor can they be imagined as the self-perception of such a being or its impression of the surrounding world.

What feelings about the world lie behind the term 'religion of salvation'? What does this evocative phrase truly mean? How can we grasp the meaning of drama in an existence reduced to the mere exchange of matter between living beings and nature? What assumptions and forebodings form the foundation of Ernst Neizvestny's sketches of Dante's *Hell*? How did fear become the universal feeling shared by all living things if life and humanity were nurtured in the embrace of 'Mother Nature'?

These questions expose the world sketched for us by science as suddenly incomplete and insufficient. In truth, science does not present us with the full picture of the world; it offers only a faithful photograph, one that lacks an entire dimension of reality.

Lacking this third, inner dimension—an absence inherent in every product of science—we encounter the weakness, or even the inability, of science to convey any ultimate or complete truth about life, and particularly about humanity. In its analyses, governed by unyielding logic, life is being deprived of life, and humanity of its essence.

The science of man is possible if he is a part of the external world or its product (if he is a thing). Conversely, art is only possible if man is distinct from nature, if he is a stranger within it (if he is a personality). In its most authentic form, art is the history of this alienation.

Thus, when it comes to the question of the origins and nature of man, art and science are in complete and irrevocable conflict. Science presents an infinite array of facts and data, particularly fossilised remains carefully collected and analysed, which lead inexorably to the conclusion of the gradual evolution of man from the animal world. Art, on the other hand, calls upon its stirring testimonies of man's arrival from the 'Unknown'—something no human heart can wholly renounce. Science points to Darwin and his monumental synthesis; art points to Michelangelo and his grandiose vision on the ceiling of the Sistine Chapel.[9]

Darwin and Michelangelo represent two entirely different conceptions of man and two contradictory truths about his origins—truths that can never cancel each other out. The former is grounded in an overwhelming wealth of irrefutable evidence; the latter is inscribed in the hearts of all people.

* * *

Man is the only subject capable of holding two contradictory truths simultaneously—and not only that. The contradictory statement about man is often the one closest to the truth.

The claim that the human body (man as a biological fact) has an animalistic nature, and even origins, originates primarily from religion, long before Darwin and Lamarck proposed the same idea. Well before any scientific theory, religion unequivocally taught that there is an animal within man. The difference lies in the scope of this assertion: science regards man as merely an intelligent animal, whereas religion sees man as an animal with a personality.

> A man, as specialists know him, is far from being the tangible, true man. They present a scheme composed of other schematic sketches, as produced by the methods of every particular science. A man is, at once, a carcass for an anatomist to dissect, a conscience for a psychologist to study, and the same personality every individual senses within themselves and recognises whenever they turn their gaze inward.

9 The idea of evolution has always been associated with atheism. The first ideas about the origin and extinction of species can be found in the works of the Roman writer and poet Titus Lucretius Carus (for example, *De rerum natura*), who is equally well-known for his atheism and advocacy of hedonistic views.

> He is a chemical compound, from which the tissues and fluids of the body are formed—a wondrous unity of cells and nourishing juices whose organic laws are studied by the physiologist. He is that combination of tissue and conscience which hygienists and educators strive to guide towards the highest possible development within an allotted time. He is *homo economicus*, ceaselessly consuming goods so that the systems turning him into a commodity can continue to function. Yet, at the same time, he is a poet, a hero, a saint. He is not only a marvellously and multiply-complex being, subjected to scientific analysis, but also an embodiment of the will, reason, and aspirations of all humanity.[10]

Let us note how the term 'human' holds a dual, almost contradictory meaning in the human mind. 'We are human' means we are sinful, weak, physical. 'Let us be human' is an appeal to remind us that we are something more—that we have certain higher duties, to act selflessly and with humanity. 'You think about the things of men'—Jesus rebukes Peter with these words, contrasting the divine with the human. Humanity, humanness, humanitarianism—all derive from the word 'human' and signify higher, moral aspirations. This dual meaning of terms tied to man's name reflects man's double nature: one rooted in the Earth, the other 'from the heavens'.

Materialists, however, will always emphasise the external aspects of existence, turning the scientific perspective into a denial of the human spirit.

'Therefore, the hand is not only the organ of labour,' Engels writes:

> ...it is also the product of labour. Labour, adaptation to ever new operations, the inheritance of muscles, ligaments, and, over vast periods of time, bones that underwent specialised development, and the ever-renewed application of this in-

10 Alexis Carrel, *Man, the Unknown* (1935).

> herited skill in increasingly complex operations, have given the human hand the high degree of perfection required to conjure into being the pictures of Raphael, the statues of Thorwaldsen, and the music of Paganini.[11]

What Engels describes is a continuation of biological, not human (spiritual), development. Painting is not a technical process but a spiritual act. The paintings of Raphael were not created by his hand but by his spirit. (Beethoven composed his greatest works after he was completely deaf.) Biological development, even if carried forward infinitely, would not, on its own, without intervention from a higher entity, produce Raphael's paintings—or even the simplest drawings left by prehistoric painters in the caves of the Sahara. What we are dealing with here are two entirely separate and distinct trajectories or two different facets of human existence.

A man cannot be reduced to mere biology, just as a painting cannot be reduced to the amount of paint used, or a poem to the syntax of its text. It is true that a mosque is constructed from a specific number of stone blocks of a particular shape arranged in a certain order, with a certain amount of mortar, wooden beams, and so forth, but that does not capture the essence of the mosque. The idea of a mosque is not fully encompassed by the details of its construction. Otherwise, what would distinguish it from a military barracks?

We could write an extraordinary, erudite, and accurate grammatical, linguistic, or orthographic analysis of one of Goethe's poems without ever approaching the essence of the poem itself. It would be akin to the difference between a dictionary of a language and a poem written in that language. A dictionary may be correct, but it has no meaning. A poem, on the other hand, possesses meaning and an unfathomable essence.

---

11 Friedrich Engels, 'The Part Played by Labour in the Transition from Ape to Man', in *Dialectics of Nature*, trans. Clemens Dutt (Moscow: Progress Publishers, 1934).

In the same way, anthropology, morphology, and physiology do not speak of the human being unless we only consider his external, incidental, mechanical, and meaningless aspects. A man, in this analogy, is the painting, the temple, the poem—not merely the construction materials from which these are made. A man is far greater than all that science combined can ever describe about him.

PRIMARY IDEALISM

According to the logic of evolution, the most primitive, unevolved type of human must have been preceded by the most evolved type of animal. However, when we compare these two neighbouring stages of evolution, it is impossible not to perceive an essential, insurmountable difference between them. On one hand, we observe packs of animals roaming in search of food, fighting for survival, or annihilating one another. On the other hand, perhaps in the same part of the woods, we encounter a primitive man, perplexed and bewildered by his unusual and incomprehensible games, mysteries, and symbols. This scene presents two entirely different creatures, and it is inconceivable that a single minor or major evolutionary leap accounts for the difference between them.

The principle of animal existence is efficiency, utility, and practicality. The principle of human existence—if he is truly human—is none of these. An animal is natural. Man is supernatural, irrational, incomprehensible, unbelievable, even rationally impossible. Without these qualities, he does not exist—at least not as a man. Man exists only to the extent that he resists the general flow of the world, the all-encompassing mechanism of nothingness and non-existence.

We say: man evolved, but this refers only to his external, mortal history. Man is also created. In a single moment, he inexplicably became aware not only that he is not an animal but also that he found the meaning of life by negating the animalistic within himself. If man is a child of nature, how is it possible that he came to stand beside her and against her?

Let us imagine his intelligence—an inheritance from his animal ancestry—developed to the highest degree. His needs would only increase, both in variety and quantity. None of these needs would diminish or disappear; rather, their satisfaction would become more intelligent, safer, and more organised. What was incidental in a primitive stage would develop into a highly evolved economy of planned systems in a civilised society. Yet, the mind itself would never conceive the idea of renouncing life, rejecting desires, sacrificing for 'the good of others', or reducing the intensity of physical living in general.

An animal has instincts that are extraordinary examples of efficiency and expediency. A man, however, possesses moral traits and non-utilitarian ethics. Animals have highly developed senses of time and are often more punctual than humans. For instance, starlings stop feeding exactly one hour before sunset, and crabs retreat to their holes and seal the entrances with mud just minutes before the tide. The waves never catch them outside. Bees, too, organise their days with surprising precision. Most flowers do not always produce sufficient nectar but offer it only during specific hours of the day. Bees gather honey at the most suitable times and in the best locations, using various markers on the ground and orienting themselves by polarised light from the sky, and so on.

All of these abilities are 'this-worldly.' They enable, support, or enhance a species' survival.

Moral principles, by contrast, both in primitive and civilised societies, reduce a man's efficacy in the competitive struggle that creatures impose on each other. Burdened by moral scruples, man could only survive thanks to his immeasurably higher intelligence compared to the species directly competing with him. If intelligence levels were equal, an animal species with 'moral prejudices' would rapidly go extinct. Man has compensated for this 'defect of power', caused by his ethics, with significantly higher intelligence and other related abilities.

This intelligence, however, has animal origins, not human ones.

> Let us open a collection of anecdotes about animal intelligence. Among the many acts that can be explained by imitation or the automatic association of images, we will also find actions that bear the undeniable mark of intelligence. These are, first of all, actions that reveal a constructive intention, whether animals are crafting rudimentary tools for themselves or using man-made objects. The animals closest to man in terms of intelligence—monkeys, elephants, and the like—are precisely those that know how to use artificial devices on occasion. Below these, we find the fox, which instinctively recognises that a trap is a trap.[12]

A chimpanzee uses a stick to reach a banana, and a bear uses a stone. A vast amount of material has been collected regarding the reception and transmission of deliberate information among bees, geese, and monkeys, in the form of 'conversation' or pantomime (as studied by the German zoologist Frisch, Professor Lorenz, and Moscow Professor I.N. Zinkin).

The long-time director of the New York Zoo, Dr William Reid Blair, also gathered fascinating observations about the intelligence and resourcefulness of animals, as well as their ability to utilise the objects around them. His general conclusion was that all animals think. Even language belongs to the natural, zoological, rather than the spiritual, side of man. Rudimentary forms of language can be found in the animal world. It has been demonstrated that linguistics—unlike music or art—

12 Henri Bergson, *Creative Evolution.*

lends itself to strict scientific examination, systematisation, and even the application of mathematical methods. This gives linguistics the clear characteristics of a science, as the object of science can only be something external.[13]

There is a clear analogy between nature and intelligence on one side, and intelligence and language on the other. Just as matter and intelligence 'mutually shape one another', the same process continues with intelligence and language through mutual correlation and interaction. 'Language is the hand of the brain' and 'the function of the brain consists in limiting our spiritual life to that which is useful in practice'. (Bergson).

Generally speaking, there is nothing in man that cannot, in one way or another, be found to some degree in higher animal species, such as vertebrates and insects. Mobility, consciousness, association, intelligence, communication, the satisfaction of needs, and even rudimentary forms of economics are evident. This side of man clearly ties him to, and originates from the animal world.[14]

However, there is nothing in the entire animal kingdom that even remotely hints at or leads to man's religion or moral prohibitions—not even traces—while both prehistoric and civilised human life is full of them. The life of animals, up until the appearance of man, seems gradual, comprehensible, and consistent when compared to the life of a savage, bound by peculiar scruples and driven by irrational beliefs and actions. When an animal hunts, its behaviour is entirely logical and rational. The vast literature on the lives of monkeys, beavers,

---

13 A negative proof of this could be the fact that abstaining from speech is encountered in some religions as a form of fasting, such as the vow of silence in certain Christian orders. It represents abstinence from a physical manifestation comparable to refraining from food and drink.

14 The Qur'an holds no different view: 'All creatures that crawl on the earth and birds that fly with their wings are communities like yourselves.' (Qur'an, 6:38)

and cats provides countless examples of animals employing completely appropriate methods to achieve their goals. Yet there is no record of an animal giving up opportunities it possessed or exhibiting 'prejudices' that are distinctly human.

Bees, the most advanced of the Hymenoptera, demonstrate an exceptionally organised collective but employ the most inhumane procedures towards an aged or exhausted queen bee: they simply expel her from the hive. No other example offers such a stark contrast between admirable order and collective organisation and the absence of what we commonly define as humanity: protection of the weak and fragile, recognition, gratitude, or scruples. Reflecting on the lives of such creatures, some express admiration and others horror at 'their implacable discipline, the synchronisation of individuals to their social functions, their unalterable schedules, and the blind, cruel punctuality that characterises them.'

Guided by instinct and focused on one clear goal—survival—an animal is therefore logical and comprehensible. Meanwhile, what does the primitive man do?

> Before starting an expedition, it is necessary that hunters, and often their families as well, submit themselves to various taboos, fasts, prayers, perform certain dances, have specific dreams, and pay attention to certain omens. When the game is within reach, they must then perform additional ritual acts. Women staying at home are also subjected to many restrictions. If these are broken, it could jeopardise the success of the hunt or even endanger the lives of their husbands.[15]

For an animal, things are what they are. Man, however, immediately created (or acquired) his imaginary world and believed in it more than in the so-called real world. An animal is typically an excellent hunter. The savage was also an excellent

15 Lucien Henry, *The origin of Religion* 1936).

hunter, and in that regard, there is no significant difference. Yet primitive man was also a tireless creator and 'producer' of cults, myths, superstitions, games, and idols. Man always sought another world, whether authentic or imaginary.

It is considered well-established that primitive men painted the animals they intended to hunt before setting off, believing this act would decisively contribute to the success of the hunt (the so-called hunter's magic). While man prayed or painted for the success of his hunt, an animal acted 'logically—surveying the territory, listening intently, or silently following the prey's trail. The initiation of a young man as a future hunter—as described by Hubert and Mauss—involved a series of elaborate ceremonies. They outlined rituals consisting of three phases: cleansing, dedication, and inclusion.

At first glance, it is evident that even without these rituals, a man—just like an animal—could become a perfect hunter. These rituals, therefore, have little to do with hunting itself. They represent something more profound and significant. In any case, it is worth noting the non-functional aspect of these rituals, which eliminates the possibility of explaining them through any purely economic lens.

In his monumental work, *The Golden Bough* (1890), J. Frazer pointed out that in primitive human consciousness, the inexplicable idea of human sacrifice became inseparably intertwined with the concept of sowing. H.G. Wells writes on the same topic:

> It was a mixture of the childish, dreamy, fairy-tale-prone primitive brain that no amount of logical thinking could ever explain. In the world 10,000 years ago, wherever there was sowing, there was human sacrifice. And it was not the sacrifice of some bad or outcast individual. It was usually a distinguished young man or woman, treated with the utmost care and respect.... Such human sacrifice, or traces of

> it, appear wherever man has reached and gone through the early stages of agriculture.

A little further, Wells continues:

A reindeer hunter (referring to Palaeolithic man) was undoubtedly a merciless hunter, a fierce and passionate creature; but he killed for reasons we can still comprehend. However, a Neolithic man, under the influence of speech and confused lines of thought, killed according to some theory, killed for monstrous and now incredible ideas, killed those he loved—out of fear and according to instructions.

In the 1862 novel, *Salammbô*, G. Flaubert describes scenes of human sacrifice in which Carthaginians, praying for rain, throw even their own children into the red-hot mouth of their deity Moloch. One might conclude, influenced by such images, that men were like animals—but this would be entirely wrong. Animals never engage in anything comparable, nor is there any phenomenon in the animal world that parallels such senseless sacrifices.

It may sound paradoxical, but the case we are discussing is a quintessentially human behaviour. It reflects the missteps and misfortunes of humanity—patterns that persist to this day in one form or another. It is humanity's enduring drama, where nations and individuals commit acts of madness, not driven by animal instincts but by the boundless fallacies of the human mind.

Sacrifice is present in all religions without exception. Yet the nature of sacrifice remains inexplicable, even absurd. It is a concept that originates from the 'other' system—the otherworldly realm. In primitive religions, sacrifice sometimes took on horrifying forms. Such sacrifices created a powerful, tangible, and painfully clear division, marking the boundary between the zoological and human eras. They represented the arrival of a principle entirely opposed to the principles of gain, necessity, and desire. Sacrifice stands as a milestone in human development, marking the beginning of the human world. For while gain is a zoological category, sacrifice is a uniquely human category. Gain would later become one of the foundational concepts of politics and political economy, while sacrifice would become central to religion and ethics.

The irrationality of primitive man sometimes manifested in incredible ways:

> One of the strange phenomena that developed in the late Palaeolithic and Neolithic ages was body mutilation. Men began cutting their bodies—removing their noses, ears, fingers, teeth, and more—and imbuing such acts with various superstitious meanings.

H.G. Wells concluded: 'No animal does anything like that.'

For comparison, we might recall the fox that gnaws off its own leg to escape an iron trap—an entirely rational act. In contrast, the self-mutilation of primitive man is entirely alien and unknown to the animal kingdom.[16]

From this, we might conclude that we are observing a phenomenon representing an evolutionary anomaly or an unexpected discontinuity in development. It suddenly appears as though evolution has reversed course, and the emergence of an 'animal with ideological prejudices' directly threatens further progress.

I refer to this phenomenon—an expression of wavering at the peak of evolution, momentarily making the zoological seem superior to the human—as the 'savage's complex.' No matter how unusual it may sound, this 'complex' is an expression of that new essence unique to humanity. It is the source of all

16 And the next difference is of the same or similar kind: an animal is dangerous when it is hungry and threatened. A human is dangerous when satisfied and powerful. Incomparably more crimes have been committed out of abundance and arrogance than out of scarcity.

later religion, poetry, philosophy, and art. This phenomenon is significant because it highlights, in its own peculiar way, the originality of the human emergence and the strange paradoxes tied to it.

These facts might lead us to conclude that animals were better equipped to carry forward the process of evolution and that primitive man—gazing at the sky and bound by moral obligations—seemed far more likely to be trampled. This almost inevitable impression of the superiority of zoological over the human at the dawn of the human era would reappear throughout history as calls to destroy idealism in the name of progress.

* * *

In this distant age when humanity first emerged from the animal kingdom, external differences—such as walking upright, developed hands, speech, and intelligence—must have been infinitesimally small and imperceptible over long periods of time. When a creature that appeared both ape-like and human began to extend its arm with a stick to reach fruit from a tree, or conveyed information to similar beings through certain sounds, it is difficult to determine precisely what it was: a human or an animal. However, the presence of any form of cult or prohibition would remove any doubt. Animal 'waited' to become human in order to begin to pray. Thus, the key distinction between humans and animals is neither physical nor intellectual. It is primarily spiritual, reflected in the existence of more or less defined religious, ethical, and aesthetic consciousness.

From this perspective, the decisive moments in the creation (or appearance) of humanity are not, as science suggests, walking upright, developing hands, or the advent of articulated speech, but rather the emergence of the first cults, paintings, and prohibitions. A savage who found joy in gazing at flowers or animal profiles 15,000 years ago and then painted them on cave walls was, in this sense, closer to being truly human (and more distant from an animal) than the contemporary epicurean who lives solely to satisfy physiological needs while constantly inventing new ones, or the average citizen of a modern metropolis, living a lonely life in concrete monstrosities, deprived of elementary aesthetic experiences and emotions.

In his book *Primeval Law*, Atkinson demonstrates how various original prohibitions can be found among savages across the world. This constant need to 'purge evil' and the awareness of the forbidden—things that cannot be touched or even looked at—appears wherever evidence of primitive human life exists. Another universal concept that dominated the minds of primeval humans was the idea of impurity and curse, leading to numerous prohibitions governing different aspects of primitive life. With the development of articulated speech, these prohibitions came under the umbrella term 'taboo', literally meaning 'not good' or 'not praised'—in other words, forbidden. 'Taboo' became the term for ethical prohibitions in early human history.

Therefore, humanity does not behave as a child of nature but as a foreigner within it. Its primary emotion is fear—not the biological fear shared by all animals, but a spiritual, cosmic, primordial fear connected to the mysteries and puzzles of existence. German existentialist Martin Heidegger considered this fear an 'eternal and timeless determinant of human existence'. It is a fear interwoven with curiosity, wonder, admiration, and dissatisfaction—emotions that may lie at the very foundation of all our art and culture.

The appearance of prohibitions and the primeval concepts of 'impure' and sublime, 'cursed' and holy, can only be explained by this particular relationship between primeval humanity and the world. If we were truly children of this world, there would be nothing within it that could be deemed holy or 'impure' to us. Such terms contradict the nature of the world as we know it. On the contrary, they bear witness to our origins from elsewhere—a place we cannot consciously remember, yet our 'inadequate' reaction to the external world, expressed through art and religion, stands as a negation of the Darwinian and, more broadly, scientific view of humanity.

Why did primitive humans, always and everywhere, respond to the world through religion? Why did they use it to express fear, anxiety, and disappointment? Why did they seek 'salvation', and from what? This aspect of humanity—the perpetual crucifixion between good and evil, the feeling of being lost, the eternal dilemmas of gain and conscience, good and evil, meaning and meaninglessness of existence, and the moral imperative that humanity is seemingly 'infected with' terminally—remains without rational explanation. Apparently, Darwinian man did not react to the world he was a part of in a Darwinian way. Even the most evolved animal species show no trace of similar concepts, dilemmas, or limitations. This primordial idealism, with its notions of the forbidden, the cursed, the taboo, and the 'secret', appears universally and without exception as an integral part of primeval human consciousness. Wherever humanity appeared, religion and art followed. Science, in contrast, is a relatively recent concept. Humanity, religion, and art have always been inseparable. This phenomenon, which might hold answers to some of the most crucial questions of human existence, has not received the attention it deserves.[17]

---

17 Ancient Greek historian, Plutarch, writes: 'We can find a city without walls, rulers, civilisation, literature, and theatre, but man has never seen a city without a place for worship and with citizens that do not practise worshipping'. Nearly twenty centuries later, H. Bergson writes: 'Human groups without science, art, and philosophy existed and still exist, but never so far has a human group without religion existed'. *The Two Sources of Morality and Religion* (1935).

From a materialist perspective, the history of humankind must appear as a process of progressive secularisation (see, for example, Reinach in his book *Cults, Myths, and Religions*). Yet no one has ever provided a fully satisfactory explanation as to why the life of primitive humans was filled with cults, mysteries, prohibitions, and beliefs, in every time and every place. Why did they seek to breathe life and personality into everything—a star, a rock, a river?[18] Why did they see the world in this way and not differently? Conversely, why does civilised humanity objectify and depersonalise everything, reducing it to the inorganic and mechanical? For thousands of years, we have strived to rid ourselves of these primeval burdens without understanding their nature or origin.

This phenomenon of inner life, or gazing at the sky—whether in admiration or fear, matters little—remains as innately human as it is foreign to any animal, and it continues to defy logical explanation. It seems, quite literally, to be 'sent from heaven'. Since it is not a product of evolution, it essentially remains beyond the influence of evolutionary forces. After studying drawings in Neanderthal caves in France, the French scientist Henri Simple concluded that the psychological life of cavemen differed very little from that of modern humans. 'Even cavemen from 70,000 BCE suffered from metaphysical dizziness, the disease of modern humanity,' stated Simple at an Archaeological Congress in Nice in 1976. This phenomenon is clearly not a continuation of biological evolution but rather a further act in the drama that began with a 'prologue in heaven'.

During the zoological history that precedes the appearance of humanity, there is nothing that would in any way predict or even suggest the emergence of cults and primitive ethics. Even if we hypothetically extended this evolution for many centuries into the future, to any given moment in time, the

---

18 'Primitive man does not know of a world without life', H. A. Frankfort, *Before Philosophy: The Intellectual Adventure of Ancient Man.*

concept of taboo or cult would still be the last thing one might expect. Animal evolution—whether already completed or envisioned—does not move towards the irrational or the supernatural. It progresses towards physical perfection and intelligence, and further towards supra-intelligence and the supra-animal, what Friedrich Nietzsche termed the *Übermensch*, who is essentially a perfected animal.[19] Nietzsche's vision is inspired by Darwin: evolution, external and zoological in its essence, is extended further, but in a direction opposite to humanity. Yet, this development is simple, logical, and deducible because it remains in line with nature. The supra-animal is the result of the 'process' and, therefore, is a being without inner life, without drama or character, without humanity. It is not *Homo* but *Homunculus*, a creature from a test tube—like the one created by Doctor Faust in his laboratory, and nature, through a similar yet slightly drawn-out process, on its own.[20] I believe Soviet poet Andrei Voznesensky must have had similar facts or thought processes in mind when he concluded that 'The computers of the future will theoretically be able to do everything that a human can—everything but two things: they will not be able to be religious or write poetry.'

* * *

Just as animals have no concept of the holy or the forbidden, they also lack the concept of beauty or aesthetic pleasure in the human sense. The thesis that some monkeys are capable of drawing—based on certain 'drawings' attributed to these animals—has been shown to be entirely unfounded. It has been

19 Nietzsche's Übermensch is freed from 'ethical prejudices'. He writes, 'Struggle against mercy, conscience, and forgiveness, those inner human tyrants; suppress the weak, climb over their corpses upwards. For you are the children of a higher kind, for your ideal is the Übermensch.' Friedrich Nietzsche, *Thus Spoke Zarathustra* 1883-1885).

20 Literature has created many similar monsters. The common trait of all these creatures is extraordinary intelligence with a complete absence of 'moral sense'.

established that monkeys can successfully imitate humans who draw, but the so-called 'monkey art', which once caused a brief sensation, quite certainly does not exist.[21]

On the other hand, it is now almost certain that Cro-Magnon humans—the first true humans—drew and carved. Such drawings have been found on cave walls, bones, and horns. The artworks in the caves of the Sahara, Spain (Altamira), France (Lascaux Cave), and the recently discovered Maszycka Cave in Poland were the result of the aesthetic thrill experienced by primitive humans. Some of these drawings are estimated to be nearly 30,000 years old. Recently, a group of Soviet archaeologists discovered a set of musical instruments carved from mammoth bones near the Ukrainian town of Chernihiv, estimated to be around 20,000 years old. Decoration predates clothing; the desire for beauty is stronger than the need for mere function, and this can be observed in dress from prehistory to the present. Costume is not simply clothing; it is an attitude. The diverse traditional garments of various nations are not merely responses to the bare needs of the day or environmental conditions. At a certain point, garments become paintings; they almost transform into poetry. While animal fur or feathers can be beautiful, their beauty is inherent and unaffected by intention, making them mere natural phenomena rather than statements.

This beauty, with its brilliance and colours, always has a certain functionality at its core. Furthermore, it is almost impossible to separate cult from art in the spiritual songs and dances that were genuine spectacles. The first carved image in stone was an idol. Religious inspiration—albeit sometimes misdirected—created those beautiful stone figures of deities and the masks found in Oceania, Ivory Coast, and Mexico, often cited as examples of art born from pure, direct impressions.

---

21 In this regard, we have significant studies by the Soviet scientist V. Bukin.

All fine art, in its origins, is idol-worshipping, and this might explain Islam's (and some other less personality-centred religions') intolerance towards this form of art. It seems necessary to travel back to prehistoric times to clearly see how art emerged from religion, or perhaps how both, combined with primitive ethics, emanate from a shared source: humanity's longing for a lost world.

This distinction from animals can also manifest as rebellion, as seen in the works of Albert Camus. Animals do not rebel against their animal fate; they are either content or indifferent. Humans, however, are rebellious animals—the 'only animal that refuses to be so' (A. Camus, *L'Homme révolté*). This rebellion is purely human and is evident in highly developed and affluent societies where civilisation, zoological in its origin, attempts to impose inhuman existential standards: order, dehumanisation, general equalisation, mass conditioning, societal dominance over the individual, and so on.

* * *

Johan Huizinga identifies yet another phenomenon: play (*Homo Ludens*, 1938). Animals also play and have fun, but only humans engage in play with an implicit underlying spiritual function and the satisfaction of an inner need. Animal play always serves a biological purpose, whether it is part of courtship rituals or the developmental needs of offspring. Animal play is instinctual and functional; human play is free and disinterested. It implies an awareness of play itself and includes certain features that give it a purely spiritual meaning: seriousness, ceremoniality, and what Huizinga calls 'aimless pragmatism'.

A special kind of game, characterised by an extremely non-utilitarian and anti-zoological nature, is *potlatch*, which is, in fact, a universal phenomenon of primitive culture. In the aforementioned book, Huizinga devotes considerable attention to this phenomenon. *Potlatch*, inherently irrational and uneconomical by nature, belongs to the same order of things as primitive art and primitive ethics, with its prohibitions, taboos, and, concepts of good and evil. I find it necessary to cite a few of the most interesting paragraphs from this book:

> The agonistic basis of cultural life in archaic society has only been brought to light since ethnology was enriched by an accurate description of the curious custom practised by certain Indian tribes in British Columbia, now generally known as the *potlatch*. In its most typical form as found among the Kwakiutl tribe the *potlatch* is a great solemn feast, during which one of two groups, with much pomp and ceremony, makes gifts on a large scale to the other group for the express purpose of showing its superiority. The only return expected by the donors but incumbent on the recipients lies in the obligation of the latter to reciprocate the feast within a certain period and if possible to surpass it. This curious donative festival dominates the entire communal life of the tribes that know it: their ritual, their law, their art. Any important event will be the occasion for a *potlatch*—a birth, a death, a marriage, an initiation ceremony, a tattooing, the erection of a tomb, etc... However, by taking part in the feast the other clan incurs the obligation to give a potlatch on a still grander scale. Should it fail to do so it forfeits its name, its honour, its badge and totems, even its civil and religious rights... In the *potlatch* one proves one's superiority not merely by the lavish prodigality of one's gifts but, what is even more striking, by the wholesale destruction of one's possessions just to show that one can do without them. These destructions, too, are executed with dramatic ritual and are accompanied by haughty challenges. The action always takes the form of a contest: if one chieftain breaks a copper pot, or burns a pile of blankets, or smashes a canoe, his opponent is under an obligation to destroy at least as much or more if possible.... Such competitions in unbridled liberality, with the frivolous destruction of one's own goods as the climax, are to be found all over the world in more or

less obvious traces. Marcel Mauss was able to point to customs exactly like the *potlatch*, in Melanesia. In his *Essai sur le don* he found traces of similar customs in Greek, Roman and Old Germanic culture. Granet has evidence of both giving and destroying matches in Ancient Chinese tradition.

In the pagan Arabia of pre-Islamic times they are to be met with under a special name, which proves their existence as a formal institution. They are called mu'aqara... Mauss neatly sums up Held's theme by saying: 'The Mahabharata is the story of a gigantic *potlatch*.' ...The mental world in which the ceremony takes place is the world of honour, pomp, braggadocio and challenge. The performers dwell in the realms of chivalry and heroism, where illustrious names and coats of arms and splendid lineages bulk large. This is not the ordinary world of toil and care, the calculation of advantage or the acquisition of useful goods.... To the best of my knowledge, anthropology seeks the explanation of the *potlatch* mainly in magical and mythical ideas. G. W. Locker provides an excellent example of this in his book *The Serpent in Kwakiutl Religion* (Leyden, 1932). No doubt there is an intimate connection between the *potlatch* and the religious preconceptions of the tribes observing it... Such a society will be animated in the highest degree by things like group-honour, admiration for wealth and liberality, trust and friendship; it will lay great stress on challenges, bettings and 'darings' of all kinds, competitions, adventures and the everlasting glorification of the self by displays of studied indifference to material values. Its purpose is the mutual exchange, by the various tribes concerned, of certain articles having no economic value either as necessities or useful implements, but highly prized as precious and notorious ornaments. The objects have a sacred value, are possessed of powers, and each has a history relating how it was first won.[22]

22 Johan Huizinga, *Homo Ludens: A Study of the Play-Element in Culture*, trans. R.F.C. Hull (London: Routledge & Kegan Paul, 1949).

To destroy goods, to express indifference towards gain and material possessions, to prioritise principle over matter—even if done hypocritically—is an exclusively human quality. Nothing comparable exists in the animal kingdom, not even traces of it. For a time, it was believed that Darwin had completed the final teaching about humanity, just as Newton had completed the final teaching about the universe. But just as Newton's mechanical vision of the universe could not endure because it failed to explain certain phenomena, so too does Darwin's theory seem destined to be 'made relative' for similar reasons. Evolutionary theory cannot satisfactorily explain the first religious phase of humanity. Nor does it offer an explanation for certain phenomena from the civilisational phase of human development.

Why is humanity increasingly psychologically dissatisfied even as its material well-being improves? Why does the 'psychological' standard decline as the material standard rises? Why is the prevalence of suicides and psychological disorders directly proportional to GDP and education levels? Why is there more humanness at the beginning of evolution than at its end? Why does progress not equal humanisation? How is it that the art of so-called uncivilised parts of the world—such as Oceania and Africa—possesses a strength and revolutionary impact that surpasses much of the art from 'cultured' areas? These are the questions!

It is difficult for the human mind to relinquish the clear and acceptable visions of Darwin and Newton once acquainted with them. Newton's world is continuous, logical, simple, and predictable—just as Darwin's human is simple and one-dimensional: a being who fights for survival, satisfies needs, and strives for a balanced, functional world. But Einstein dismantled Newton's illusion, and now pessimistic philosophy and the failures of civilisation are dismantling Darwin's. Humanity is unpredictable, inexplicable, dissatisfied, steeped in doubt and fear—'curved', as Einstein would say. The philosophy of humanity awaits its overturn, its 'Einsteinian shift', having spent too long under a linear Darwinian vision. A new understanding of humanity will relate to Darwinian man as Einstein's universe relates to Newton's. If it is true that we are elevated through suffering and dulled through pleasure, it is because we possess a soul—and therein lies the difference between us and our animal ancestors. Neither is humanity 'tailored' according to Darwin, nor is the universe tailored according to Newton.

DUALISM OF THE LIVING WORLD

Can we produce life, and will we ever be able to? Does this ambition even lie within the scope of human capabilities? The answer is: yes, we can—if we can understand it. But can we even comprehend life?

Biology is not a science about the essence of life, but rather about the phenomenon of life, insofar as it is presented to us as an object, as much as life is a product. Here, we encounter the same dualism previously mentioned between animal and human, but now it is one level lower, in the matter–life relationship. Once again, we see on one side uniformity, quantity, repetition, causality, and mechanism, and on the other side originality, quality, growth, spontaneity, and organism. Life does not manifest as a mere extension of matter—neither in a mechanical nor dialectical sense—nor as its particularly complex and highly organised form. In some respects, life even contradicts the premises of our understanding of matter. It expresses a nature that is fundamentally opposed to matter.

According to the latest understanding in biology, entropy plays a crucial role in defining life. All the laws governing matter ultimately reduce to entropy—universal disorganisation, the tendency of any system to move towards the lowest degree of order and energy. Conversely, the defining attribute of living systems—the one from which all others derive—is their opposition to entropy, a state of 'anti-entropy', the ability to create complexity from simplicity, order from chaos, and to maintain a system, even temporarily, at a higher energy level. Every material system moves towards higher entropy, while every living system follows the opposite course. They are turned 'back to back' because, as Soviet cyberneticist Kuznetsov once said, 'life means moving against the wind of mechanical laws'.

The author of these lines is not a biologist and must therefore limit himself to quoting authorities in this field. The inability of biology and psychology to offer deeper insights into the very essence of their subjects—life and psyche—is a striking fact that cannot be overlooked. By acknowledging this fact, the author merely wishes to highlight that this failure was not unexpected. In 1950, André George conducted a survey for *Nouvelles Littéraires*, asking biologists, doctors, surgeons, and physicists a single question: *What is life?* He noted that their answers were almost universally characterised by uncertainty and caution. Pierre Lepin replied: 'Mystery remains complete. Our ignorance makes every explanation we could possibly give about life less clear than the instinctual knowledge we have of it.' Jean Rostand,[23] perhaps the greatest living biologist of his time, provided the following response: 'If we say that we truly know only the things we make, then at present we do not know what life is. We are not even capable of providing an entirely accurate definition of the phenomenon of life.'

> It is by avoiding the rapid decay into the inert state of 'equilibrium' that an organism appears so enigmatic; so much so, that from the earliest times of human thought some special non-physical and supernatural force (*vis viva, entelechy*) was claimed to be operative in the organism, and in some quarters is still claimed... How does the living organism avoid decay? Every process, event, happening – call it what you will; in a word, everything that is going on in Nature means an increase of the entropy of the part of the world

23 Died in 1977.

> where it is going on. Living organisms counteract this tendency, aka stay alive by continuously consuming negative entropy from their surroundings. What an organism feeds upon is negative entropy.[24]

French palaeontologist Teilhard de Chardin writes in the same vein:

> Indeed, despite many obstacles, this curve that leads from big molecules to multicellular beings continues uninterrupted: this curve is the exact one where (separate from coincidence and big numbers) life events and indeterminants, self-editing and consciousness appear. The question follows from this setup: is there some sort of connection between this mysterious movement of the world towards states ever more complex and inward and the other movement (the one far better studied and well-known) that drives this world towards states ever more simple and outward.... The essential puzzle of the whole Universe is maybe trying to fit into this question and get formulated for future scientific inquiry.

Alexis Carrel, in *Man, the Unknown*, states:

> The spontaneous tendency of cells to build organs, as well as the social behaviours of certain insects, are among the fundamental facts we have observed; we will not find an explanation for these in the world of our current understanding.[25]

Distinguished biologist Kurt Goldstein writes:

> However, to find that solution, can we act in this regard the way we are used to doing when it comes to inanimate nature? Are we allowed to divide a specific object, then observe the smallest particles created by that division, and from these attempt to reconstruct the object—in our case, an organism—in the same way we do in other natural

24 Erwin Schrödinger, *What is Life?* (1944).

25 Carrel, *Man, the Unknown* (1935).

> sciences? This method has long been imposed upon biological research, or rather, it has seemed the ideal of biological research. In truth, it has yielded only marginally satisfying results. But then, how do we proceed? Here, at the outset of our presentation, we can make only one negative statement: that method is unsatisfactory one way or another.

After noting the correlation between the subject and the method, Goldstein concludes:

> Instead of following the traditional rules of researching lower forms before higher forms, and simple forms before complex ones, we should adopt the opposite approach when studying the phenomenon of the organism. Therefore, by taking the human being as our starting point, we shall attempt to analyse the life and behaviour of other living creatures.[26]

Karl Jaspers, in *General Psychopathology* (1934), reflects on this 'reverse' nature of life:

> In psychopathology, our genetic understanding (or perception of meaningful connection) soon reaches its limits. (We can call this process 'psychological explanation' if we like, but then we must keep it clearly distinct, as of a different order from objective causal explanation, which is the perception of causal connection in the strict sense.) In psychopathology, psychic phenomena appear suddenly as something entirely new, in a way we cannot understand at all. One psychic event follows another quite incomprehensibly; it seems to follow arbitrarily rather than emerge. Stages of psychic development in normal people, psychic phases and episodes in abnormal people are all incomprehensible events and appear as purely temporal sequences. It is equally difficult to understand the whole range of a person's psychic development and its full meaning in genetic terms. We can only resort

26 Quotes from Goldstein's book: *The Organism: A Holistic Approach to Biology Derived from Pathological Data in Man.*

> to causal explanation, as with phenomena in the natural sciences, which, as distinct from psychological phenomena, are never seen 'from within' but 'from the outside' only.[27]

In continuation, Jaspers points out the difference between understanding (*verstehen*), which is achieved through psychological 'interpenetration', and explaining (*erklären*), which represents the discovery of objective cause-and-effect relationships through the method of natural sciences, concluding: 'Here, it is a matter of ultimate sources of knowledge, which differ profoundly from one another.'

Louis de Broglie, winner of the Nobel Prize in Physics in 1929, writes: 'It is therefore probable that it is impossible to give a complete explanation of life using our current physical-chemical knowledge.'

Swiss biologist Émile Guyénot advocates the important distinction between life and physico-chemical processes, explaining:

> Physicists should be aware that we biologists, who have invested so much effort into expressing life in physical and chemical formulas, have found something that cannot be solved, and that is life itself. Life has found an organised form—not once, but millions of times, over billions of years. There is a constructive ability that escapes any physical and chemical explanation.

André Lwoff, winner of the Nobel Prize in Medicine in 1965 (a French biologist distinguished for his research on hereditary mechanisms in viruses and bacteria), stated:

> Life can be defined as a characteristic, manifestation, or state of an organism. An organism is an independent system of mutually dependent structures and functions that is capable of self-replication.... It is often said that viruses

27 Let us recall Hegel's maxims: 'Matter is outside itself. Spirit has its centre within itself. Spirit is existence contained within itself.'

> are the connection between organic substances and living matter. In fact, there is no such thing as living matter. A cell element, such as protein, enzyme, or nucleic acid, is not alive. Only an organism is alive, and an organism represents much more than the sum of its parts. We have succeeded in synthesising proteins and nucleic acids of viruses in vitro. But we cannot speak of synthesising life from these because, in all such research experiments, one substance is necessarily borrowed by the virus—genetic material specific to nucleotides.... Life was born spontaneously at some point. It is easy to synthesise certain ingredients of proteins or nucleic acids, but so far it has been impossible to create an organism itself.... For now, it is beyond our powers to reconstruct even a single bacterium. [28]

Famous experimental psychologist Ivan Pavlov expresses similar scepticism:

> Humanity has been investigating psychological phenomena—those relating to spiritual life and the human soul—for thousands of years. It is not only specialist psychologists who deal with this question, but all of art, literature, and every form of psychological exploration of human life. Thousands of pages have been filled with demonstrations of human inner life, yet we have not achieved any success with these efforts; we have not discovered any law that governs the psychological life of humans.[29]
>
> The methods that organs use to build themselves are foreign to the human mind.... All of that material resulting from one single cell, it is as if an entire house would arise out of a single piece of magic brick that would eject a whole series of other bricks out of itself. Then these would join together to form walls, windows, roofing tiles, coal for heating, and water for the kitchen and bathroom—all without waiting

28 From an interview in *Le Monde* magazine in 1965.

29 Ivan Pavlov, *Psychologie experimentale.*

> for an architect's plan or the arrival of masons. Organs are developed using the means and methods that fairies used in children's tales from times past. Our mind cannot find itself in the world of inner organs.... It constructed its own model based on the cosmic universe, not on the complicated inner mechanism of living creatures.[30]

And further:

> We have yet to grasp the organisation of our body, its nutritional, nervous, and spiritual energy. The laws of physics and chemistry apply fully to inanimate matter but only partially to humans. We must completely discard the illusions of the nineteenth century, the dogmas of Jacques Loeb, and the childish physico-chemical ideas of the human being that many physiologists and doctors sadly still believe in today.

Life is a wonder, not a phenomenon.

A human eye consists of the eyeball, inserted into the eye socket coated with fat. Its protective apparatus includes the upper and lower eyelids, eyelashes, eyebrows, mucous membranes, and commissures. Eye movement in all directions is enabled by the motor apparatus, consisting of four rectus and two oblique eye muscles, and facilitated by the tear apparatus (lacrimal gland, lacrimal sac, and lacrimal ducts and canaliculi), which maintains moisture levels in the eye socket and protects the eye from infections.

The eyeball is composed of three main membranes: first, the solid and opaque sclera, which transitions into the transparent cornea; beneath the sclera lies the choroid, rich in blood vessels that provide oxygen and nutrients to the eye; and the third, inner membrane—the retina (neural tunic)—which contains the receptive apparatus for vision: light-sensitive cells in the shape of rods and cones, where the optic nerve fibres begin. The inside of the eyeball is filled with an elastic

---

30 Carrel, *Man, the Unknown* (1935).

and transparent vitreous body (vitreous humour). The biconvex lens is located in front of the vitreous humour, attached to the ciliary body by fine fibres (zonules) and positioned behind the iris. Light rays pass through the cornea into the eye, refract through the lens, and project onto the retina, forming reversed images of objects, which are then transferred by the optic nerve to the visual centres in the brain. Each eye receives the image of an object from a different angle. Nerve signals travel to subcortical visual centres and then to the occipital cortex, where visual perception is formed. A single, plastic image of the object is created by combining images from both eyes.

Tears, secreted by the lacrimal glands, are indispensable for eye function. They maintain corneal moisture and contain lysozyme, an enzyme that dissolves microorganisms, protecting the eyes from infections. The activity of the lacrimal glands is regulated by the seventh cranial nerve (*nervus facialis*). As a bactericide, human tears surpass pharmaceutical products, destroying over 100 different pathogens, even when diluted up to 6,000 times.

The liver performs numerous functions: it secretes bile as an exocrine gland, stores iron and vitamin B12, and detoxifies substances through complex processes of oxidation, reduction, hydrolysis, and conjugation. Numerous processes of intermediary metabolism also take place in the liver. It also regulates blood glucose levels by storing glycogen.

Blood transports nutrients to various body parts, carries oxygen from the lungs to tissues, removes waste, distributes hormones and antibodies that serve as the body's defence, and participates in regulating bodily temperature. White blood cells destroy foreign matter and bacteria that enter into an organism.

The brain consists of the forebrain (with two large cerebral hemispheres), the diencephalon, the midbrain, and the hindbrain (including the pons—*Varoli's bridge*—and the medulla oblongata). It is enveloped by three membranes: *dura mater* (hard), *pia mater* (soft), and the *arachnoid* (connective). The brain tissue consists of grey and white matter. The grey matter contains nerve (ganglionic) cells, while the white matter contains the endings of motor and sensory nerve fibres. The nuclei of most sensory and effector cranial nerves are located in the medulla oblongata and the pons. The spinal cord plays a major role in carrying out reflex actions and transmits nerve impulses from the spinal cord to the higher cortical centres of the brain and vice versa.

The cerebellum regulates balance and muscle tone. The midbrain includes the cerebral peduncles and a plate with four colliculi, which are involved in visual and auditory reflexes. In the anterior two colliculi, the fibres of the visual pathway cross, which are involved in the reflex of the pupil of the eye, while the posterior colliculi are part of the subcortical auditory centre. The midbrain area contains the nuclei of cranial nerves, with the most important being the substantia nigra, the red nucleus, and the nuclei of the eye motor nerves.

The midbrain directly transitions into the small diencephalon. The main part of the diencephalon consists of the visual colliculi, which serve as collectors of fibres directed towards the centre, transmitting impulses from most of the body's receptors. The grey matter in the cerebrum forms the surface or cortex of the cerebral hemispheres, where subcortical nerve clusters are found: the striatum and the corpus callosum. In higher mammals and humans, the so-called corpus callosum is particularly developed, with its fibres connecting the two hemispheres. The cortex of the cerebral hemispheres coordinates the entire highly complex activity of nerve elements, thus enabling the realization of higher mental functions, especially the mechanism of conditioned reflexes. The average weight of the human brain ranges from 1300 to 1450 grams and contains fourteen–fifteen billion nerve cells.

Animals possess tools far greater and more perfected than many human-made ones: car headlights mirrored in birds' night vision, the violin in grasshoppers, the dulcimer in crickets and an entire set of traps, snares, nets, loops, adhesives, suckers, etc. André Tétry devoted an entire book to these.[31] Evolution, it seems, did not develop blindly or mechanically, as Darwin envisioned (because natural selection acts precisely so). The principle of utility evident in evolution suggests an inherent meaning that cannot be found in matter alone—meaning always implies awareness of a goal.[32]

The rattlesnake possesses an unusual ability to perceive and respond to infrared rays. Scientists from the University of Colorado have established that this highly sensitive 'infrared detector' is located on the snake's head and consists of very thin nerve branches with specific cells that change according to the light that falls on them. Experiments have shown that the snake's reflex is triggered as quickly as 35 milliseconds after the emission of a light impulse, a record speed of reaction for a biological system.

Similarly, sharks possess highly sensitive electrical 'antennae' in their noses, enabling them to detect food hidden in the sand at the bottom of the sea. All marine organisms produce weak electrical waves, which sharks detect through these antennae.

Dr Aleksandr Gorbovsky, a member of the Soviet Academy of Sciences, revisits an old idea—supported by Einstein—that the very structure of matter and the universe possesses mysterious features we attribute to reason. Here are a few interesting excerpts from his analysis:

> A whole multitude of termites, thousands and thousands of them, participate in building the termite mound. Then, after the construction work is done, a very complex foundry

---

31 See André Tétry, *Les outils chez les êtres vivants* (1948).

32 See Lucien Cuénot, *Invention finalité en biologie* (1941).

arises, with a surface greater than 100 cubic metres and a height of about 3–4 metres, with a well-constructed system of passages, ventilation ducts, food storage units, and special rooms for larvae.

The following experiment has been conducted: a termite mound whose construction had just begun was divided into two parts, completely separating the termites. However, despite this separation, the construction continued successfully, with all the lines, canals, rooms, and storages in both parts built identically—with mutual junctions.

One could assume that each termite was precisely informed about the work its counterpart did in the neighbouring section and then replicated it exactly! Yet, it knew nothing about the fate of its counterpart, nor could it communicate with it. Let us try to explain this phenomenon. It is clear that each termite individually is incapable of receiving complete information about the construction of the entire mound. Each unit can only know the part of the process in which it is involved. Therefore, it can be concluded that the repository of all information is the termite population as a whole. Thus, we now speak of knowledge—Great Knowledge—that only exists within a community whose members belong to the same species.

But this is not an isolated phenomenon. When a swarm of grasshoppers flies, they follow a strictly specified route. If we separate one grasshopper from the swarm and place it in a closed box, it immediately loses its sense of direction and begins to panic, rushing aimlessly in every direction.

However, if we place the box back in the centre of the moving swarm, the captive grasshopper immediately finds its bearings and persistently rushes in only one direction—the direction of its swarm!

In other words, when it comes to independent organisms, Great Knowledge (collective knowledge) appears only at

> the level of the community and does not exist at the individual level.
>
> It was long believed that a flock of migratory birds, which travels to warmer regions annually, was led by an older, more experienced bird. But facts have disproved this assumption. Japanese ornithologist, Professor Yamamoto Hirosuke, discovered that a flock of birds flies without a guide. If, by chance, a single bird is found at the front, it does not mean it is leading the others. Sometimes, a weak, featherless chick can be seen at the head of the flock. According to Yamamoto Hirosuke, in six out of ten cases, a flock of birds is led by a young bird that only hatched that summer.
>
> It is very clear that such a bird does not 'know' the traditional flying route and cannot lead older, more experienced birds who know the route well.

Gorbovsky continues:

> It is well known that, biologically, the birth ratio of male and female individuals is almost equal. But if that normal ratio is disturbed and one sex becomes dominant, a spontaneous process of equalisation occurs. If females are in the minority, more females will be born; if males are in the minority, their numbers will increase proportionately. This process continues until the sex ratio is balanced.
>
> It is, however, clear that an individual organism cannot influence the sex of its offspring at will. In other words, we are once again faced with a phenomenon that suggests a certain lawfulness. Once again, we encounter a directed action, an external influence whose source lies outside any independent organism.
>
> Humanity knows this phenomenon well. Demographers call it the 'phenomenon of wartime.' In times of war and immediately afterwards, when there is a significant loss of

men, their numbers soon increase proportionately, restoring the disrupted balance.

A couple of examples I cited earlier are taken from the closest biology textbook I had at hand. Religion explains these true wonders of nature through the Highest Mind—God. All scientific explanations, however, reduce to the same stance: that all of these phenomena simply came into existence on their own. A greater superstition could hardly be imposed upon the human spirit. Asking me to accept that something as perfect and complex as the human eye or brain has emerged by accident or on its own is akin to asking me to accept the entirety of Greek mythology as truth. We might prefer to conclude with the thought of the great Islamic thinker, Abu Hamid al-Ghazali: 'All wonders are natural, and all of nature is wonderful.'

* * *

So, what is the situation with this famous 'self-organisation of matter', with the supposed spontaneous emergence of highly complex tools that fill the living world? Let us attempt to illustrate this with the example of the self-creation (accidental formation) of a single protein molecule, which serves as the material basis for every known living form on Earth.

Swiss physicist Charles Eugène Guye attempted to calculate the probability of one protein molecule forming by pure chance. It is known that a protein molecule consists of at least four different elements. For simplicity, Guye assumed a molecule composed of just two elements, made up of 2,000 atoms with an atomic weight of 10 and a dissymmetry of 0.9. Under these simplified conditions, Guye calculated the probability of a protein molecule originating by chance as 2.02×10^{321}.

When observed in the context of the time and size of our planet, this result suggests that the probability of forming just one Guye's molecule would require 10^{243} billion years, assuming a frequency of 500 trillion (5×10^{14}) oscillations per second. This far exceeds the estimated age of our planet, which is approximately 2 billion years, and completely excludes the possibility that life emerged by chance in that time.

The calculation was later repeated by Manfred Eigen from the Max Planck Institute for Biophysical Chemistry in Göttingen, Germany, a Nobel Prize winner in Chemistry (1968). Eigen demonstrated that neither our planet nor all its water would be sufficient to generate even a single protein molecule by pure chance. Even if the entire universe were filled with chemical substances continuously combining over the ten billion years since its formation, it would still be insufficient for the creation of a specific protein molecule. Confronted with this fact, Eigen proposed the hypothesis of evolution before life or 'life before life', as it came to be known—essentially admitting that nucleic acids possess some life-like properties. In any case, the presence of a principle of order, selection, and adjustment within matter—opposed to chaos and entropy—cannot be reconciled with the traditional definition of matter.

British scientists Sir Fred Hoyle, former President of the Royal Astronomical Society, and Professor Chandra Wickramasinghe from the University of Cardiff proposed that life did not originate on Earth but was 'imported' from the depths of space via interstellar dust clouds. According to them, biological activity in the cosmos began long before the formation of Earth.

Russian author R. Balandin writes:

> Even if a million laboratories worked on earth for millions of years synthesising chemical compounds by chance, the probability of creating life in a test tube would remain minimal. According to J. Holden's calculations, such a chance occurs in 1.310×10^{30} of all possibilities.

This is the state of affairs regarding the self-organisation of a single protein molecule, which is to a living organism what a brick is to a completed building. How, then, can we explain the perfection of the human eye, even when applying the 'highest level' principles of matter's self-organisation?

* * *

Science, particularly molecular biology, has succeeded in reducing the vast gap between animate and inanimate matter to an almost infinitesimal one. Yet, to those knowledgeable in the field, this seemingly small gap remains vast and hopelessly insurmountable. Underestimating or ignoring this gap is unscientific and aligns with the tendencies of official materialism.

How do we explain the following paradox: if, during an excavation, we find two rocks arranged in a certain way or polished for some purpose, we conclude that this is the work of humans from the distant past. But if we find a human skull next to that same tool—infinitely more perfect than the stone implement—we do not make the same assumption that it is the construction of an intelligent being. Such a perfect skull or skeleton, we are told, came into existence by accident or through random processes, without any guidance from reason or awareness. Is not human denial of God sometimes capricious?

The narrow-mindedness of modern humanity is most evident in its conviction that everything is clear and understood. Its wisdom is merely the sum of its knowledge combined with an immense amount of ignorance it fails to recognise—or worse, treats as knowledge. Even when faced with the greatest mysteries, modern man behaves with confidence and conceit. He fails to see a puzzle where one exists, and therein lies the clearest reflection of his colossal ignorance and prejudice.

Swallows from Central Europe fly to distant African lands each autumn, only to return in spring to the exact same roof where they left their nest. How do they know not only that they must go, but precisely when to embark on this distant journey? How do they find their nest again, under the roof of one house among thousands, in a city of millions?

Our conceited ignoramus smoothly responds to this question: it is simple—an instinct guides them. Or it is natural selection; the swallow species that 'figured out' they should migrate to warmer areas in winter survived. The species that did not figure that out were destroyed. In constant battle with environmental conditions, in which this bird evolved, swallows gradually realised that they should migrate if they wished to survive. Their migration instinct is a result of this wisdom gathered through thousands of generations, etc.

The issue is not the vacuousness of the answer itself; it is that our conversational partner believes they have provided an explanation, thereby dismissing the puzzle—the very foundation of inquiry and the pursuit of truth. A false answer is as dangerous as a fake medicine. It does not cure and, in the meantime, prevents further attempts; it fosters a false sense of certainty. It is precisely because Einstein saw a puzzle where others believed all was explained that we now have the general theory of relativity.

After all, the purpose of all art, philosophy, and religion is to direct human attention towards puzzles, mysteries, and questions. It awakens our consciousness, not necessarily to provide knowledge, but to transform our unrecognised ignorance into recognised ignorance. This distinction is what infinitely separates a wise man from a simpleton. Both may know equally little about a hidden question, but unlike the wise man, the simpleton mistakes his ignorance for knowledge and behaves as though everything is clear to him. In short, he is blind to the problem—in this case, blind to the miracle. (This dynamic often has tragic consequences in real life: simpletons act with confidence, while wise men behave like Hamlet and ponder endlessly—sometimes giving the former a considerable advantage.)

This state of mind is the exact opposite of the spiritual state of meditation, for meditation arises where the world is full of questions, mysteries, and secrets. There is no meditation where 'everything is clear'. Plato said that the feeling of wonder is the source of all philosophy, and Jaspers observed that 'to wonder means to strive for knowledge'. The feelings of mystery and meditation are intertwined. Religion and meditation converge at this point—it is a congruent state of the spirit. Ignoring mystery is one of the key characteristics of practical atheism.

The life of the 'mass man' is shaped by the absence of meditation. Such a person notices no puzzles or mysteries anywhere. He neither wonders nor feels astonishment; he is not gripped by the fear of the unknown. In a word, he does not live through his spirit. When faced with a question, he labels it, names it, and then continues living under the delusion that the problem is solved by this mere act. Terms like instinct, self-organisation of matter at a higher level, and complex forms of highly organised matter serve as such labels.

We cannot understand life solely through science because life is as much a wonder as it is a phenomenon. 'A tree surprised me to admiration', says painter Jean Dubuffet. Wonder and admiration are the highest—and perhaps the only—forms of our perception and understanding of life.

MEANING OF HUMANISM

'To aim for pleasure and run from pain'—two great representatives of materialist thought, Epicurus in antiquity and Holbach in the West, define the foundations of all life and the ultimate basis of not only human but also animal behaviour with this one lapidary sentence. Materialism will always seek similarities between humans and animals, while religion will always emphasise their differences. The purpose of many cults and religious prohibitions is to underline or emphasise this distinction. In some cases, we observe a distinct materialist interest in proving the animalistic nature of humans—an interest that transcends mere pursuit of truth.[33]

Darwin did not turn man into an animal, but he did reintroduce awareness of humanity's animal origins. Corresponding moral and political conclusions naturally followed from this new awareness: that human collectives are herds (swarms, hives) in a civilised form; that civilisation is humanity's sobering up, its conquest of nature, its transcendence of biological existence—living through the senses rather than through the spirit.

Evolution erased the contradiction between nature and culture by establishing continuity between animal and human.

---

33 A good example of this is the persistent insistence of materialists on the state of unlimited sexual relations in the prehistory of human society, when every woman belonged to every man, and every man to every woman. Engels explicitly admits that there is no direct evidence that such a state ever existed, but continues to insist on this thesis. See F. Engels, *The Origin of the Family, Private Property and the State* (1884).

Religion, starting from an entirely opposite premise, reinforced this contradiction. Since the act of Creation, humanity—and with it the entirety of culture—has been in inevitable conflict with the entire flow of human history. This is where the schism between culture and civilisation began. 'Man is an animal that refuses to be one.' (A. Camus)

The essence of the religious stance lies precisely in this negative fact, in this 'great rejection' (A.N. Whitehead). It is as though religion commands: observe what animals do and do the opposite—they devour, you fast; they copulate, you abstain; they gather into herds, you isolate yourselves; they seek pleasure and avoid pain, you expose yourselves to hardship. In a word, they live through their bodies—you live through your spirit.

This refusal of zoological positioning—this 'negative striving'—is entirely inexplicable from a rational or Darwinian standpoint, yet it remains an authoritative fact of human life. It may be a human curse or privilege, but it is the only real truth about human existence. Remove this human 'rebellion', and human life vanishes instantly. Without it, there is no religion, art, poetry, sacrifice, or drama—only existence, mere functioning, meaningless and void.

A complete parallel and absolute incompatibility exist between a human and an animal. The similarity between human and animal lies in the biological, constitutional, and therefore mechanical aspect. However, absolute incompatibility exists in the essential, spiritual view. An animal is innocent, sinless, and morally neutral—just like an object. A human is never these things. From the moment of the 'humanisation of the animal', from that dramatic 'prologue in heaven' or 'fall to Earth', humanity has had no option for animal innocence. Man is 'set free' without the possibility of return, making every Freudian solution irrelevant. He cannot be both man and animal; he can only be man or not-man.

If man were merely a more perfect animal, his life would be simple and devoid of puzzles. But because man is the 'worm of the earth and child of the sky', because he is created, he is a creature of discord—incapable of 'Euclidean harmony'. Not only all the profound truths but also all the terrible fallacies of human life are rooted in the fact of Creation. It is not only humanity's greatness, morality, striving, and tragedy that stem from it, but also its dilemmas, dissatisfactions, curses, atrocities, and wickedness.[34] An animal knows none of these, marking the significance of this epochal moment.

The problem of Creation is essentially the question of freedom. If you accept that man has no freedom, that all his actions are predetermined—whether by internal or external forces—then God becomes redundant for explaining and understanding the world as you perceive it. But if you recognise freedom in man, if you make him responsible, you also—implicitly or explicitly—acknowledge God. Only God can create a free being, and such freedom can only be bestowed through the act of Creation.[35] It cannot arise as a product of evolution.

Freedom and product are disparate, opposing concepts. No product, whether emerging suddenly or through evolution, can possess freedom. Neither God nor an artist constructs a personality—they create it. The one who constructs produces not a personality, but a schematic poster-man. Personality cannot be constructed.

I know what a portrait would mean without God—it simply would not exist. Perhaps humanity, sooner or later—by the end of this century or after a millennium of civilisational

34 Compare: '(By the soul) and He Who proportioned it, and inspired it with discernment between its right and wrong...' Qur'an, 91:7–8

35 A man who is truly aware of his freedom simultaneously becomes certain of the existence of God. Freedom and God are inseparable. Furthermore: 'If the certainty of freedom contains within itself the certainty of God's being, then there is a connection between the denial of freedom and the denial of God.' (Karl Jaspers, *Introduction to Philosophy* (1951))

progress—will produce its imitation: a robot or a monster remarkably similar to its creator. Such a human-like machine might resemble a human in many ways, but one thing is already certain: it will not be free. It will only be able to perform the tasks programmed into it by its creator.

Herein lies the greatness of God's creation—the uniqueness of this act, incomparable to anything that has occurred in the universe before or after. A free creature began to exist in one neon of eternity. Without this divine touch, humanity would not exist as the result of evolution, only a higher form of animal—a super-animal—a monster with human intelligence and a human body, but without heart or character.

His intelligence would be even more efficient and ruthless if stripped of moral scruples. Some have imagined such creatures as beings from distant planets; others have seen them as products of our civilisation on some notional level. One such creature appears in Goethe's *Faust*, but it is the quasi-human Homunculus, not a man. It is important to note that there is no analogy between the amorality and soullessness of a Homunculus and the immorality of even the most deviant man. A man may act against moral laws, but he cannot—like a monster—exist outside the moral sphere, beyond good and evil; he cannot be 'disconnected'.

In practical moral experience, a man's ability to sin seems more apparent than his striving for righteousness. His capacity to sink to the depths of sin often appears greater than his ability to rise to the heights of virtue.[36] Negative characters always seem more truthful than positive ones, and the poet who portrays a negative character is invariably at an advantage over one who seeks to depict a hero. In any case, man is either good or evil, but never innocent—and that is perhaps the ultimate meaning of the biblical story of original sin. Humanity

36 '... indeed, the soul is inclined to evil.' Qur'an, 12:53

is not inherently sinful, but neither is it innocent. From the moment of expulsion from heaven, Adam (humanity) could no longer be innocent in the way that an angel or an animal is. He must choose, exercise his freedom, and be either good or bad—in other words, be human. This capacity for choice, regardless of its outcome, represents the highest form of existence possible in the universe.

Man has a soul, but psychology is not a science of the soul. There can be no science of the soul. Psychology addresses a certain domain of the illusory inner world—the part of the external world that is transient, destructible, and found within the human being; the part that is faceless and universal. This is why we have psychophysiology, psychometrics, psychohygiene, and the physics of the psyche. The possibility of quantitative psychology confirms the thesis of the external, mechanical, and quantitative—therefore non-spiritual—nature of thoughts and feelings.

The animalistic and the human can form a whole precisely because psychology concerns itself not with the soul, but with the manifestations of the psychological. The renowned psychologist John Watson writes:

> Human psychology, as a behaviourist understands it, must be modelled on the objective and experimental psychology of animals, borrowing from them its subject matter, methodology, and goals, so that there are no two psychologies—human and animal—separated by an iron curtain, unaware of each other and having radically different subjects, methods, and goals, but one unique psychology that takes its place among the natural sciences.

This quote speaks for itself. In the East, they would say that psychology is a science of *nafs* but not of *ruh*. Psychology operates on the biological level, not the individual (personal) level. There are three circles: mechanical, biological, and personalistic, corresponding to three degrees of reality—matter, life, and personality.

Scientific thought will always attempt to impose its method upon the spiritual realm, inevitably introducing and reinforcing absolute causality—thereby negating freedom, which is the essence of the soul. Our effort to 'study' the soul must inevitably lead to the negation of the subject matter. It is impossible to escape this vicious circle, which explains why psychoanalysis is inherently tied to atheistic conclusions, starting from its very method.

* * *

The equality and brotherhood of men are possible only if God created man. Human equality is a spiritual fact, not a natural (physical or intellectual) one. It exists as the equal moral value of each human being, as human dignity, and as the unalienable worth of every human personality. Conversely, as physical, intellectual, and social beings—as members of groups, nations, classes, and political systems—humans are profoundly unequal, a fact we ignore in vain.

Deny the spirituality of man—this fact of religious nature—and you lose the realistic foundation of human equality, reducing it to an unsupported phrase that crumbles when faced with the undeniable facts of human inequality, or worse, with the natural human drive to dominate and be dominated, to be unequal. Once the religious approach is abandoned, the void it leaves is quickly filled by various forms of inequality—racial, national, class-based, political...[37]

---

37 A characteristic example in this regard is the debate that took place in China in 1974 about the fourteenth century novel *Water Margin*, better known globally through Pearl Buck's English translation under the title *All Men Are Brothers*. The novel, considered one of the most valuable works of Chinese classical literature, is a story about a peasant rebellion in the early twelfth century against the imperial administration. Because of its message of universal human brotherhood, it was cited as an 'instructive negative

Human dignity cannot be derived from biology, psychology, or science in general. It is a question of spiritual nature. Science, with its 'objective observation', is more likely to establish human inequality than equality, making 'scientific racism' a plausible and logical outcome.[38]

The ethics of Socrates, Pythagoras, and other ancient thinkers, at its best, does not lag behind the ethics of revealed religions (Judaism, Christianity, Islam). However, the difference is clear: only the ethics of revealed religions unequivocally postulate the equality of all people as God's creation.

In antiquity, a man was strongly bound to his community, state, nation, or class. Even a mind as extraordinary as Plato's could not discard the notion of necessary human inequality. Conversely, revealed religions established the common origin of all humans and, therefore, absolute equality and equal rights, forming the cornerstone of their worldview. This idea has had immense importance for all subsequent spiritual, ethical, and social developments of humanity.

The connection between human equality and the concept of immortality has not been thoroughly explored, but the history of ethics leads us to conclude that the idea of human equality is always tied to the concept of immortality. Religions and moral systems that lack clear notions of immortality also lack

---

example' of a non-class-based approach, as 'all men are not brothers', as emphasised in this debate.

In Hungary, on the other hand, according to a normative act of the Ministry of Education (1976), all schoolchildren were categorised in such a way that a simple review of school documents could determine the children's class origin (six categories, from 'a' to 'f'). Public reaction to this classification, however cautious it may have been, showed that it was perceived as a measure of division and discrimination. Some people always seem to have ideas of distinction and inequality swirling in their minds.

38 Evolutionism, for example, cannot in any way be reconciled with the idea of equality, nor with the concept of natural (inalienable) human rights. Even the 'Égalité' of the French Revolution has a religious origin (see Chapter IX of this book).

the concept of equality. Without God, humans are evidently and hopelessly unequal.

Nietzsche claimed that religion was invented by the weak to deceive the strong. Marx claimed the opposite. If religion is indeed an 'invention', Nietzsche's version seems more convincing, as the weak, oppressed, and less capable could only base their demands for equality, freedom, and dignity on religious grounds. Everything besides religion—even science—implacably confirms human inequality.

In practice, only religion sees equally worthy human quality in all humans and views them all the same. Why are the most crippled, disabled, sick, and impoverished always found near all the temples we enter? The temple alone opens its doors to those exiled from the feasts of the world—from places where name, lineage, wealth, education, and ability matter. It declares these people who have nothing to show or prove—these 'poor spirited'—equal and equally worthy, for even factory gates admit only the healthy and educated, while the sick and illiterate are left outside. But in a temple, a poor blind man can stand beside a king or a potentate—and may even be deemed greater than him, as illustrated in the Qur'an (Surah 'Abasa).

The greatest cultural and humane significance of temples lies in this constant testimony of equality. Meanwhile, the most profound and moving purpose of art is to recognise humanity in the broken, to find greatness in the small and forgotten, and to reveal the human soul—equally worthy and exalted in every person. The lower the social and physical standing of the hero, the greater and more striking this discovery becomes (think of Quasimodo, Fantine, Jean Valjean).

The greatness of Russian classical literature lies precisely in this.[39]

---

39 A text by Virginia Woolf is dedicated to this matter. She writes, 'The soul is the main character in Russian artistic prose. Delicate and subtle in Chekhov,

Therefore, and above all, humanism is not charity, forgiveness, or tolerance, even though it generally results in all of these. Humanism is an affirmation of the human being and their freedom, a confirmation of their worth as a human—nothing more, nothing less.

Everything that degrades the human personality and reduces it to the level of objects is inhuman. For example, it is human to hold a person responsible for their actions and to punish them accordingly. It is inhuman to demand that they repent, revise their attitude, 'improve', and then be pardoned. It is more humane to persecute people for their convictions than to coerce them into renouncing them by giving them the chance of pardon in exchange for 'sincere attitude'. Thus, there are punishments that are human and pardons that are entirely inhuman.

Inquisitors claimed they burned a man's body as a price to save his soul. Reducing a human to the function of producer and consumer, even if it guarantees every individual a place in production and consumption, is not humanism but dehumanisation. It is inhuman to subject people to dressage, even if it results in them becoming 'correct' and disciplined citizens.

Education can also be inhuman if it is one-sided, orchestrated, or indoctrinated; if it does not teach but offers ready-made solutions; if it prepares people solely for a function without broadening their horizons and thereby expanding their human freedom. Every manipulation of people, even if done with their best interests in mind, is inhuman. Thinking on behalf of a person and freeing them from all duties and obligations is equally inhuman.

---

it is deeper and greater in Dostoevsky, prone to fierce and frenzied fevers, yet always dominant. Dostoevsky's novels sow whirlwinds, swirling sandstorms, jets of water that hiss and gurgle, drawing us in. They are, through and through, composed of the soul.' (Virginia Woolf, 'The Russians and Their Outlook')

Humanity obliges—it does not free one from obligations. That is why God affirmed humanity in the highest degree by giving it the choice of two paths and threatening severe punishment.[40] We can only affirm the human being by following this divine example, by imitating the Creator: let us leave them the freedom to fight and choose, rather than fighting their battles and making their decisions for them.

Without religion and its 'prologue in heaven', there is no authentic belief that humanity is the greatest good. Without it, there is no faith that humanity is even possible or that it truly exists. Atheist humanism is a contradiction because, as Berdyaev stated:

'If there is no God, there is no man.'

If there is no man, humanism becomes an empty phrase devoid of real substance. Those who deny the Creation of humanity and reject the introduction of the primordial mystery cannot comprehend the true meaning of humanism. Such individuals will always reduce humanism to the production of goods and their distribution 'according to needs' because they have lost the fundamental compass.

It is an immense achievement to ensure that all people are fed, but as history has shown in wealthy societies, this alone does not guarantee a better or more humane world—especially not if certain individuals' ideas of general levelling, uniformity, and depersonalisation prevail at all levels.

In such a world, as described by Aldous Huxley in *Brave New World*, there would be no hunger, and equality, uniformity,

---

40 'We have certainly created man to live in struggle... Did We not give him two eyes, a tongue, and two lips, and guide him to two paths? But he did not choose the uphill path. And do you know what the uphill path is?—It is to forgive a slave, or to feed the hungry during a shortage, or to take care of an orphan of close kin or a poor person in great distress, and then to be among those who believe and exhort one another to patience and compassion.' Qur'an, 90: 4- 17

and stability would prevail in every aspect. Yet, all of us—whether consciously or instinctively—reject this vision as an example of total dehumanisation.

'A man is a product of his environment'—this foundational materialist stance forms the backbone of all subsequent inhuman theories in law and sociology, as well as the practices of human manipulation that culminated in the monstrous forms of Nazism and Stalinism in our century.

All other seemingly good and acceptable theories that prioritise society over the individual, and reduce the individual to serving society fall into the same category. A human being cannot serve anything—they cannot be a tool. Everything must serve humanity, and humanity must serve God. This is the first and the ultimate meaning of humanism.

CHAPTER 2

CULTURE AND CIVILISATION

A TOOL AND A CULT - TWO HISTORIES

Two contradictory facts are tied to the appearance of man: the first tool and the first cult. The first tool was a piece of wood or a rough-hewn rock—a fragment of nature. The crafting and use of tools represent the continuation of biological evolution, external and quantitative, which we can trace from the simplest life forms up to humanity as the perfect animal. Walking upright, the perfection of the hand, thought, speech, and intelligence are different degrees and stages of this evolution, which remains zoological in character.

When man first used a rock to crush a hard fruit shell or to throw it at an animal, he did something remarkable—but not entirely new, as his animal ancestors had already attempted and succeeded in similar feats. However, when he placed that rock before himself as a symbol of a spirit, he did something unprecedented in all of evolution—a phenomenon that would become a universal and indispensable part of human habitation everywhere on Earth. Likewise, when a man 'drew a line around his shadow in the sand and made a first painting that way' (Leonardo da Vinci), he embarked on an 'impossible activity' exclusive to humanity, something that no animal—regardless of evolutionary advancement—could ever achieve.

From a biological perspective, the appearance of man can be explained by the zoological history that preceded him. Yet, from a spiritual perspective, his emergence cannot be derived from or explained by anything that came before him.

Humanity came from another world—'from heaven', as religion vividly expresses it.

A cult and a tool represent two human natures and two histories. One history is the human drama that begins with the 'Prologue in Heaven' (Gospel, *Faust*) and develops through the triumph of the idea of liberty (Hegel) to culminate in the Last Judgement, as a moral sanction of history. The other is the history of tools—of objects—which will culminate in the classless society: an entropy akin to the rest of the material world.[41] These two histories relate as cult and tool—or, identically, as culture and civilisation.[42]

---

41 Compare: 'The changes of humanity follow the changes of tools.' (Pierre Lecombe, *History Seen as Knowledge*) Or vice versa: 'All history flows towards Christ and comes from Him.' (Hegel, *Philosophy of History*) It is evident that Lecombe and Hegel do not have the same concept of history here.

42 And etymologically, culture is related to cult (Latin: *cultus* and *cultura*). Both words derive from the common Indo-European root *kwel*—to move, to turn. Civilisation is linked to *civis*—citizen.

DUALITY REFLEX

Few terms have been more confused and conflated than culture and civilisation.

Culture began with the 'prologue in heaven'. Through religion, art, ethics, and philosophy, it will always concern itself with humanity's relationship to that heaven from which it came. Everything in culture is either an affirmation or denial, a doubt or memory of this heavenly origin. All of culture is marked by this mystery and flows from a constant striving to solve and comprehend it.

Conversely, civilisation is the continuation of zoological, one-dimensional life—the exchange of matter between man and nature. If human life differs from that of any other animal, it is a difference in degree, level, and organisation. Here, there is no man with his dilemmas from the Gospel, *Hamlet*, or *Karamazov*—only an anonymous member of society (a continuation of the pack) who exploits natural resources and modifies his surroundings through labour to suit his needs.

All of culture is religion acting upon man or man acting upon himself, just as all of civilisation is intelligence acting upon nature, upon the external world. Culture is 'the art of being human', while civilisation is the skill of functioning, producing, managing, and perfecting objects. Culture is 'ceaselessly creating oneself', just as civilisation is ceaselessly changing the world. It is the opposition of man and object, humanism vs. *choséité* (literally, 'thingness', objectification).[43]

43 From the French word chose–thing. The expression is Durkheim's. It refers to a method that seeks to examine a certain phenomenon objectively, externally, 'as a thing'.

Religious beliefs, drama, poetry, games, folklore, folk wisdom, mythology, moral and aesthetic codes, political and legal elements that affirm personal value and freedom, tolerance, philosophy, theatre, galleries, museums, libraries—this is the uninterrupted order of human culture, whose first act played out 'in heavens', between God and humanity. It is 'climbing up the holy mountain whose peak ceaselessly evades, walking through the darkness with the lights of a fiery torch that a man carries' (A. Malraux, *Antimemoires*).

Civilisation is the continuation of technical, not spiritual, development—just as Darwinian evolution is the continuation of biological, not human, development. Civilisation represents the development of forces already present in our animal ancestors; it is the continuation of natural, mechanical, and therefore unconscious and meaningless elements of our existence. For that reason, civilisation is neither good nor bad in itself.

Man must create civilisation just as he must breathe or eat—it is an expression of necessity, of lack of freedom, just as culture is the constant feeling of choice, the expression of human freedom.

Human dependence on matter has constantly increased with civilisation. It has been calculated that each American—man, woman, and child—consumes around 18 tonnes of various materials annually. By constantly creating new needs—and even more, developing the need for the unnecessary—civilisation intensifies the exchange of matter between man and nature, promoting external living at the expense of internal life.

'To produce in order to gain; to gain in order to waste'—this is the nature of civilisation. Conversely, every culture, by its religious nature, seeks to reduce human needs or at least the degree to which they are satisfied, thereby increasing inner freedom. This is the ultimate meaning of asceticism and the various forms of abnegation found in all cultures—taken to an absurd form in the 'vow of impurity' (whether of a monk or a hippie, it matters not).

Opposed to the Buddhist maxim 'destroy your desires', civilisation, governed by seemingly opposite laws, has embraced the slogan 'create more and more desires.'[44]

The true meaning of these contradictory demands is understood only by those who grasp that neither is accidental. Both affirm humanity as a creature of discord, reflecting the duality of human nature—the contradiction between culture and civilisation.

Humanity is the bearer of culture, while society is the bearer of civilisation. The aim of culture is governing the self through nurture; the aim of civilisation is governing nature through science. Man, philosophy, art, poetry, morality, and beliefs belong to culture. State, science, cities, and technology belong to civilisation. Its instruments are thought, speech, and the alphabet.[45] Culture and civilisation relate to one another as the heavenly and earthly empires, as *Civitas Dei* and *Civitas Solis*—one is drama, the other utopia.

Tacitus recounts how barbarians treated slaves with much greater kindness than the Romans. Ancient Rome, in general, is an excellent case for highlighting the difference between culture and civilisation. Pillaging wars, *panem et circenses*, the soullessness of the ruling class, the facelessness of the masses, lumpenproletariat, false democracy, political machinations, the exile of Christians, Nero and Caligula, imperialism and dictatorship, gladiatorial games—all these are not enough to dispute Roman civilisation, but one must ask: what remained of its culture?

'Hellenic soul and Roman intellect—it is the difference between culture and civilisation.'[46]

---

44 In a recent article in the New York Times, this motto is called 'the first commandment of the new era'.

45 Marshall McLuhan showed how writing influences differences in the way of thinking and the representation of life: 'The application of the alphabet creates and encourages the habit of perceiving everything surrounding man in visual and spatial terms—and particularly in terms of uniform space, uniform time, constantly and continuously.'

46 Oswald Spengler, *Decline of the West* (1926).

The Romans leave us with the impression of civilised barbarians, and Rome stands as an example of a highly developed civilisation devoid of culture. Mayan culture might serve as an opposing example. From what we know of the life of the ancient Germanic peoples and Slavs, it seems they were culturally ahead of the Romans, much like the Native Indians were more 'cultured' than their white conquerors and colonisers.

The European Renaissance provides a striking example of this differentiation. It has been demonstrated that this period of human history—arguably the most vibrant culturally—resulted in decline from a civilisational perspective. Europe witnessed a true economic revolution in the century preceding the Renaissance, marked by increased production and consumption, the expansion of markets, and population growth. However, during the two centuries known as the Renaissance era (1350–1550), many of these gains were significantly reversed.

Entirely consumed by the human visage and focused wholly on humanity rather than the world, the Renaissance appeared indifferent to 'real-life' developments. While the greatest artworks of Western culture were being created, Europe experienced general stagnation and, in many cases, clear regression—including population decline across much of the continent. England's population stood at around four million in the mid-fourteenth century, but by the following century it had fallen to only 2.1 million. The population of Florence dropped from 100,000 to fewer than 70,000 during the same period.

There are evidently two kinds of 'progress' that, in principle, have nothing in common.[47]

47 This 'unscientific' state of mind during the Renaissance can be illustrated by an interesting fact about the prevalence of superstitions, not only among ordinary people but also among artists and humanists. 'Astrology was most valued by free thinkers, and it was in fashion in a way it hadn't been since ancient times.' B. Russell, *History of Western Philosophy* (1946), p. 485.

EDUCATION AND MEDITATION

Civilisation forms, culture elevates. The former requires studying, the latter meditation. Pondering—meditation—as the inner effort to know oneself and one's place in the world, is a completely different activity from studying, educating oneself, and gathering knowledge about facts and their relations.

Meditation leads to wisdom, gentleness, inner peace—a form of Greek *katharsis*. It means turning to mysteries, diving into oneself to reach religious, moral, or artistic truth. Conversely, studying is turning to nature to understand and alter the conditions of existence.

Science employs observation, analysis, examination, experimentation, and control, while contemplation signifies pure awareness—even a suprarational way of awareness in Neoplatonism. Contemplative observation is 'freed from want and desire' (Schopenhauer), meaning an observation without function, devoid of interest—something science can never be.

Contemplation is not the stance of a scientist, but that of a thinker, poet, artist, or ascetic. A scientist may also experience moments of contemplation, but not in the capacity of a scientist—rather, as a human being and an artist (for all humans are artists to some degree).

Meditation grants power over oneself, while science grants power over nature. Our formal education builds civilisation, but it does not, in itself, contribute to culture. As much as we study, repeat, and follow scientific disciplines today, people once pondered just as deeply before.

'Wise men of Laputa, deep in thought, did not even notice or hear those who disturbed them with their questions.'[48]

Legend has it that before his enlightenment, Buddha sat by the riverbank for three days and three nights, so deep in thought that he lost all sense of time. Xenophon left us with a similar story about Socrates:

> One morning, he was pondering something he could not solve, and he refused to give it up. He remained deep in thought from early dawn until midnight, standing motionless as if nailed to the ground. Around midnight, people began to notice him, and whispers spread through the astonished crowd that Socrates had stood there pondering since dawn. Finally, some Ionians brought out their sleeping mats after dinner and slept under the stars just to observe him, to see if he would remain standing the whole night. He stood there until the next morning, and when dawn broke, he prayed and went on his way. [49]

The prophet of European civilisation, Galileo, was obsessed throughout his life with the problem of falling bodies, while Tolstoy spent his life pondering man and his destiny. If an aeroplane or parachute designer had to study and experiment extensively, then Buddha, Socrates, Seneca, Al-Ghazali, Rumi, Ferdowsi, Shakespeare, Dostoevsky, and Hugo had to think deeply and experience their inner worlds.

To study and to think are two different activities. The former led Newton to discover the law of gravity; the latter led Beethoven to create the *Ninth Symphony*. The contrast between man and the world, soul and intellect, or culture and civilisation, is once again reflected in the contrast between meditation and study.

In the end, we find the world and people in nature—in fact, we find everything except ourselves, our own Me, our

48 J. Payot, *The Art of Being Human.*

49 Xenophon, *The Symposium*, p. 220.

personality. It is precisely through that Me that we are connected to infinity. Through our Me, and only through it, we feel freedom and gain a glimpse into another vast world that we also inhabit simultaneously. Only I can bear witness to myself that there is a world of spirit and freedom. Without that Me, without myself, I am left without the only and final witness of a world beyond the natural world. Without me, everything else is external and manifest.

Meditation is that dive into oneself—an attempt to reach the road to truth about one's life and existence in general through one's own being. It does not attempt to solve the problems of society or humanity. It concerns the questions that a person asks themselves.

Strictly speaking, meditation is not a function of intelligence. A scientist constructing a new type of aeroplane or solving the details of a project for a bridge or other structure in his head is not meditating. He thinks, questions, checks, and compares, but none of these—either individually or combined—is meditation. A monk, a poet, a thinker, an artist—they meditate. The latter strive to reach one single great truth, one ultimate secret. This truth means both everything and nothing: everything to one soul, nothing to the rest of the world.

Therefore, meditation in its essence is a religious activity. According to Aristotle, the difference between reason and contemplation is the difference between the human and the divine. In Buddhism, prayer literally consists of contemplation, and it is confined to that. Christianity has contemplative monastic orders—a completely legitimate phenomenon. Spinoza speaks of contemplation as both the highest form and the highest goal of morality.

Education alone does not cultivate humanity. It does not inherently make people better, freer, or more humane; it makes them more capable, efficient, and socially useful. As historical practice demonstrates, educated individuals and nations can be manipulated and serve evil more effectively than less educated ones. The history of imperialism is a series of true stories of civilised nations waging unjust, exterminating, and subjugating wars against less educated, more backward nations defending their freedom. The level of civilisation of the aggressor had no impact on their goals or methods—only on their efficiency and the speed at which they defeated their victims.

TECHNICAL AND CLASSICAL EDUCATION

But education is not an unambiguous phenomenon. If we observe it more carefully, we will notice two distinct tendencies within it, both equally significant and independent. School education in civilised society is far too intellectual and scientific, and insufficiently humane and humanist. Using common terms, we could say that it is too technical and not classical enough.

It is entirely possible today to imagine a young man who has passed through all levels of education, from kindergarten to university, without ever being told that he should be a good and righteous person. He first learned how to write and calculate, then studied physics, chemistry, ethnology, geography, political theories, sociology, and a whole spectrum of sciences. He memorised countless facts and, in the best-case scenario, learned how to think—but he is not enriched. We hear less and less about history, art, literature, ethics, and law in schools.

Compared to civilisation, technical education appears both as its cause and its consequence. This form of education prepares a member of society (a social unit) and is tailored to that purpose in all its forms. It is oriented towards a clear goal, interested and engaged in subjugating nature and the external world. Classical education, on the other hand, begins and ends with the human—it is 'purposelessly purposeful'.

The dilemma between technical and classical education is not a technical but an ideological question. Behind it lies an attitude, a philosophy. The contrast between culture and civilisation, with all its consequences, is projected in these two educational systems. A Christian society will always lean towards classical education, while a socialist society will lean towards technical forms. This principle, understandably, suffers many deviations in practical life, but the main tendency remains and is realised through all necessary corrections. A comparison of school curricula in the USSR, France, China, or Japan—especially regarding the amount of artistic education, history, law, ethics, literature, Latin, and Ancient Greek, etc.—would confirm this hypothesis.

A specific form of technical education is specialisation. Let us first establish that intelligence, science, and industry form one line and stand in mutual causal relation. Science is the result of intelligence, just as industry is nothing but an applied form of science. All three are conditions and forms of man's coping with nature and the external world. Specialisation is a tendency aimed at ever greater and more thorough integration of the individual into the social mechanism. It degrades personality but strengthens society, making it more efficient. Society assumes the role of a whole, and man becomes a mere part of the social mechanism—an ever-diminishing part. The automation of labour and the depersonalisation of man as the subject of labour tend towards the ideal state of utopia in their progressive movement.

The expansion of education is dizzying. For example, in 1900, there were a total of 24,000 teachers in all US colleges and universities combined; 49,000 in 1920; and by the end of the twentieth century, it was estimated there would be 480,000. In 1900, there were 238,000 students enrolled in all those colleges and universities, 3,377,000 in 1959, and ten years later, this number rose to 14,600,000. Total educational expenses increased from a symbolic 270 million dollars in 1900 to 42.5 billion dollars in 1970.[50] The expansion in

50 Data from the Office of Education, U.S. Department of Health, Education, and Welfare.

socialist countries is no less impressive, though they started from lower positions.

The two greatest scientific powers in the world—the US and the USSR—are also the two greatest military powers, but they are not the most cultured countries. These two nations spend the most on research and education (USSR 4.2 per cent and US 2.8 per cent of their GDP). An average American above the age of twenty-five had about 10.5 years of education by 1960, followed by a Briton with 9.5 years, and a Soviet citizen with five years.

But what kind of education is this? Regularly, it follows the typical civilisational model. In communist countries, education is strictly indoctrinated, orchestrated, and subordinated to the interests of the ruling ideology and political system. In capitalist countries, it is largely adapted to the demands of the economy and serves the industrial system. In both cases, education is a function and a service, and this tendency dominates despite the lofty proclamations about the 'multifaceted development of human personality' and the 'humanist orientation of education', etc.

We will corroborate these claims with two sufficiently authoritative sources. Lenin explicitly pointed out that education should not be 'neutral', objective, or apolitical. At the First Congress of Soviet Education on 25 August 1918, he proclaimed, 'Our work in the school domain aims to destroy the bourgeoisie, and we openly declare that there is no school outside politics—such a claim is a lie and hypocrisy.' Indoctrination remains the principle of the Soviet educational system to this day.

Famous American economic theorist and probably the leading expert on the industrial system today, John K. Galbraith, writes:

> Of course, modern higher education is thoroughly adapted to the needs of the industrial system... The great renown

that pure and applied science and mathematics have lately is merely a reflection of the needs of the technostructure... while the lesser renown of art and humanities and the smaller support they receive is a reflection of their subordinate role... Business and technical schools are in demand because of their utilitarian character... The industrial system has inspired a vast expansion in education. We can only salute that. However, if the tendencies are not clearly pinpointed and resisted, the system will only support those forms of education that serve its needs the most and question its goals the least.[51]

What are the common characteristics of school systems everywhere? Above all, they include rigorous selection leading to destructive competition, the artificial 'specialist' language that most disciplines develop, and the rigidly functional architecture of school buildings, which serve exclusively the measures of utilitarianism and hygiene. All of this occurs because the school serves the bureaucracy and the highly competitive industrial system, for which it must prepare experts who will best serve and further develop these mechanisms. Calls for a 'humane school', which can occasionally be heard, remain, for now, mere wishful thinking.

If we were to assess the value of the cultural content in school education, we might say that the school is a constituent part of civilisation; it contributes to culture only to the extent that it is not mere training, if it develops critical thinking, and if it leaves room for man's spiritual freedom. A school that serves and enforces ready-made ethical and political solutions is barbaric from a cultural standpoint. It does not create free personalities but subjects, and as such, it may contribute to civilisation, but it sets back culture.

51 J.K. Galbraith, *The New Industrial State* (Boston: 1967), pp. 339–41.

"MASS" CULTURE

Considering these observations, the reader can easily find the right place for the phenomenon of so-called mass culture. Is it really culture, or just another aspect of civilisation? The subject of every culture is man as an individual, as a personality, as a 'one-of-a-kind individuality'. The subject (or object) of mass culture is a group, a mass, or 'man-mass'.[52] A man has a soul; a mass only has needs. That is why every culture is the elevation and refinement of man, whereas mass culture is the satisfaction of needs. Culture tends towards individualisation; mass culture pulls in the opposite direction – towards spiritual uniformity. Mass culture parts ways with ethics, even culture, at this point. Mass culture educates, but it does not raise. It pushes toward depersonalisation with its serial production of 'spiritual goods', copies, kitsch, and trash, and a lack of sense of the individual. Unlike authentic culture, mass culture narrows human freedom precisely with this tendency of uniformisation because 'freedom—it is opposing uniformity' (Horkheimer).

One of the well-spread fallacies is the failure to distinguish between mass and folk culture, which is a great injustice for the latter. Unlike mass culture, folk culture is authentic,

52 The concept of the 'man-mass' was introduced into literature by José Ortega y Gasset. The mass is a group of anonymous, dehumanised individuals. A group of people, when it loses its personality, degenerates into a mass. The man-mass is the ultimate product of bare civilisation—a state in which there are no longer doubts or 'prejudices' of culture.

active, and direct. It does not know kitsch and trash, which are exclusively urban products.

Folk culture is based on a consensus, an inner concordance, participation, while manipulation is the dominating principle of mass culture. Rituals, games, and songs are common to one village or a tribe. There are no performers on one side and listeners or observers on the other. Once the ceremony begins, everyone joins in and becomes a participant. Mass culture gives us a complete reverse example. People are strictly divided into 'producers' and 'consumers' of cultural goods. Does anyone still think that they can influence the content of a TV programme if they do not already belong to a small group of content creators of the said programme? So-called mass communication devices—press, radio, and television—are in fact devices of mass manipulation. We have editorial staffs that create programmes, made of a small group of people, on one hand and a passive auditorium of millions of people on the other.

One survey in 1971 found that an average Englishman spends between 16 and 18 hours a week in front of his TV (data from Tendencies of Society, statistical annual magazine of the English government). It has been especially noticed that television is steadily supplanting its cultural equivalent, literature, everywhere. One in three Frenchmen does not read any books ever, while the French nation spends the entirety of its leisure time in front of TV—these are conclusions from a survey done for *Le Point* magazine in 1975 that show us that for more than 87 per cent of the population, watching TV programmes is the main 'cultural' entertainment, with opera and ballet at the end of the list. A survey done during the 'Book Week' in 1976 in Japan indicated that the situation is the same there. About 30 per cent of Japanese do not read books or even newspapers at all, while the average Japanese spends around 2.5 hours in front of the TV daily. Professor Horikava from San Francisco University claims that the level of the generation entering adulthood now is below university criteria. He explains it very simply: television replaced literature and thinking, it decreased inner activity and restrained intellect in general. It serves ready solutions for all of life's problems.

Our time gives examples of how mass culture devices—radio, film, television—if monopolised by authorities, can serve to create false idols and mass delusions of the worst kind. There is no need anymore to use brute force to rule a nation against their will. Now it can be done in a 'legal way', by paralysing national will, serving ready 'truths' to the tired masses of people and using work, rallies, and cheap and vulgar entertainment to take away their time to think and try to form their own judgement about people and events.

Psychology of masses has taught us—and practice has confirmed—that it is possible to make people believe myths detached from reality through persistent repetition.[53] The psychology behind mass communication devices is designed to subdue not only the conscious mind but also the instinctive and emotional parts of individuals, creating a habit of perceiving enforced choices as one's own.[54]

---

53 Until 1945, the Japanese were taught that the Mikado was a descendant of the Sun Goddess and that Japan was created before the rest of the world. This myth was repeated over several generations, even by university professors to their students. This Japanese case now belongs to the past. New myths in the form of leader cults exist in Russia, China, North Korea (the cults of Stalin, Mao Zedong, Kim Il-sung, etc.). These myths generally follow the same model. For example: 'Every word of our respected and beloved leader Comrade Kim Il-sung has deeply penetrated our hearts, just as water seeps into thirsty soil... We will resolutely continue to carry out the great plan for building communism set forth by our respected and beloved leader Comrade Kim Il-sung,' (Kim Jong Hui, 'Everything the people love is good'). In the yard of a factory, a stone is displayed in a glass sarcophagus, on which the 'respected and beloved leader Comrade Kim Il-sung' sat during a conversation.

54 On this issue, we recommend the outstanding book by Đuro Šušnjić, *Ribari ljudskih duša* (*The Fishermen of Human Souls*) (Belgrade, 1977).

Totalitarian societies everywhere saw their opportunity in television and swiftly exploited it. Thus, television has become a threat to freedom more dangerous than police forces, prisons, or concentration camps. Future generations may be appalled by the torment endured by today's generation, subjected to the limitless influence of this unchecked power—if, indeed, their own ability to think freely does not become entirely eroded. Just as constitutions were once written to limit the absolute power of rulers, a new constitution may be necessary to restrain this new danger that threatens to impose the worst kind of spiritual slavery.

Mass culture is characterised by a spiritual state that Johan Huizinga termed 'puerilism'. Huizinga observed that modern man behaves immaturely and childishly in the negative sense of the word, akin to the mental stage of adolescence: banal pastimes, a need for intense sensations, a proclivity for mass parades and sloganeering, an absence of genuine humour, an influx of trash, and extreme expressions of hate, love, criticism, or praise.

Finally, there is a contrasting attitude towards machines and technology. Culture exhibits a 'fear of machines', an instinctive rejection of technology ('Technology is the first sin of culture'—Nikolai Berdyaev), rooted in the belief that machines inevitably shift from manipulating objects to manipulating people. This sentiment is echoed in the warnings of Tagore, Tolstoy, Heidegger, Neizvestny, Faulkner, and others. Conversely, Marxist thinker Henri Lefebvre argued: 'The highest degree of freedom that man can achieve will be in a society where technology develops all its possibilities—a communist society.'

A society modelled on utopia finds an ally in machines and technology. Technology facilitates, rather than hinders, the manipulation of people and objects. It promotes conformism and uniformity through education and mass media (press, radio, TV), necessitates collective cooperation and centrally managed mechanisms, and ultimately promises complete control of society (or authorities) over individuals through direct or indirect surveillance of their actions, conversations, or thoughts. Therefore, if technology poses a threat, it is to the free individual, not to the anonymous member of a collective whose function is to produce and consume, perfecting methods and techniques of production and consumption.

THE COUNTRY AND THE CITY

Poets speak of the 'hell' of the metropolis, Marxists of the 'idiocy of country life' (*Manifesto*). Rejection of cities, no matter how impractical it might seem, is a purely human reaction, as every human is a poet to some degree. Today, as in the past, protest against the city and urban civilisation arises from religion, culture, and art. Early Christians viewed Rome as Satan's kingdom, heralding the end of the world and Judgement Day.

Religiousness decreases in proportion to city size,[55] coinciding with the concentration of urban elements that alienate humans. The larger the city, the less sky is visible above it, the fewer flowers and natural elements remain, while smoke, concrete, and technology dominate. The larger the city, individuality also erodes and the city dweller becomes increasingly part of the mass. Moreover, larger cities experience higher crime rates. Religiousness is inversely proportional to city size, while criminality is directly proportional. Both phenomena share a common cause and correlate with what we might call practical, 'lived aesthetics'.

A villager has the daily privilege of gazing at starry skies, blooming meadows, rivers, plants, and animals. He maintains direct, daily contact with nature and the elements. Rich folklore, wedding customs, folk songs, dances, and games—often

55 According to a survey, 12–13 per cent of the population in Paris attends mass, 20.9 per cent in Lyon, 28.5 per cent in Saint-Étienne, etc.

participated in rather than merely observed—offer cultural and aesthetic experiences largely absent in urban life. The average citizen of a metropolis is exposed to suffocation of everything beautiful and self-grown. He most often grows up in uniform apartment blocks, is bombarded with passive knowledge from mass communication devices and surrounded by the unattractive uniformity of mass-produced objects. Even the innate sense of rhythm found in all primitive nations is nearly extinct in modern man.

The belief that city dwellers have more opportunities for artistic and aesthetic experiences is one of the strangest fallacies of our age. Concerts, museums, and exhibitions—visited by only a small fraction of the urban population—cannot compensate for the daily, perhaps unconscious but profoundly stirring aesthetic experiences of villagers witnessing a breathtaking sunrise or the awakening of nature in spring. The majority of the urban population finds its strongest thrills in the naturalist atmosphere of football or boxing matches. Everything surrounding villagers is vibrant and elemental; everything surrounding city workers is lifeless and mechanical. In this differing spiritual climate and aesthetic experience, rather than in material living conditions or levels of education, lies the explanation for the religiousness of villagers and the atheism of city dwellers.[56] Religion belongs to life, art, and culture; atheism belongs to technology, science, and civilisation.

56 It is not economic insecurity either. The worker is no more secure regarding his existence than the peasant. The market is as fickle and uncertain as the sky. Marx showed how the worker feels the market as a fetishistic force over which he has no control.

WORKING CLASS

As a product of cities, the working class is most affected by the negative impact of so-called pure civilisation—that is, civilisation with the least amount of culture. Factories dull and oppress personality. A sociologist writes: 'Subjected to rigid discipline and the manufacturing process, workers transfer the habits they acquire in the factory into their own organisations. They tend to transfer their authority to bureaucracy that they create spontaneously and control insufficiently, which plays a conservative role both in the capitalist and socialist world.'[57] Herbert Marcuse states that workers in developed capitalist systems (meaning where the impact of technology and factories is the strongest) have ceased to be a revolutionary force. The working class is an example of a manipulated group—flattered, invoked, and spoken for, but rarely consulted. The two largest working classes in the world, those in the US and USSR, have almost no real influence on the political structures in their countries or the decisions those structures make.

One of the outward forms of this state, besides alienation from religion and art, is poverty of thought—in fact, a complete theoretical sterility within the workers' movement, recognised even by communist writers such as A. Gorz, R. Garaudy, L. Basso, S. Malle, and others.

57 There are even serious indications of the strong influence of the underground and the mafia in the leadership of some American trade unions.

Famous Marxist writer György Lukács said in an interview with the correspondent of the Italian magazine *Il Contemporaneo* in 1965: 'Since Marx died, nobody except Lenin has made any theoretical contribution to the problems of capitalist progress', and then, reflecting on the Stalinist period in the USSR, he added: 'Every free thought was suffocated, and personal stances were declared to be theoretical law. One whole generation came of age based on this perversion of theoretical meaning.' Truly, after Marx—who did not himself come from the working but from the bourgeois class—we can barely find any remotely valuable and original idea that originated from the working class, with the exception of workers' self-management in Yugoslavia, which represents a unique and original direction despite all its hardships. In any case, this idea represents a departure from the clichés and dogmas with which official Marxism shackled the progress of working-class thought.

The strikes that occasionally shake capitalist economies are almost exclusively economic in character and end with compromise agreements about salary increases. Since the process of economic development did not lead to the material impoverishment of the working class (pauperisation), instead of waging class wars, it found ways everywhere to negotiate the conditions of class peace with the antagonist groups in society.[58]

The traditional form of the working class—the class of oppressed factory proletarians, as Marx saw it and believed would exist 'until that class abolishes itself'—was only a temporary form. Physical labour is gradually being taken over by

58 According to data from a Swedish institution (1978), in a number of the largest capitalist countries (USA, UK, Italy, Canada), strikes accounted for less than 1 per cent of total working hours annually over the last five years (1973–1977); in Sweden, it was six minutes on average per worker annually, and in Switzerland, the amount was negligible.

machines, and man's activity is moving towards the control and management of large automated systems.[59]

The development of science and technology— 'development of means of production'—therefore did not bring about the rule of the working class but rather its gradual abolition as such. This development did not hand power over to the manual worker but is instead transferring the brunt of production and social impact gradually to technical intelligence. The last traces of idealism and revolutionary romanticism are disappearing. Technocracy—rational and soulless rule, the final expression of a consequential civilisation—emerges on the scene.

59 According to one analysis, a worker operating a fully automated machine actively and specifically intervenes only one hour out of a total of forty hours per week, while for the remaining thirty-nine hours, he more or less oversees the machine. Development in this direction is very rapid, and automation is becoming the dominant mode of work in an increasing number of industries. Marx, a great dialectician, either did not foresee this development or failed to draw the appropriate conclusion from it. In any case, he viewed the phenomenon of the working class statically, rather than dialectically.

RELIGION AND REVOLUTION

Revolution is never merely an event in the domain of civilisation, society, economy, or politics. Every true revolution embodies a moment of faith—a state of fervour, justice, striving, sacrifice, and death—a feeling transcending interest and existence. Even when a revolution is antireligious in its aims, it remains a form of religious expression due to people's participation—a human drama. Anyone who has participated in a revolution or observed it closely has witnessed these ethical elements. They see it as an epic rather than a mechanical overturn or mere change of government machinery. This might explain why workers in modern capitalist countries are unable to spark revolution, as Marcuse noted, and conversely, why poets, artists, and religious individuals can be inspired by revolutions that are ostensibly atheist in their declarations. From within, as a lived experience[60] rather than a mere process, revolution is a drama gripping people with something only religions comprehend. Politically and pragmatically, of course, it can have entirely different meanings and goals.

Every community enters a 'religious state' when gripped by heightened fervour, solidarity, and shared destiny, where people feel like brothers or comrades. Arthur Rubinstein recounts:

---

60 In the famous poem 'The Twelve' by Aleksandr Blok, the Red Guards are led by Christ. This is how the poet sees it. The poem was written shortly after the revolution and was attacked by the official criticism of the time as being religious. We do not know how much the minister of culture at the time, Lunacharsky, managed to defend Blok by claiming that it was 'just a vision based on tragedy and biblical pathos.'

> During the Victorian era, full of wealth and snobbery, no one attended concerts. The French attended concerts only on Sundays, and halls stayed empty on other days. However, on the eve of World War II, a renowned English pianist performed for free in museum halls, consistently drawing full audiences. I gave more than 50 concerts in various cities during the Mexican revolution, when trains were being blown up and people ruthlessly killed. The halls were sold out in advance, and people paid for tickets with gold. Yet, during peaceful times in that same Mexico, it was a struggle to attract even a small audience.

A society incapable of religion is also incapable of revolution. Regions of strong revolutionary turmoil are those where religious feelings remain alive. The sense of brotherhood, solidarity, and justice—religious in essence—is channelled through revolution into the pursuit of earthly justice and utopia.

Both religion and revolution are born in pain and suffering and perish in prosperity and comfort. Their true existence lies in their striving. Their 'achievement' is their death. As they are realised, both religion and revolution create institutions and structures that ultimately suffocate them. Official structures are never revolutionary or religious.

If revolution ever had enemies in religion, they existed only within institutionalised religion—churches, clergy, and hierarchies—representing fake religion. Conversely, pseudo-revolutions—those reduced to structures or bureaucracies—found allies in equally institutionalised and inauthentic religion. Since it started lying and betraying itself, revolution was able to find a common language with fake religion.

PROGRESS AGAINST HUMAN

According to American scientist J. Robert Oppenheimer—the inventor of the American hydrogen bomb—humankind made greater technical and material progress in the last forty years than in the previous forty centuries. From 1900 to 1960, the distances accessible to man increased from 10^{26} to 10^{40}, temperatures from 10^5 to 10^{11}, and pressure from 10^{10} to 10^{16}. Within thirty years, electric motors with batteries will replace piston engines, and steamships will be supplanted by atomic-powered ships. The day is approaching when electric cables beneath roads will power vehicles.

Jean Rostand predicts biology's magical powers: humanity will transform itself by manipulating hereditary substances from highly intelligent individuals. The artificial production of DNA—the chemical foundation of heredity—will open unlimited possibilities. Custom-designed children may become a reality. In addition to its own ten billion cells, the human brain could be augmented with a few more billion of cells through transplantation or production processes. Organ and limb transplants from corpses will become routine, and discoveries in brain chemistry may allow humans to fulfil their centuries-long striving to extend life by reducing sleep. Advanced economic possibilities in developed regions already enable shorter workweeks—soon potentially thirty hours per week and nine months per year.

In 1965, the USA had sixty-nine million cars, sixty million televisions, and 7.7 million motorboats and yachts, spending thirty billion dollars on vacations—almost an entire national income of India (population 300 million people). Two-fifths of personal goods in the USA are luxury items, and wealthy countries—a third of the world—collectively spend fifteen billion dollars annually on cosmetics. The living standards in these countries have increased fivefold since 1800 and are projected to quintuple again in 60 years. After such an optimistic vision, the question remains: will life be five times fuller, happier, or more humane?

The answer is decidedly negative. The USA—the world's wealthiest nation—records about five million serious crimes annually and the crime rates surged 178 per cent between 1960 and 1970, outpacing population growth (13 per cent) fourteenfold. In 1964, a crime occurred every twelve seconds, a murder every hour, a rape every twenty-five minutes, a robbery attack every five minutes and a car theft every minute in USA, according to data from FBI's Annual Report.

It is the tendency that is particularly worrisome: there were 3.1 murders per 100,000 citizens in the USA in 1951, five murders in 1960, and already nine in 1967. This means that the number of murders tripled in sixteen years. West Germany had around two million registered crimes in 1966, and that number rose to 2,413,000 in 1970. The number of intentional murders in England rose by 35 per cent during the last decade, and in Scotland, violent crimes have risen by a whole 100 per cent. The number of murders in Canada doubled from 1962 to 1970 (exactly 98.2 per cent), which was significantly influenced by the abolition of the death sentence in 1962. The French have placed the fear of violence at the top of their daily concerns in the last few public surveys. The number of thefts alone has risen by 177 per cent in a decade (1966–1976, official data of the French government). The number of all types of crimes has doubled in Belgium in a decade (1969–1978), and so on.

The Seventh International Congress of Criminologists held in Belgrade (September 1973) concluded that the current moment in the world is characterized by 'a dizzying rise in crime that spans all meridians.' In an attempt to explain the causes of this situation, American criminologists described the planet as 'an ocean of delinquency', resigned to the pervasive criminality. The 1970 UN Report on the *World Social Situation* highlighted that in one highly industrialised, unnamed country, the number of youths under twenty handled by police rose from one million in 1955 to 2.4 million in 1965.

OUN General-Secretary stated in a 1972 report titled *Prevention and Suppression of Crime*: 'Some of the most developed countries have the most serious crime issues.... Despite material progress, human life has never been less safe than today. Criminality, with its various forms of personal or public violence, theft, deceit, fraud, corruption, and organised crime, represents a serious cost of modern living and an expensive counter-reward for progress.'

Soviet psychiatrist N. Hodakov's research highlighted the terrifying post-WWII expansion of alcohol use, particularly in civilised countries. Alcohol sales doubled between 1940 and 1960, increased 2.5 times by 1965, 4.3 times by 1970, and 5.5 times by 1973. Alcoholism among women and youth surged. The British charity 'Offered Help' reported over 400,000 alcoholics in England in 1971, including 80,000 women. Half of these women later required psychiatric care, and a third faced suicide risk. France led Europe in per capita alcohol consumption, followed by Italy and the USSR. West Berlin recorded the highest alcohol-related mortality rate globally in 1971, with 44.3 deaths per 100,000 people, followed by France with 35 then Austria with 30.

Alcoholism has become, above all, an issue for wealthy and educated circles in our century. If alcohol—or narcotics—are an escape and a defence mechanism, what kind of escape are the rich and educated searching for, and what are they defending themselves from? We used to associate alcoholism with poverty and backwardness, which gave us hope. Now, the confusion is complete: 'For reasons that can hardly be established and identified, the symptoms of these social ills are more openly expressed in Sweden than in any other country', a Swedish expert on the matter writes. Faced with the fact that every tenth Swedish citizen, man or woman, suffers from chronic alcoholism, the Swedish government has begun applying consecutive drastic tax increases on alcoholic beverages, but the effect remains minimal.

The brutal surge in pornography follows similar trends, with France, Denmark, and West Germany leading in production and consumption. Paris had 250 cinemas dedicated to pornography and pornographic films accounted for more than half of the repertoire of all French cinemas in 1975. Public workers were confused. The famous psychiatrist, Professor Blanchar, tries to explain this phenomenon:

> Ruling ideology is increasingly suppressing the personality, directing man to automatic routine according to the formula: sleep – metro – work. While this does guarantee a certain standard of living, it robs man of all real experiences and excitement. Everything is prepared in advance, even vacations are organised and happen according to a plan that participants cannot change at all. Because of that, the majority feels the instinctive need to escape from themselves and to experience something else at a cheap price. That need is misused through pornographic films.

Even games of chance experience their 'progress' in civilisation. They too follow the general trend of vices—alongside alcoholism, pornography, kitsch, trash, and other troubles.

The greatest gambling metropolises of the world are found in regions of top-tier civilisation: Deauville, Monte Carlo, Macao, Las Vegas. A giant casino is being built in Atlantic City, where one hall alone can accommodate 6,000 players. Data tells us that the French spent 115 billion francs on games of chance in 1965, while Americans spent fifteen billion dollars on them in 1977 (American government data). One in three Hungarians plays the lottery. It has been found that Sweden has, proportionally, the greatest interest in games of chance, measured by invested funds per capita, followed by Israel and Denmark: a curve that fits the curve of the degree of civilisation with only minor deviations.

According to official New York police data, more than 23,000 young people abused heroin and other heavy narcotics in 1963, but that number is estimated to be over 100,000. More than half of the students at Hunter College in New York were found to have smoked marijuana, which is often considered the first step towards heavier narcotics.

It is precisely in these countries of prosperity and abundance that a sad new generation appeared after World War II. They usually have everything but do not want anything. They are beatniks or so-called 'beaten generation' that preaches the philosophy of meaninglessness; *halbstarkers*—minors prone to crime, and finally, hippies who detest reality, mock every order and rule, and whose manners and understandings spread like a plague in almost all major cities of the world.

It is entirely wrong to characterise the rebellion of the youth in the USA or France (1968) as political or ideological, misled by slogans and outer manifestations. The rebellion is of a moral kind—in the USA against so-called 'organised America' and the 'establishment', and in France against its 'structures'. In both cases, it is a rebellion against certain civilisational aspects. (Hugo La Malfa: 'It was a resistance to consumerist ethics of industrial society.') Unable to explain this rebellion amidst abundance, they named it 'rebellion without cause' (an irrational rebellion of the youth – A. Malraux), which it is if we ignore its moral dimension.

Arthur Miller, a competent expert on modern USA, explains youth delinquency:

> All delinquents have one same mood: they are suffocated in boredom.... To drag around not expecting anything is the closest thing to dying.... The problem of youth delinquency is not just a problem of big cities but rural areas too; not only a capitalism problem but a socialism problem too; it is not limited to poverty, wealth shares the same issue; it is not a racial problem or recent immigration issue or purely American problem. I believe that in its current form it is the product of technology that destroys the very concept of man being of value as he is.. In short, the spirit has disappeared. Maybe the brutality of the two world wars chased it away from Earth.... Or the technological process itself sucked it out of the human soul... Many people rarely mix with others, except as buyer to seller, worker with boss, rich with poor and vice versa – shortly, as factors that are being manipulated in some way, but not as essentially valuable individuals.[61]

How does one explain the fact that the number of suicides and psychological ailments is in direct proportion to the level of civilisation? 'The fact that is of special importance psychologically is that the better off people are, the more they are dissatisfied,' noted one American psychologist. This phenomenon—especially evident in developed countries without

61 There is no doubt that television has also made its sad contribution here. In informing the British public about the results of a six-year study on the topic of whether violence on television encourages violence in real life (the study was completed in 1977), William Belson stated that the answer is unequivocally affirmative. Someone calculated that the average American child sees 18,000 murders on television before finishing high school.

typical class-related social issues—shakes the very foundations of the belief in progress.

Out of every 1,000 people in the USA, four are hospitalised in psychiatric clinics (for the state of New York, that number is 5.5). More than half of the beds in all US hospitals are occupied by the mentally ill. Hollywood is the city with the highest number of psychiatrists per capita in the world. According to an official report from the American Public Health Organisation in 1968, every fifth American has experienced a nervous breakdown or was on the verge of having one. This conclusion is based on irrefutably proven materials, with examinees selected in such a way as to represent 111 million adult American citizens aged nineteen to seventy-nine.[62]

A grim record in the number of suicides, alcoholics, and mentally ill individuals is held by Sweden, which also ranks first globally in national income, literacy, employment rates, and social insurance. In 1967, Sweden recorded 1,702 suicides, an increase of 9 per cent from 1966 and 30 per cent from 1960. The World Health Organization in Geneva published a ranking of countries by suicide rates in 1968. That year, the top eight countries in this ranking were: FR Germany, Austria, Canada, Denmark, Finland, Hungary, Sweden, and Switzerland. Suicide is the third leading cause of death for people aged fifteen-forty-five (after cardiovascular diseases and cancer). In the World Health Organization Report for 1970, it is

62 Ten years later, a special Mental Health Commission, established by a decision of the President of the United States, concluded in its September 1977 report that the problems of this nature among Americans were 'worse' than previously believed and that at least one-quarter of the population suffers from the consequences of serious emotional stress. From a study prepared by the National Institute of Mental Health (1977), it is evident that in 1976 alone, over 31.9 million Americans received treatment for mental health issues of various types; that eight million out of fifty-four million American children need help for psychological disorders; that at least ten million people have problems related to alcoholism; and that the number of heroin users exceeds 500,000.

unequivocally stated that this phenomenon is 'parallel to industrialisation, urbanisation, and a reduction in family size.' The same report contains the following statement: 'The high suicide rate in Finland corresponds with a high percentage of depressive ailments, alcoholism, and violence.'

If we examine this phenomenon within a single country or milieu, we find that it rises with the level of development and education. In former Yugoslavia, the number of alcoholics and suicides is directly comparable to the degree of development. In Slovenia (literacy 98 per cent), there are 25.8 suicides per 100,000 citizens, whereas in Kosovo (literacy 56 per cent), the rate is only 3.4 per 100,000 citizens—making the ratio 7 to 1 (data for 1967). The suicide rate in British universities is three to six times higher than the national average, and at Cambridge University, it is even ten times greater than the average among young men of the same age within the broader British population (data from Die Zeit). Research in this area, conducted by Dr Anthony Rail, head of the health service at Sax University, has shown that material conditions are not the cause, as all English students are either children of wealthy parents or recipients of national scholarships.

It would be entirely wrong and unfair to conclude that these phenomena are exclusive to Western civilisation. Rather, they represent phenomena and laws that express the very nature of civilisation itself. What has been stated here regarding the USA, Germany, England, or Sweden is equally applicable to Japan, despite its geographical remoteness and vastly different cultural milieu (see: Anasaki, Crisis of Japanese Culture). The issue is a phenomenon that, depending on conditions, may undergo certain modifications but does not alter the fundamental tendency. Some differences in Japan arise from the resilience and strength of its cultural traditions and the stability of Japanese families.

It is difficult to confidently establish all of the causes of the phenomena we have discussed. Nevertheless, the issue of drug and narcotic use spreading among young people has increasingly directed researchers towards the parental home. Psychiatrist Dr Vladeta Jerotić writes:

> Disturbed family environment or completely destroyed family that direct young individual to neurotic development inherently directs it to seeking wrong mechanisms to defend themselves from this neurosis... The decay of patriarchal community and familial hearth, which is a common occurrence in the world today, contributes to the inner climate of dissatisfaction that then has two exits into the outer world: as rage and revolt or as passive, resigned and in time apathetic state created by drug abuse.[63]

Roger Rawel, the director of the Centre for Sociological Research at Harvard, has recently suggested founding a special committee within the US Senate to study the impact of technology on man and society. 'Thanks to modern conditions, human life will be prolonged for nearly three decades, but it will be a boring and empty life,' he said.

Contrary to the materialistic view, civilisation and comfort do not suit human nature. Generally speaking, the social gap is greater in Catholic than in Protestant countries. For example, income differences in France are twice as large as those in England and West Germany and three times as large as those in the Netherlands. However, the number of mental illnesses and suicides presents the opposite situation. The 'material' human is made of is not the one, or not just the one, that nineteenth century science and evolutionist biology thought it was. Humans are simply not meant to live solely through their senses. 'Unfulfilled desires create pain, but fulfilled ones create satiation.' (Schopenhauer) Comfort and the consumerist mentality attached to it are weakening (and even breaking) adherence not only to religion but also to any other value

63 Dr Vladeta Jerotić, NIN, 9.2.1969.

system.[64] Far from being the meaning of our lives, civilisation might become the meaninglessness of our existence.

The impossibility of choice—this fatal characteristic of civilisation—is nowhere expressed as clearly as in our helplessness to stop the production of weapons of mass destruction or the terrifying rhythm with which the civilised part of humanity destroys the natural conditions for life in its own environment. It is the clash of mechanical versus organic, artificial versus natural principles in human life.

The Brazilian forests are retreating ten to fifteen kilometres yearly, faced with the invasion of civilisation. The rich green vastness is being conquered by desert. More than 80 per cent of fresh water in the USA has been polluted with industrial waste. The smoke from the huge copper-smelting works in Ducktown, Tennessee, has transformed the once fertile soil into a 20,000-hectare desert. The concentration of copper acids and fumes in the London smog killed more than 4,000 people in a single day in 1952. Factory chimneys and cars in the USA emit 230 million tonnes of various dangerous compounds yearly. Thermal plants alone emitted 114,000 tonnes of sulphur fumes and more than eighty-two million tonnes of ash into the air in France in 1960. These numbers were twice as high in 1968 despite myriad protective measures. Every city in the Ruhr region is covered with about 27,000 tonnes of industrial dust yearly. Lung cancer mortality has risen fifty-fold in the past twenty years in US cities shrouded by smog. That increase is forty-fold in England and Switzerland over the past fifty years. During one study in Tokyo, the blood of pedestrians at the busy Janaga traffic crossing was found to contain two to seven times higher levels of lead than normal. The main cause of this: exhaust fumes from cars. Since its invention, the car has killed more people than all the wars of

64 'You gave them and their forefathers to enjoy, but they forgot to remember You.' Qur'an, 25:18

this century (data from American highway expert Norbert Timan at the International Conference on Road Safety, held in Paris in 1976).

How do we save ourselves from this 'progress'?

Without leaving civilisation, one cannot see any force within it capable of contradicting all these phenomena. Furthermore, in the value system accepted by civilisation, there is not even a single argument that can be raised against the invasion of pap, pornography, and alcohol. It is the same feeling of powerlessness and resignation that is evident in the attitude of American criminologists in the face of an impending tide of crime. In fact, it is the powerlessness of science against evils that possess not only social but also a clear moral dimension. Challenging civilisation is impossible from within, only from outside—that is, from culture. Religious and ethical upbringing and the family are obviously a way out. However, science cannot resort to religion, nor can civilisation return to the traditional family. From a civilisational viewpoint, the circle is closed.

PESSIMISM OF THEATRE

It is particularly symptomatic that an ominous philosophy is emerging from the wealthy, developed regions of the world (Ibsen, Heidegger, Mailer, Pinter, Beckett, Marcuse, O'Neill, Bergman, A. Camus, Antonioni, etc.). There is still some optimism left in scientists, as they mainly engage with the outward appearance of things. Thinkers and artists, however, are troubled—especially the latter.

On the surface, it seems that pessimism begins with the advent of complete literacy, social insurance, and reaching a national income of 1,000 dollars per capita. Scandinavian philosophy at the turn of the twentieth century is profoundly pessimistic. According to it, human destiny is hopelessly tragic, with darkness and void as the final results of human efforts to find an exit. This philosophy arose in countries where there were no illiterate citizens even at the start of the century, while the southern part of Europe enjoyed the 'bliss of ignorance' (in 1906, Bulgaria and Serbia had 70 per cent illiterate citizens, Spain 63 per cent, Italy 48 per cent, Hungary 43 per cent, Austria 39 per cent, etc.). One is tempted to ask whether there is a connection between Sweden's social insurance—now the most advanced in the world—and the pervasive sense of despair and loss. Does the feeling of material security give birth to the feeling of social alienation?

Contrary to the apparent external dynamism—essentially the dynamism of social and political life—civilisation is characterised by a delayed inner rhythm of life. The theatre of the absurd is a faithful representation of the lives of people in the most developed societies today. Comfort is external, while meaninglessness is the inner experience of life within civilisation, producing a dialectic: the greater the comfort and abundance, the stronger the sense of being lost and of life's meaninglessness. Conversely, primitive societies, though poor and marked by stark social differences, exhibit a remarkable vitality and fullness of feeling, as attested by all available evidence. Folklore—'the literature of primitive society'—in particular conjures up an extraordinary life force and emotional richness in the primitive individual. This impoverished society does not experience feelings of being lost or without meaning.[65]

The civilised world discovers its 'human tragedy' primarily on the theatre stage. Some residual optimism remains in cheap comedies and old-fashioned musicals, but serious plays exude pessimism. Theatre continually strips away the halo of perfection that science keeps placing on civilisation. While science relentlessly presents data on product abundance, mass production indices, energy, and human capability, art reveals scenes of human destruction, intellectual and moral poverty, violence, bestiality, and existential emptiness. Theatre invariably depicts an aggressive, helpless man prone to vice, situated in a wealthy world amid all its riches and power.

Poets are humanity's sensitive antennas. Judging by their fears and doubts, the world is not moving towards humanism but overt dehumanisation and alienation. Yasunari Kawabata, a Japanese writer, Nobel Prize laureate for literature in 1968, and one of the most striking personalities in contemporary Japanese literature, committed suicide in 1971. Another great

65 A Gallup survey titled, *The Opinion of the Entire Humanity*, conducted in 1976, showed that, in contrast to the scepticism of the inhabitants of developed countries, the poor nations of South America and Africa view the future optimistically.

Japanese novelist, Yukio Mishima, ended his life in the same way in 1969. Thirteen Japanese novelists and other writers have committed suicide since 1895, among them the famous author of Rashomon, Ryunosuke Akutagawa (died in 1927). This 'tragedy in sequels' of Japanese culture, lasting for the past seventy years, coincides with the incursion of Western civilisation and its materialist worldview into the traditional culture of Japan. Whatever else it may be, civilisation will always have an inhuman character and pose a threat to humanity in the eyes of poets and tragedians.

A year before his death, Kawabata wrote, 'People are separated from each other by a concrete wall that prevents any flow of love. Nature is being suffocated in the name of progress.' Kawabata places the theme of human loneliness and alienation in the modern world at the centre of his novel *Snow Country* (1937).

All the great representatives of culture perceive this failure and defeat of man in civilisation in the same way. André Malraux asks what the final result of the hopes and optimism of the nineteenth century is, and then answers: 'It is a devastated and bloody Europe, but not bloodier than the human it hoped to create.' (spoken at a UNESCO conference in 1946). Paul Valéry saw a similar image right after the First World War. Writing in 1919, he states:

> There is a lost illusion of a European culture and the proof of the helplessness of knowledge to save anything; there is a science that is deathly wounded in its moral ambitions and dishonoured by the atrocity of its applications; there is idealism that took a difficult victory; thoroughly battered, responsible for its dreams; a disappointed, beaten, crushed realism, under the weight of crimes and mistakes; greed and abnegation equally ridiculed, faiths mixed up in different times; cross against cross, crescent against crescent; there are sceptics confused as well by the events so fast, so heavy, so startling

> that play with our thoughts as a cat with mice; sceptics lose their doubts, find them again, then lose them once more and no longer know how to use these turns of their spirit.

Nihilism and the philosophy of the absurd are the fruits of the richest and most civilised parts of the world. This philosophy speaks of a 'world without a future', of a 'psychologically disassembled and disintegrated individual', of a 'world of deaf-mute silence', etc. It is certainly not a poisonous philosophy, as some have labelled it. In fact, it is profoundly insightful and instructive. It expresses human resistance and the refusal to accept a world that develops and grows contrary to one's own image of it. It is the rebellion of man against the one-dimensional world of civilisation (A. Camus, *The Rebel*; Herbert Marcuse, *One-Dimensional Man*). In this sense, some have called modern nihilism a certain form of religion—and not without reason, as we shall see. Both religion and nihilism represent the negation of materialism, and they grasp this world with the same sense of dread. Both share the primeval anxiety of gazing beyond the grave, desperately trying to find a way out of a world in which man is a stranger (A. Camus, *The Stranger*). The difference is that nihilism cannot find the exit, while religion believes it has found it.

Once the failure of civilisation to solve the problem of human happiness with its science, power, and wealth is understood and accepted, it will exert an enormous psychological influence on humanity. This realisation will mark the beginning of an awakening and a re-examination of some of our elementary and widely accepted beliefs. The scientific fallacy about humans will be among the first under attack. For if civilisation is unable to solve the problem of human happiness, it means that the religious idea of human origins is true and the scientific one false. There is no third option.

NIHILISM

Let us return once more to the common points between nihilism and religion. This connection reveals contemporary nihilism as a form of religion within civilisation. Nihilism is not a negation of God, but a protest against the absence of God—or, as Beckett put it, a protest against the absence of man, the impossibility of man's existence, and his unachievability under current existential conditions. This stance implies not a scientific but a religious vision of man and the world. The man envisioned by science is both possible and achieved. But 'all finite is inhuman'. Sartre's famous line that 'man is a useless passion' is religious both in tone and meaning, for in materialism there is no passion or uselessness no uselessness because there is no passion. Materialism frees itself from the risk of meaninglessness and vanity by rejecting any higher purpose. In a materialist view, the world and man have practical goals and functions, even if purely zoological. To claim that man is a futile longing is to acknowledge an incompatibility between man and the world—an acknowledgment shared by every religion at its core.

Sartre's uselessness and Camus' absurd assume a search for purpose and meaning—a search that, unlike the religious one, ends in failure. This search is religious because it signifies a rejection of the worldly human life and its mere function. Every search for God is an act of religion, but not every search results in finding. Nihilism is disappointment—not in the world's order, but by the absence of God from the universe.

Everything becomes futile and meaningless if man dies forever (compare with Qur'an, 23:115).

The philosophy of the absurd does not speak of religion literally, but it clearly expresses the belief that man and the world are not created in harmony. It voices an anxiety that is religious in all its phases except in its final conclusion. Man is a stranger in this world, both to nihilism and religion—but while he is hopelessly lost for the nihilist, he remains a stranger with hope of salvation for the religious.

Albert Camus' thoughts can only be understood as those of a disappointed believer: 'In a world where illusion and light are suddenly gone, man feels himself a stranger. It is an exile without exit, considering there are no memories of a lost home nor hope of finally reaching some promised land.' Or: 'If I were a tree among trees… this life would have sense, or even better, this problem would not have been set because I would be a part of this world. I would be this world that I am now defying with all of my consciousness.' And: 'Everything is allowed since God does not exist and man dies.'

This last statement bears no connection to the shallow and confident atheism of rationalist thinkers. On the contrary, it is the subdued curse of a muted soul, exhausted by the search for God and unable to find Him. It is an 'atheism of despair'. Existentialism shares religion's stance on moral freedom. The French writer Simone de Beauvoir states:

> In the beginning, man is nothing; it is up to him to make himself good or bad, based on whether he accepts freedom or rejects it… Freedom absolutely sets its goals, and no foreign power, not even death itself, is capable of destroying what freedom has set…. If the game is not lost or won beforehand, then it is necessary to fight and take risks every single minute.[66]

66 Simone de Beauvoir, *L'existentialisme et la sagesse des nations*, 1953.

Even Sartre's duality of being (*être-en-soi* and *être-pour-soi*—'being-in-itself' and 'being-for-itself') is a clear negation of materialism.[67]

The Beatniks (or hippies) are, in a certain sense, a continuation of existentialism—its practical expression and application. Their protest against progress—regardless of its extreme and absurd forms—is the greatest merit of this movement, making it an authentic cultural phenomenon of our age. Such a challenge to progress could have originated only within a philosophy that is, at least in its basic premises, religious.

This critique of civilisation is not a call to reject it. Even if we wished to, we could not cast away civilisation. But what is both necessary and possible is to debunk the myth of civilisation. Dispelling that myth is the condition for further humanisation of the world and the greatest task of culture.

67 Or his acknowledgment of consciousness: 'Everything that happens in consciousness cannot be explained by anything outside of it, but only within consciousness itself.' (J. P. Sartre, *Esquisse d'une théorie des émotions*). And what can be said about *Huis Clos*, Sartre's play, which tells us that everything that truly exists, exists only as a relationship between man and man. Only the names are new, the essence is old and easily identifiable.

CHAPTER 3

PHENOMENON OF ART

ART AND SCIENCE

There is an order in a machine and an order in a melody. These two orders cannot be reduced to each other, even in the deepest analysis. The first represents a spatial, quantitative combination of relations and parts with respect to nature, logic, and mathematics. The second holds a combination of tones in a certain sequence, as found in the structure of a melody or a poem. These two orders belong to two different realms: science and religion—or, from this standpoint, science and art.

The existence of another world (another order of things), different from the natural world, is the basic premise of every religion and every art. If there were only one world, art would be impossible. In fact, every piece of art is a declaration, an impression of a world to which we do not belong, from which we have not sprouted, but into which we have been 'cast'. Art is nostalgia, or 'remembrance'.

Someone once called art 'the call for the creation of man', while the final conclusion of every science must be: man does not exist. Art is therefore in natural opposition to the world, including all of science—its psychology, biology, and Darwinism. Essentially, it is a religious opposition. Religion, morality, and art stem from the same family tree that begins with the act of Creation. Darwinist negation of Creation, by circumventing this act, becomes the most radical denial of religion, ethics, art, and even law. For if man is indeed 'tailored according to Darwin', if he is not merely the vessel or scaffolding for his spirit, his 'I', then art has no purpose, and poets and tragedians are merely deluding us and writing nonsense.

It is at this point that the first, and perhaps most decisive, concordance between art and religion occurs, as well as the absolute, irrevocable schism between science and art. Of the three degrees of reality known and possible in our universe—matter, life, and personality—science deals only with the first, while art deals exclusively with the last. Everything else is either an illusion or a misunderstanding, for when science turns to life and humanity, it finds only what is dead and impersonal within them.

Science and art relate to each other as quantity relates to quality. Auguste Comte defined mathematics, the queen of sciences, as 'indirect measurement of quantities', while Giacometti defined art as 'exploration of the impossible and the doomed attempt to grasp the essence of life.' One concerns the relation of sizes, the other the relation of values. In the material world, there is only quantity, and all quantities are comparable. Quality, in this realm, is merely a form of quantity. In *Dialectics of Nature*, Engels observes that 'it is impossible to change the quality of a body without adding or subtracting matter or movement—that is, without a quantitative change to that body.' This quantitative principle in nature is expressed in Pythagoras' words: 'Number is the essence of all things, and the organisation of the universe is a harmonious system of numbers and their relations.' Or, as Mendeleev stated: 'The chemical attributes of elements are periodic functions of their atomic weight.' In the natural world, there is only this quantitative—and therefore illusory—quality.

No two identical men exist, just as no two different rocks exist. What is the difference between two water molecules? Their position in space. If we assume that space is infinite, this difference loses all specificity. Causality, dialectics, and matter are identical. Proving dialectics in a material world is tautological. Precisely because there is no quality in nature, the science of nature is possible. It is impossible to base any science or opinion on quality.

Nature can be beautiful or frightening, convenient or chaotic, meaningful or meaningless, but only in relation to a subject—in relation to man. Otherwise, objectively speaking, these qualities do not exist, and nature remains completely homogeneous and 'indifferent'.

When faced with a song, melody, or painting, we stand face to face with the secret called quality, in the metaphysical sense of the word. For example, how could one use quantity to explain the difference between an original painting and its forgery? The original possesses the quality of beauty, and 'every copy is ugly'. The difference between them is obviously not a matter of something being added to or taken from the forgery in a quantitative sense. The difference lies in the personal touch between the work of art and the artist. Quality can only be found in relation to personality.

Science and art stand in relation to each other like Newton, the oracle of the mechanical universe, and Shakespeare, 'the poet who knew everything about man.' Newton and Shakespeare—or Einstein and Dostoevsky—represent gazes facing opposite directions, two completely separate and independent 'knowledges' that neither proceed from nor depend on each other.

The question of human destiny, loneliness, transience, and death; the question of the meaning or meaninglessness of existence and the way out of these dilemmas—none of these will ever become subjects for science. Yet art cannot escape these topics, even if it wanted to. Poetry is 'knowledge' about man, just as science is knowledge about nature. These two forms of knowledge are parallel, simultaneous, and independent, just like the two worlds they represent. One approach uses intelligence, analysis, observation, experimentation, and experience of the material world, 'the sum of things and processes connected by causal relations.' The other dives into the human inner world, its hidden corners and secrets, where we understand—or perhaps merely sense—through excitement, love, and suffering. Here, there are no rational, scientific discoveries.[68]

This inner, organic nature of art is reflected in another specific fact: the impossibility of organising teamwork in an artistic endeavour. A piece of art is always tied to the artist's personality. Just like creation, like 'the making of a man' (Michelangelo), it is the fruit of one soul and, as such, an indivisible act. Cooperative teamwork among scientists is possible in scientific fields because the subject of science is prone to analysis, separation, and division, as it is composed of details. Science, as a whole, from its earliest beginnings until today, is merely a continuation—a mechanical carrying on. This is impossible in art. Two painters could not have created the ceiling of the Sistine Chapel, regardless of it being a lifelong work. The same applies to poetry or music. Art concerns something unique, simple, and indivisible—something that cannot be halved without ceasing to live.

68 From this perspective, we associate philosophy with science, rather than with art. For, although their subjects differ, both science and philosophy share the same method—the rationalistic one. Every form of reasoning, whether scientific or philosophical, leads to the same or similar conclusions. The eighteenth-century rationalist philosophers developed the so-called 'geometric' (also called axiomatic) method of presenting philosophical theories. Its creator is considered to be Baruch Spinoza, who presented his main work *Ethics* (1677) using the 'geometric' method, similar to Euclidean geometry, i.e., by formulating definitions, axioms, and theorems derived from them. The same system was applied by Malebranche, who derived all his teachings about the world from a small number of evident and widely accepted propositions, while Christian Wolff deduced his entire system, encompassing cosmology, ontology, theology, psychology, law, and logic, through rationalistic deduction. Philosophy, even when addressing the human being and morality, inevitably remains in the realm of nature, and therefore can apply methods of mathematics, geometry, and rationalistic deduction. However, for this reason, philosophy often remains devoid of knowledge of the true essence of life.

The claim that teams of architects achieve remarkable results today (Bauhaus, S.O.M. in the USA and others) is largely a misunderstanding. A building, as a product of construction, technique, and utility, is subject to teamwork, but the style, idea, and artistic side of architecture are always the work of one person—an artist.

Wherever it goes, science discovers the equal, compatible, immovable, and uniform, while art is 'continuous new becoming' (Jean Cassou). Serial production belongs to industry (which is applied science); original work belongs to art. 'A village potter strives to bring a dozen simple pots into existence, while a Greek ceramicist strives for the existence of the Canosa amphora.' (Étienne Souriau) Science discovers; art creates. The light of a distant star existed long before science discovered it. The light that an artwork suddenly casts upon us was created by art itself in that very moment—without it, that light would never have been born. Science deals with the existing; art is the coming into existence itself—the birth of the new.

Science tells correct things; art says truthful things. Consider a portrait or an artistic painting of a landscape. How correct are they? Yet, they are always more truthful than a photograph of that face or landscape. Science creates 'psyche' out of soul and 'root cause' out of God, just as contrived, insincere academic art creates a poster-like, anonymous individual out of a living, free personality. Both represent the same degradation at their core, achieved by eliminating the inner dimension of freedom. All biological or psychological analyses are more or less correct, and with enough time and resources, they may become entirely correct. However, they are not truthful because, in both cases, the essential phenomenon is lost from the overall picture: in the first case, life; in the second, soul.

From this standpoint, all exact sciences are false sciences. Art neglects facts (often deliberately) in its pursuit of truth about a given subject. This is confirmed, in its own way, by so-called abstract art, which strives to give shape and colour a purely spiritual meaning by removing any resemblance to the external world. This is what Whistler called 'ridding the painting of every external interest.'

Science aims to know the laws and use them. A work of art, on the other hand, 'reflects the cosmic order of things without questioning it.' The father of European science, Francis Bacon, clearly highlights the functionality or utilitarianism of science: 'True knowledge is only that which increases man's power in the world', while Kant speaks of the 'aimless purposiveness' of the beautiful.[69] A song is neither functional nor utilitarian, nor is it 'a social order', as Mayakovsky claims. French painter Dubuffet dismantles that favourite fallacy bluntly: 'Art is, in fact, uncomfortable, useless, antisocial, dangerous. And if it is not all that, it is just a lie, a mannequin.'

Science, no matter how deep or complex, has never felt the insufficiency of language, yet art has always sought out other, 'supralinguistic' tools precisely because of its inner, spiritual tendency. Language is the 'hand of the brain', and the brain is part of our physicality—our mortality. The word, united with the alphabet as a means of continuing human experience, became the most powerful instrument of science. The alphabet suits language, language suits thought, and all three are moulded by intelligence—yet entirely inadequate, almost incapable, of expressing the movement of the soul.[70]

There is no way to retell Beethoven's *Ninth Symphony*, nor to translate *Hamlet* into scientific language or reduce it to a series

---

69 It has been shown that war is the main driving force of scientific progress. Periods of intense scientific discoveries and technological advancements coincide with periods of war or sharp confrontations. The last great war and its continuation in the bitter peace that followed (the Cold War) are convincing evidence of this claim.

70 Bryen: 'Painting is the complete absence of speech, a special visual world in which the painter serves himself. It is a world unto itself, a metaphysical phase that criticism cannot explain, as it is forced to grapple with language.'

of psychological or ethical questions. The failure of the analytical approach should, at last, reveal something to us. While working on *King Lear*, Peter Brook spoke of the play as 'a mountain whose peak will never be reached or conquered.' To reach the essence of the spiritual, one must transcend terms and language.

A peculiar multilingual play of words appears in the works of James Joyce (*Ulysses*). Similar untranslatable expressions can be found in the Qur'an at the beginning of some surahs. Morality, metaphysics, and belief are passed on through tradition, expressed in drama or the silent language of dance and ritual. The ancient Japanese *Kabuki* ballet—according to legend, invented at the dawn of time—or *mudras*, the fascinating finger and hand gestures in classical Indian dance, surpass the expressivity of any speech. Language is inadequate and unfit to convey what these forms of art communicate to the spectator. There is evidence suggesting that dance is older than language. In fact, the perfection of ancient dances parallels the utter imperfection and underdevelopment of early language.

This impossibility of reaching art through rational or logical means is not limited to certain branches or movements within art. The common belief that realism is closer and easier to understand than impressionism or surrealism is largely a fallacy—if we are speaking of the true essence of art and not merely superficial impressions of the artwork. The true secret of the *Mona Lisa* is no less enigmatic than Picasso's *Les Demoiselles d'Avignon*, which launched the Cubist revolution in European painting. The essence of a work of art is as unfathomable as the concept of piety or the sense of inner freedom, and all efforts to capture it on a rational level—like attempts to define life itself—have remained fruitless.[71]

---

71 Let us listen to this definition by Hauser, which seems to exist only to demonstrate the failure of any definition of a work of art: 'A work of art is form and content, confession and deception, play and message, it is close to nature and far from nature, purposeful and purposeless, historical and ahistorical, personal and suprapersonal at the same time.' (Arnold Hauser, *The Philosophy of Art History*, Zagreb, 1977)

ART AND RELIGION

All of these efforts, regardless of the fact that they remain incomplete and even unsuccessful, still lead to the anticipation of the essential connection between art and religion. 'Poetry is the fruit of spirit touching reality that is unspeakable on its own and touching its source: God.' (Maritain)

> Every poem owes its pure poetic character to the presence, meaning, and unifying action of one mysterious reality that we call 'pure poetry'. (Monk Bremond, *Pure Poetry*)

> Poetry shows itself as direct knowledge of the terrible secret that our life, taken by the cosmic mystery, sets for itself. (Roland de Peneville, *Poetic Experience*)

A poet is an oracle discovering the key to the former festivals. (Rimbaud)

> Art as creation, in particular poetry as a way of existing, strives to become a form of replacement for the holy… Whether it appears as knowledge or as an application of life (or both at the same time), poetry in every way exalts man above his human limitations; it becomes a holy activity. (Gaétan Picon)

> Most people would not have an opinion about painting, sculpture, or literature any more than they have about architecture… if they did not have the feeling of transcendence that every religion is based on, when faced with the darkness of infinity, a birth, a death, or even some personality. (André Malraux, *Voices of Silence*)

Many believe that Kafka's novels can only be interpreted as religious parables, while Kafka himself said that he saw his questions as a form of prayer. 'The universe is brimming with signs that we do not understand.' (Franz Kafka)

One of the famous surrealists, Michel Leiris, states:

> I no longer believed in anything—in any case, I did not believe in God, not even in another world—but I gladly spoke of the Absolute, the Eternal... I faintly hoped that a poetic miracle would intervene to change everything and that I would enter Eternity alive, defeating my human destiny with my words.[72]

One way or another, it is the same human longing. The difference lies only in which of them takes the central place in any particular case. Religion places Eternity and the Absolute at its centre, morality places Good and Freedom, and art places Man and Creation. Ultimately, they are all different aspects of the same inner reality, expressed and sensed through a language that may be insufficient but is the only one at our disposal.[73]

There is a fundamental unity at the core of both religion and art. The origin of drama is religious, both in its themes and its history, with temples serving as the first real theatres, complete with actors, costumes, and audiences. The first dramas were ritual performances in ancient Egypt, dating back to the 3rd and 2nd millennia BC. The famous ancient Greek drama developed from choral songs in honour of the deity Dionysus. Theatres were built near Dionysus's temples, plays were performed during Dionysian celebrations, and they were seen as part of the 'divine service' (Bloch). The origin of theatre, like all of culture, is undoubtedly rooted in ritual, with clear principal and historical evidence of this connection.[74]

---

72 Michel Leiris *Manhood*, 1963.

73 See more in: Jules Monnerot, *La Poésie moderne et le sacré* (1945).

74 See: Zdenko Lešić, *Teorija drame kroz stoljeća/Drama theory through centuries* (Sarajevo 1977).

Drama, not theology, is the medium through which true religious and ethical problems of man and humanity are expressed. One can clearly sense the dual nature of the mask, which evokes both religion and drama simultaneously. Likewise, the first painting, sculpture, poem, and dance were integral parts of rituals, only later separating from the cult to exist independently. When a primitive man painted an animal he intended to hunt (so-called 'hunter's magic'), painting for him was a form of worship—a prayer.

The roots of the famous Japanese *gigaku* ballet reach into the distant past, to 'the time of the creation of the world', according to Japanese beliefs. These ancient performances were a blend of song, dance, and mimicry, symbolically depicting the metaphysical journey that the souls of the deceased must undergo. These performances share much with religion, both in their antiquity and in their subject matter. Similarly, in pre-Islamic Arabic tradition, the poet (shair) was a privileged figure, endowed with power through his connection to magical forces. The terrifying and exalted words of poets were believed to possess supernatural power, capable of saving or destroying lives.[75]

Gabriel Zaida, who recently compiled an excellent selection of Mexican Indian poetry, writes in the foreword of his book that 'the general and common characteristic of Mexican Indian poetry is the symbolisation of eternal life, and the relationship with the totem—a plant, animal, or natural phenomenon—is almost always transformed into a magical, religious ritual.'[76]

The unity of art and religion explains the famous mystery of the *Song of Songs*, a purely worldly text of great artistic value, being included in the Bible. If religion and art are strictly

75 Nerkez Smailagić, *Uvod u Kur'an/Introduction to Translation of Meaning of Qur'an* (Zagreb 1975) pg. XXVI.

76 Gabriel Zaida, *Omnibus de poesia Mexicana* (1971).

divided, this inclusion is inexplicable. But if one accepts their intrinsic unity, the problem disappears, and there is nothing surprising about the *Song of Songs* finding its place within a religious text. After all, this 'mystery' concerns only biblical analysts; believers have never questioned its presence.

Art is the daughter of religion, just as 'science is the daughter of astronomy' (Bergson). For art to thrive, it must continually return to this source—and, as we can see, it does exactly that.

Architecture has reached its highest levels of inspiration in the construction of temples, across all cultures without exception. This holds true for the ancient temples of India and Cambodia, older than 2,000 years, mosques throughout the Islamic world, temples in the jungles of pre-Columbian America, and the churches and chapels of twentieth century Europe and America. None of today's great builders and architects have resisted this challenge. Frank Lloyd Wright designed the Beth Sholom Synagogue in Elkins Park, Pennsylvania; Le Corbusier designed the Notre Dame du Haut in Ronchamp (completed in 1955) and the Dominican Monastery in Éveux, France; Mies van der Rohe designed the Chapel of the Illinois Institute of Technology (1952); Alvar Aalto designed the Lutheran Church in Vuoksenniska, Finland (1959); Wallace Harrison designed the First Presbyterian Church in Stamford (1959); Philip Johnson designed the Kneses Tifereth Israel Synagogue in New York (1954); Rudolph Lendy designed the Lutheran Church of St Paul in Sarasota, Florida (1959); Oscar Niemeyer designed the Church of St Francis of Assisi in Pampulha, Brazil; Eduardo Torroja designed the Herald Chapel in the Pyrenees (1942); and Félix Candela designed the La Virgen Milagrosa Church in Mexico (1953), among others.

A complete list would be too long. Through its tireless construction of temples, architecture—even though the most functional and least spiritual of all branches of art—confirms its sacred character.

Art repaid its debt to religion even more clearly through painting, sculpture, and music. The greatest works of art in the Renaissance are almost without exception centred on religious subjects, embraced with parental hospitality by churches across Europe. Is there a church in Italy or the Netherlands that is not also a gallery? The paintings and sculptures of Michelangelo represent a certain continuation of Christianity—'the Gospel in colour and stone.'

Two of the greatest composers of the twentieth century, Debussy and Stravinsky, created works with clear religious content (Debussy: *Le Martyre de saint Sébastien—The Martyrdom of St Sebastian*; Stravinsky: *Symphony of Psalms, Mass, Canticum Sacrum*), while Chagall painted 15 of his great canvases on biblical themes. Olivier Messiaen, a leading composer of piano music and a representative of the musical avant-garde of the 1950s, also created a series of works inspired by religious meditations (e.g. *Twenty Contemplations on the Infant Jesus*).

The most impressive ballets of Maurice Béjart, the greatest contemporary ballet composer of the twentieth century, are inspired by Wagner's mythology and Far Eastern mysticism (e.g. *Bhakti, Boléro, Les Vainqueurs*, etc.). Mondrian, one of the fathers of abstract painting (and a member of the Theosophical Society of the Netherlands!), saw asceticism and sanctification in art—a tool to reach the 'supreme truth'—while his equally renowned compatriot Jan Toorop developed a religious and moral conception of painting through his symbolism and mysticism.

Yves Klein drew inspiration from Zen Buddhism, meditating on immaterial cosmic energy—a painterly continuation of Bergson's philosophy of intuition. For Klein, art is a pure outpouring of vocation, a kind of divine revelation (his most daring composition, *Cosmogonies*, was painted with the help of rain and wind). The idea of the so-called 'world theatre' also clearly points to the sacred nature of its symbolism.

'Our century is marked, in all fields of creation, by the emergence of an all-encompassing symbolism of sacred thought and feeling,' notes one writer. However, as we have seen, this is not a new or temporary tendency but a permanent state emerging from the very nature of art. Everything in true art—if we exclude all that is mediocre—is precisely this: suprarational and sacred.[77]

Art communicates truths as profound and enigmatic as those conveyed by religion. Consider an ancient Japanese fresco, the intricate arabesques adorning the Court of the Lions in the Alhambra, a Melanesian mask, a Ugandan tribal dance, Michelangelo's *The Last Judgement* in Sistine Chapel, Picasso's *Guernica*, or listen to Debussy's *Le Martyre de saint Sébastien*, or an African American spiritual. Each offers an experience as ineffable and transcendent as prayer. Doesn't every piece of abstract art seem as irrational and non-scientific as a religious ritual? In a sense, painting is ritual on canvas, and symphony is ritual in sound.

Art is not primarily the creation of beauty, for 'the opposite of beautiful is not ugly but a lie.' One might not claim that Aztec masks, Ivorian masks, or Alberto Giacometti's slender, eyeless figures are conventionally beautiful. However, they express an authentic quest for truth, representing, in various ways, an anticipation of cosmic events tied to human destiny or a sense of transcendence.

This intrinsic connection between religion and art is also evident in the intentional, 'professional' dishevelment of artists and the so-called 'holy impurity', a form of physical neglect present in certain religious orders, especially within Hinduism and Christianity. Artists and monks are often viewed

77 The example of the eighteenth century is not the only one in this regard, but it is certainly the most striking due to the pronounced contrasts: the thought was anti-religious, life secular, and art explicitly religious (this is the era of Bach).

similarly by the general populace. Though it may seem surprising at first, monasticism and bohemianism share a foundational philosophy. For monks, it's a vow; for artists, a lifestyle. In both cases, the essence is the same: emphasising the spiritual meaning of life and disdain for the material, external, and conventional—essentially, a genuine religiosity. The term 'dervish', the Muslim equivalent of a monk, literally means beggar. 'Live as lilies in the field' or 'as birds in the air' (Gospel)—this astonishing religious injunction finds its most practical embodiment among artists.

It now seems entirely natural that religion and art have shared similar fates throughout history. They have often experienced comparable degrees of freedom and restriction in various contexts. There's a discernible pattern: the extraordinary advancement of science and education in the Soviet Union was accompanied by a marked decline in artistic creation across almost all fields, while the opposite was true during the Church's dominance in medieval times. In such scenarios, the prevailing philosophy of the ruling system is profoundly engaged with religion, either through fervent support or outright rejection. Despite the constraints of the medieval era, the atmosphere was imbued with religiosity, allowing art to feel 'in its element'.

Conversely, despite formal declarations of freedom of faith and creation, atheistic and materialistic philosophies can deprive art of its *élan* and freedom. It is the nature of atheism to suffocate art, just as it is the nature of religion to inspire it. Even open-minded atheism stifles art, while even authoritative religion sets it free. When Pope Julius II 'persecuted' Michelangelo during his work on the frescoes in the Sistine Chapel, he effectively 'compelled' him to fulfil his destiny. State persecution of artists, however, always has an opposite aim: to force them to abandon their mission.

Artists did not feel the totalitarianism of the Church in the medieval era (scientists did), and it seems that scientists in the

Soviet Union felt the totalitarianism of the existing government the least. The renowned Italian school achieved its best works at the height of the Inquisition and the persecution of scientists and thinkers at the end of the Middle Ages. Soviet science accomplished significant results in atomic energy and space exploration under Stalin and Zhdanov.[78] All the pressure was borne by Soviet art because—being art—it belonged to another world, another order of things.

The Church once tried to turn science into a servant of theology; in the Soviet Union, they attempted to turn art into an official of politics. When an authoritative body declares that Socialist Realism is the only correct direction in Soviet art, it is a dictate (and delusion) akin to when the Church, from its high council, 'establishes' that Earth is the centre of the universe. The difference is that the first dictate is directed at art and the second at science. But rather than a dictate, it is a misunderstanding—a natural misunderstanding.

Atheism will never have an essential understanding of art; religion will never understand science. Picasso can go to the Soviet Union, but his painting cannot. The Soviet Union accepts his political stances but does not accept—cannot accept—his art, because art, regardless of the conscious desires and beliefs of the artist, remains what it is: a sacred message, a testimony against the finality and relativity of man, news about a cosmic order of things; in one word, a cosmic perspective that contradicts the vision of a materialist universe without God, both as a whole and in each of its parts.

The reasons are essentially the same for placing the Christian novels of Fyodor Dostoevsky and the paintings of his compatriot Marc Chagall on the index in the USSR. There is a certain

78 A. A. Zhdanov, Stalin's close associate, secretary of the CPSU Central Committee, known as the protagonist of the persecution of painters, philosophers, writers, musicians, and other public figures in the USSR after World War II.

tragedy akin to that of Bruno and Galileo in the misfortunes of Pasternak and Solzhenitsyn, but by reverse logic. Zhdanovism and the Inquisition are parallel phenomena 'of the same kind'. Zhdanovism is an inquisition against artists and thinkers in the name of state atheism, and the Inquisition is Zhdanovism against scientists in the name of the Church as an organised religion. Zhdanovism is a reversed inquisition.

ART AND ATHEISM
(ART IN USSR)

One of the law-like patterns of 'state atheism' is the phenomenon of general recession of art in Russia simultaneous with extraordinary expansion of education. The tempo of education that is recorded in communist countries surpassed everything that has ever been registered in this field up to then. According to some data, there were more than 60 million people attending some kind of school in the USSR in 1965.[79] But as we have seen, it is the naked education whose 'civilisational' character is only increased by the uncritical political and ideological indoctrination. Culture and art are clearly lagging behind in this typical country of civilisation. This is true particularly for the relation between public rule and the man—citizen, or even more precisely, the question of human freedom as the basic question of culture.

According to official understanding (all the understandings are official there), the literature in the USSR should be the tool of daily agitational-political pressure on masses. Different literary groups were liquidated by the decision of the Central Committee of the Communist Party of the Soviet Union in 1932 and a singular Union of Soviet Writers was established. This liquidation turned very literal. Out of 700 writers present in the First Congress of Soviet Writers in 1934, only 50 of them were alive for the next Congress held in 1954. Most

79 Roger Dale mentions this in his *History of Education*.

of them died in Stalin's purges (data from *Encyclopaedia of Lexicographic Institute*, Zagreb, binder 5, pg. 641). Socialist realism was declared the only correct direction (method) in Soviet art. As an expression of this 'engaged' art, the so-called 'production novel' emerged in the USSR, which deals with industrialisation and kolkhoz. Theory of anti-heroism in Soviet literature was condemned at a Congress of Soviet Writers in 1965, and it was concluded that 'deep patriotism and heroic acts are the characteristic of Soviet literature.'

'Of all the arts, film is the most important for us,' used to say Lenin, but the fact is that film is less art than all of the phenomena that carry that name. If art has to serve someone or something—ideology or authority does not matter—then film is the most convenient form to be put in the position of hireling. R.N. Yurenev, Soviet film critic, declares in one of his monographs about Soviet comedy films that Stalin did not tolerate the showing of clashes, hardships, and imperfections in movies about contemporary topics. Instead, he would ask for scenes of feasts, weddings, rallies, folk dances, and choir songs. Since Stalin watched all the movies before their public screening, he would give directives that would turn into laws. The consequences were the decrease in production of movies and the emergence of an illness known as 'fear of satire'.

'Don't worry man. Think about the size of the universe—Andromeda is a few million light years away—you will understand how insignificant you are, your suffering and your confusion,' I have heard these words countless times. But I always believed in the opposite: the only significant thing, the only real happening, is the man and his drama on Earth. Without man, without his fear, admiration, dilemmas, good and evil, everything is meaningless. What will the universe signify when the last human eye observing it shuts down? God says it clearly too: man was the purpose (not the world).

In the nineteenth century, Russia, despite being a poor, barely literate, and disorganized country, gifted the world with luminaries such as Pushkin, Gogol, Chekhov, Tolstoy, Dostoevsky, Tchaikovsky, and Rimsky-Korsakov. However, by the mid-twentieth century, the Soviet Union struggled to produce artists and writers that would be of comparable stature to the great protagonists of Russian culture in its very beginnings on the world history scene. Notable figures who did emerge, nurtured by the profound spiritual genius of the Russian people, regularly found themselves at odds with the system—Pasternak, Solzhenitsyn, and Voznesensky among them. The Russian land is indeed fertile, but its atmosphere is suffocating for poets and artists.

Following the revolution, there was an advance in Russian science and a recession in the arts. Soviet Russia produced physicists, atomic scientists, statesmen, and organisers, but not poets, painters, or musicians of the same calibre. This lag is particularly evident in the field of philosophy, which remains virtually void, save for professors and officials in philosophical institutes. The contemporary Soviet Union lacks a single philosopher on par with Heidegger, Marcuse, or Sartre. Soviet 'philosophers' do not measure up to their compatriots who have devoted their intellectual energies to science, technology, or politics.

The saturation with the formula of so-called socialist realism is palpable. To counter the evidently waning audience interest, authorities resort to grandiose slogans such as 'The plateau on which the flag of socialist realism is raised is high and marvellous.'[80]

Writers like Grigurko, Boiko, Malychev, Tarasov, and Sushinsky—largely unknown in Europe, even in the USSR—are lauded by official state critics for their focus on contemporary

80 The slogan was displayed at a retrospective exhibition of Soviet academicians in Manezh in early 1974.

'production' themes. They depict the construction of large industrial projects and 'reflect the life of the working class and village labourers' in their works. These creations adhere to the 'soczakaz' system, or social order.[81]

Academician Korzhev acknowledges that 'unfortunately, our exhibitions often feature works that merely replicate already established characters,' while poet Boris Oleynik laments the monochromatic portrayal of life, drabness, superficiality, and mediocrity: 'The sky of Soviet poetry has stars of pale glow; there is no true poetry—only verses and the imitation of poetry.'

A group of Soviet writers—including A. Voznesensky, Bella Akhmadulina, Vasily Aksyonov, and Fazil Iskander—describe the literary landscape in the USSR in a recent publication (*Almanach*, 1979) as a 'chronic ailment identifiable as a fear of literature and a gloomy inertia that induces a state of quiet and stagnant dread.'[82]

This adverse attitude towards art is equally evident in architecture. Civilisation has propelled architecture towards functionalism and stark 'tecture' worldwide, but the 'artificial cities' (or new urban areas) in socialist countries represent the bleakest, most faceless urban developments ever constructed. They exude achromatism and drabness. Various justifications are offered for this—such as vast needs, insufficient funds, and industrial construction—but these reasons often prove unconvincing. Many beautiful structures were erected during times of greater poverty, and aesthetically pleasing buildings can be constructed from prefabricated elements.

---

81 'Soczakaz' – a term in the USSR for artwork produced on commission, characterized by stereotypicality and a lack of true inspiration.

82 "This 'Almanac' is more widely known for the sharp polemic between a group of American writers (Albee, Miller, Updike, etc.) and the management of the Moscow Writers' Union due to the ban on publishing the 'Almanac' and administrative measures against its authors."

The underlying issue is a conscious or unconscious inner stance, a hidden question: if humans lack souls, why should cities possess them? In any case, regarding art, one must distinguish between the Russian people and the Soviet regime. The former are imbued with religious and artistic fervour; the latter adopts an anti-religious and, consequently, anti-artistic stance.

People's interest in literature is vast, almost 'hysterical', as Vasiliy Aksionov put it. This phenomenon deserves examination. One might find that it was a way of expressing 'unlived' religiousness of the Russian man and experiencing it through literature and poetry what is denied through religion. Art becomes a substitute for repressed religion in the enforced atheism.

THE CONCRETE WORLD OF ART
(ARTISTIC AND SOCIOLOGICAL APPROACH)

Culture has art; civilisation has science, or more precisely: sociology. Sociology is a faithful reflection of the soul—or soullessness—of civilisation. The difference between artistic and sociological approaches reflects a fundamental division of the world and that pursuit directed in opposite directions: one that will discover a personality inside a man in the first case, and in the second case, after all analysis, view him merely as a member of society or part of the mass.

There is no 'average man' to a poet. It is a lie, a fabrication. There is only a concrete man, a certain personality, and sociology finds only the common and quantitative in man and real life, while it remains blind to what is real and what is the only thing existing: the living personality, unrepeatable and incomparable with any other. Because there are no men or humankind for art. There is only man next to man in an infinite row, completely definite concrete personalities, portraits as a painter would say, that cannot be added up nor made into a median case or some average value. 'One man died, and another, and another...,' declares the poet.[83] What value would a portrait have if one did not catch those few lines that make the portrayed face 'most itself', one and unique, different from all the other faces? Sociology strives to find the general and the common, while art seeks the particular and the individual.

83 Bašeskija in his *Chronicle* (Mehmed Fatih Bašeskija, Ljetopis).

A man resists 'systematisation'. Elisabeth Noelle writes about the spontaneous repulsion of the public against examinations based on quantitative methods, against numbers, general characteristics, templates, standards.[84] No one wants to be 'an average Frenchman', an average citizen. The resistance to sociology is certainly most pronounced in poets and artists.[85]

Rainer Maria Rilke writes:

> The house, public fountain, well-known tower, even their own suit, their coat still had immensely greater significance for our grandparents; they were far more reliable; nearly every object contained a tiny part of a certain personality, every object had something human saved in it. Today we have hollow and meaningless stuff coming from America and piling up, objects that create the illusion of life.... A house in the American sense, an American apple or the grapes from there have nothing in common with a house, fruit or grape that bears the fruit and thoughts of our ancestors in them. (*Letters Around a Garden*).

Another poet, W.H. Auden, in 'Under Which Lyre', writes:

> Thou shalt not answer questionnaires
> Or quizzes upon World-Affairs,
> Nor with compliance
> Take any test. Thou shalt not sit
> With statisticians nor commit
> A social science.[86]

---

84 Elisabeth Noelle, *The Invaluable Man*, Nuremberg (1961).

85 This aversion of poets towards statistics and sociological studies received an appropriate 'dialectical' explanation from Marxists. According to this explanation, it is about the artist's fear that the 'silent agreement' about their service to the bourgeoisie might be revealed before the eyes of the world?! See: Rene Barbier, 'The Anti-Sociological Stance of Writers and Artists,' *Kultura*, Belgrade, No. 19/72.

86 W. H. Auden, *Nones* (1951).

Science and philosophy discuss the outer world or man—but always and about all things in general—in principle. As for art, things do not exist in general; they exist specifically. Art does not talk about man in general, but always about a certain man: Oliver Twist, Evgeniy Onegin, Fyodor Karamazov. The linden tree that the poet mentions is not the linden tree in general sense that botany talks about; it is the fragrant treetop in the garden of the poet's home—the same one under whose shade he dreamt his boyhood dreams. Art strikes us as more truthful because, indeed, all things that exist are individual. Here are a few examples that illustrate this claim:

A multitude of faces appear in *War and Peace* (1887). All of them are completely specific personalities, characters. Here is how Tolstoy describes one of them, the character of diplomat Bilibin:

> He was one of those, who, liking work, knew how to do it, and despite his indolence would sometimes spend a whole night at his writing table. He worked well whatever the import of his work." "Bilíbin liked conversation as he liked work, only when it could be made elegantly witty. In society he always awaited an opportunity to say something striking and took part in a conversation only when that was possible. His conversation was always sprinkled with wittily original, finished phrases of general interest. These sayings were prepared in the inner laboratory of his mind in a portable form as if intentionally, so that the very people with whom he conversed would carry them from drawing room to drawing room. His thin, worn, yellowish face was all covered with deep wrinkles, which always looked so clean and carefully washed, like the tips of one's fingers after a bath. The movements of those wrinkles formed the main play of his facial expression...

Or the character of Olivia Pentland in *Early Autumn* (1926) by Louis Bromsfield:

> If she had a rival in all the crowd that filled the echoing old house, it was Olivia Pentland--Sybil's mother--who moved about, alone most of the time, watching her guests, acutely conscious that the ball was not all it should have been. There was about her nothing flamboyant and arresting, nothing which glittered with the worldly hardness of the green dress and the diamonds and burnished red hair of Sabine Callendar; she was, rather, a soft woman, of gentleness and poise, whose dark beauty conquered in a slower, more subtle fashion. You did not notice her at once among all the guests; you became aware of her slowly, as if her presence had the effect of stealing over you with the vagueness of a perfume.

If the topic is an object, it is not an object in general. It is always a very specified object. It might be a pencil case, as in Richard Llewellyn's novel *How Green Was My Valley* (1939). Here is that description:

> There is a beautiful box, it was, too. About eighteen inches long, and three wide, with a top that slid off, and a piece cut out for your thumb to press it through the groove. On the top tray, three lovely red pencils, new, and without the marks of teeth, with sharp points, and two pens green, with brass holders for nibs, and at the end a little pit for a piece of rubber. The top tray was fast on a pivot, and you pushed it round to come to the second tray, with five more lovely pencils, three yellows, and a red and a blue. Under that one, another then, with dividers, a comcass, a ruler, a box for nibs and drawing-pins, a couple of ivory angles, a drawing pen, and crayons. And all so good you wished it had more trays again underneath.

If the topic is a situation, then it is again one specific, unrepeatable situation:

> For example, Saturday, about four in the afternoon, on the end of the timbered sidewalk of the new station yard, a little woman in sky blue was running backwards, laughing,

> waving a handkerchief. At the same time, a Negro in a cream-coloured raincoat, yellow shoes and a green hat, turned the corner of the street and whistled. Still going backwards, the woman bumped into him, underneath a lantern which hangs on a paling and which is lit at night. All at once there was the paling smelling strongly of wet wood, this lantern and this little blonde woman in the Negro's arms under a sky the colour of fire. (J. P. Sartre, *Nausea* (1938))

Or again, an extraordinarily pure and clearly sculpted character from the same novel:

> It is one-thirty. I am eating a sandwich in the Cafe Mably, everything is more or less
>
> normal. Anyway, everything is always normal in cafes and especially the Cafe Mably,
>
> because of the manager, M. Fasquelle, who has a raffish look which is positively
>
> reassuring. It will soon be time for his nap and his eyes are pink already, but he stays quick and decisive. He strolls among the tables and speaks confidently to the customers. 'Is everything all right, Monsieur?'

Or the landscape:

> It was about eleven o'clock. The sun shone somewhat to the left and behind him and brightly lit up the enormous panorama which, rising like an amphitheatre, extended before him in the clear rarefied atmosphere. From above on the left, bisecting that amphitheatre, wound the Smolénsk highroad, passing through a village with a white church some five hundred paces in front of the knoll and below it. This was Borodinó. Below the village the road crossed the river by a bridge and, winding down and up, rose higher and higher to the village of Valúevo visible about four miles away, where Napoleon was then stationed. Beyond Valúevo the road disappeared into a yellowing forest on the horizon.

> Far in the distance in that birch and fir forest to the right of the road, the cross and belfry of the Kolochá Monastery gleamed in the sun. Here and there over the whole of that blue expanse, to the right and left of the forest and the road, smoking campfires could be seen and indefinite masses of troops—ours and the enemy's. The ground to the right—along the course of the Kolochá and Moskvá rivers—was broken and hilly. Between the hollows the villages of Bezúbova and Zakhárino showed in the distance. On the left the ground was more level; there were fields of grain, and the smoking ruins of Semënovsk, which had been burned down, could be seen.

And a description of interior for the end:

> Pierre well knew this large room divided by columns and an arch, its walls hung round with Persian carpets. The part of the room behind the columns, with a high silk-curtained mahogany bedstead on one side and on the other an immense case containing icons, was brightly illuminated with red light like a Russian church during evening service. Under the gleaming icons stood a long invalid chair, and in that chair on snowy-white smooth pillows, evidently freshly changed, Pierre saw—covered to the waist by a bright green quilt—the familiar, majestic figure of his father, Count Bezúkhov, with that gray mane of hair above his broad forehead which reminded one of a lion, and the deep characteristically noble wrinkles of his handsome, ruddy face. (Tolstoy, *War and Peace* (1887))

These examples, taken at random from books I had at hand, are not unique to the works of Tolstoy, Sartre, Bromfield, or Llewellyn. They illustrate a phenomenon central to the very essence of art: the more an artist adheres to this intrinsic law of all art—being concrete, individual, personal, unrepeatable, original, unique—the greater the artist he is. Intelligence and science aim toward the pole that marks everything as equal, striving to establish uniformity in all that exists. Art, conversely, holds that each entity is singular, an original; nothing repeats itself—neither character, situation, nor landscape—and throughout eternity, there is nothing identical or congruent. This belief is inherent in the nature of art, just as uniformity, repeatability, and identity are fundamental assumptions, or even conditions, of all science. In the spectrum ranging from the mechanical to the personal—where one end represents lifeless matter with its laws, and the other end embodies life with personality as its highest expression—the further we move from the mechanical, the more freedom, uniqueness, and creativity we encounter, culminating in the originality that signifies personality. Conversely, moving away from personality leads to increased conditioning, law-like patterns, and homogeneity, until only the abstract, identical, and mechanical remain at the opposite pole.

FIGURE AND PERSONALITY
(THE DRAMA OF THE HUMAN FIGURE)

Art is profoundly engaged with the concept of personality. *War and Peace* features 592 characters and *The Divine Comedy* presents a world teeming with personalities none of whom are overshadowed or lost 'in a mass'; each soul stands alone, depicted with such realism in their responsibilities and sins that the scene of the Last Judgement, with billions of souls who lived and died seems plausible and tangible. The frescoes on the ceiling of the Sistine Chapel, illustrating scenes from the Book of Genesis, showcase a multitude of faces, each entirely individualised, embodying the essence of the figure.

What transforms a face into a figure is individuality, inner life, and freedom. A figure is more than just a human face; it reflects the striving inherent in the visage. The relationship between figure and nature parallels that of spirit and matter, quality and quantity, awareness and inertia, drama and utopia. A figure opposes nature by being free, unique, and, in a sense, immortal. Nature embodies sameness, homogeneity, compatibility, and causality. In contrast, a figure represents individuality, spontaneity, freedom, and the miraculous. Religion speaks of the soul, while art speaks of the figure; both are expressions of the same concept. Religion addresses the soul, and art endeavours to reach it, to 'bring' it into our perception.

Even in primitive art, it is evident that the most crucial element of a composition is the head, while the body, reduced to a supporting role, is depicted schematically or entirely overlooked. Sculptures of heads found in Jericho, dating back to 6000 B.C., indicate the Neolithic belief that the centre of the spirit—soul—resides within the head. The colossal stone figures on Easter Island focus entirely on the faces, with the body and nape omitted. As the Bible states, 'God breathed into man's face the spark of His spirit.'

Throughout history, great artists—from Phidias and Praxiteles to Raphael, Michelangelo, Da Vinci, Rodin, Meštrović, and Picasso—have been captivated by a singular grand theme: the human figure and its inner world. The renown of the Mona Lisa stems from its portrayal as perhaps one of the most successful attempts to 'paint' the enigma of inner life.

In recent years, American art, particularly painting, has experienced what some describe as a 'return to the drama of the human figure'. However, for art, this is a perpetual recurrence. Thus, the subject of every artwork, regardless of external ascriptions or intended uses, remains inherently spiritual and personal, never social or political. While the plot and external decor may be social, art invariably addresses the moral dimension of phenomena. Art is spiritual, even when it engages with the corporeal. Misled by appearances, some have labelled Rubens as 'the painter of the body' and Rembrandt as 'the painter of the soul', yet every painter endeavours to depict personality—that is, the soul.

The essence of every drama—which can be attributed to its religious origins—ultimately lies in the relationship between inner human freedom and the determinism of the external world into which one is cast. As Charles Lamb observed 'In certain of Shakespeare's characters, the plot concerns us comparatively little; the motive, the hidden soul in its perverted greatness, seems so real that we pay attention solely to that, and the crime becomes insignificant.'

Eugene O'Neill echoes this sentiment: 'What will I do with action? Characters are enough for me.' Similarly, Martin Buber (Author of *Me and You*) asserts, 'This character is never an object; in art, it only exists as Me and You.' This perspective fosters a continual effort to dissolve the barrier between creator and observer, integrating the audience as direct participants in the creative process. For instance, American painter Robert Rauschenberg sought to engage viewers actively in his works. In certain African villages, when a group of dancers comes to perform, the surrounding spectators gradually join in, erasing the distinction between performers and audience. No one remains outside the performance; all become participants—subjects. This exemplifies the principle of unity among the artwork, artist, and audience, a principle rooted in the metaphysical nature of art.

This principle primarily reflects art's unique stance towards what is commonly termed 'objective reality'. This so-called 'objective reality', which materialist science and philosophy have elevated to an absolute, serves as a backdrop, an illusion, and a false deity for both art and religion. The sole reality acknowledged by art is the human being and their relentless endeavour to affirm and save themselves, and not get lost in 'objective reality'. As previously discussed, every painting represents an audacious attempt to depict the miracle we call the figure. A personality amidst lifeless nature or an alien, faceless world—and the ensuing conflict from this fundamental relationship—forms the foundation of every painting. Without this content, art devolves into mere skill. This distinction elevates Rembrandt's renowned portraits above equally skilful, yet superficial fairground paintings. Even when such conflict is not overtly highlighted, it remains inherent, as every portrait strives to reveal an authentic human essence—consciousness, individuality, and freedom—standing in stark contrast to nature and the world.

This soul is not the psyche referenced by scientists; it is the true soul, the *rūh*, the bearer of human dignity and responsibility, as mentioned in the Qur'an. In essence, it is the soul that all religions, prophets, and poets speak of. This distinction separates Carl Jung's psychological types from the characters in Dostoevsky's *Crime and Punishment*. The former are monsters, superficial and two-dimensional; the latter are living beings, torn between sin and freedom—God's creations, true characters. Some critics have rightly noted that Dostoevsky's novels lack traditional development, catharsis, genesis, or temporal progression. Everything transpires within the soul, which is timeless. Actions and events require time; what occurs within the soul belongs to eternity, not temporality. In the inner world, time does not flow. Everything that transpires (what truly occurs in *The Idiot*) could unfold in a single moment.

ARTIST AND HIS WORK

Thinking about this weird, irrational, unnatural (or supernatural) side of art, emerging from its metaphysical origin, we will understand at once that artwork, as something materialised, as a fact in the outer world, is not the original goal of art. On the contrary, the creation itself is the goal, and the artwork is its inevitable byproduct. The essence of art is striving, and it is found inside, in the soul, not in the world. Art remains what it is, without everything that follows it, even without the concrete artwork. Without this creator's striving, art is not art anymore. Pollock painted by walking over canvas or waving tubes of paint above canvas. Rauschenberg started one of his phases from a row of completely white empty canvases of different sizes, and Yves Klein published a map of monochrome sheets in Madrid in 1954. The American pianist John Cage, in a composition titled '4'33"', sits at the piano for that duration without playing. Hamlet's 'inaction full of action' or the famous poverty of plot in the plays of Anton Pavlovich Chekhov is of the same kind. Some of his plays contain completely silent scenes. Nothing else happens on the stage, but the drama continues, the action unfolds 'within'. Because hope, regret, rage, humiliation, shame, and despair are not events; they are experiences. There are scenes in Japanese Noh drama in which an actor does not make the tiniest move in twenty or so minutes. He is expressing his inner turmoil during that time. This brings a view inherent to art, the emphasis of internal and subjective and negation of external and objective to its final, absurd consequences. A monochrome canvas in Art Informel can only be understood as an absolute negation of the external world. This negation cannot be expressed more clearly or more radically. Painting, the activity itself—*Action Painting*—and not the painting as an object, is the meaning and goal of art. An artwork can be unrealised, unmaterialised, can remain in a state of aspiration, but it cannot turn into production, into series. It must retain its attribute of being unique, as an important condition. Nonexistence of even this one unique piece does not bring into question the existence of 'work', but the copy or multiple copies always represent its negation. That is how we reach the paradox: artwork is destroyed by multiplication. What is left in the end is the artist's aspiration or intention as the last verifier of the artwork, the intention that is verified externally by a signature; 'Everything that an artist puts out – is art,' proclaims Schwitters. That is why bicycle parts, put next to each other by the hand of Picasso and authenticated by his signature, turn into an artwork (*Bull's Head* found in Galerie Louise Leiris in Paris).

It is at this point, in the aspiration, the wanting, conscious attitude of the subject that moral, art, and religion touch once more. 'Righteousness is not that you turn your faces toward the east or the west...' (Qur'an, 2:177), and the intention (or aspiration) remains the irreducible value of human actions, regardless of it not changing their significance or consequences in the external world. Art is creation, the activity itself, just like moral is that which gives a failed attempt or a sacrifice in vain the value in the eyes of every man. When we extract everything unimportant and accidental from art, moral, and religion, when we strip them to their essence, we will find aspiration, longing, or intention—in a word, freedom—as their final and authentic content. Religion, moral, and art in that way have one thing as their final quintessence: pure humanity. Even the works that are recurring by their nature are renewed through the artist's personality. Arthur Rubinstein said on one occasion that Beethoven's *Fourth Concerto*, which he performed countless times, was never the same piece when he performed it. Meyerhold advocated for a theatre that would only perform one piece—*Hamlet*. It would be set by different directors, and it would always be a new piece, claims Meyerhold. It is possible only because art is not in the art piece; it is in the inner life and personality of the artist, and this personality is freedom itself. The result: the experience of artwork is always different and new in some way both for the artist and the audience.

Therefore, speaking about artwork, we speak of the artist, the man who created it. Picasso used to say that looking at Cézanne's paintings always made him interested in Cézanne's enthusiasm and the fervour he had when he painted them. He says: 'It is not important what a painter does, but what a painter is.' According to him, an artwork is only significant as a gradual revelation of the artist's personality. Even an artist's moral personality is reflected in his work. 'A bad man cannot be a great poet' (Boris Pasternak), because his work—that is, he himself. We find this identification in common speech too. We say *It is Cézanne, Dürer, Rubens* instead of saying the name of the piece. When we say *Rembrandt* instead of *The Night Watch*, everything is said about that painting. That is the essence; the rest is circumstance. Art belongs to our inner world of truths, not to the external world of facts. This is why we can differentiate between sincere and insincere art, between a song from inspiration and a song by order. This is why 'every copy is ugly' (Alain). The difference between an original and a copy, if you recognise it, only exists from the standpoint of creation. There is no difference from the objective standpoint, or there is less and less of it. The situation is similar with kitsch. All the attempts to objectively define it remain incomplete. This is why Abraham Moles probably made the highest breakthrough when he discovered that kitsch is 'a relation between a man and an object, not the object itself. An adjective, not a noun.' No artistic painting or direction is fake or true by itself. Only an artist's attitude towards the world and his own work can make it fake.

Repetition, specialisation, or academicism are fake regardless of the direction or genre to which the artwork nominally belongs, because they are void of sincere inspiration and freedom, which is an irreplaceable condition of inner life in art. 'Every academicism means dying' (Jean Cassou). Insincere artists bring a stillborn artwork to the world. It is as when I pray to God. A prayer without enthusiasm or inner presence is nonsense in every world and every consciousness. Academicism in art is what pharisaism or formalism is in religion.[87] Primary significance of creation itself, as a movement of the soul, and secondary significance of the work of art as a fact in the external world is also manifested in the creation of incomprehensible works of art. Here we must first point out that there are no completely comprehensible works of art. Because 'a work of art is primarily an inner problem, a secret, an issue of faith' (French sculptor Adam) and as such it is a confession, only partially and conditionally comprehensible and meant for others. 'Only one man in the world understands my paintings, and it is me,' says De Chirico, one of the leading Italian painters, the founder of so-called metaphysical painting. Every work of art is autobiographical in a certain sense. The dramas that tragedy writers create, if they are sincere, are only fragments from the drama of their own lives. 'Even though I do not describe my personal life anywhere, all the characters in my novels speak about my life,' says Ignazio Silone. Poetry

87 "Notice how everything is reversed in civilisation. Things here have objective value. The railways and roads to the American West Coast were built by adventurers, greedy bankers, and entrepreneurs, but their motives and means had no impact on the significance of these structures, which changed the life of America and served the welfare of millions of people."

is a monologue, an often quiet monologue. It is the complete truth only for the poet and his world. What is Alberto Giacometti trying to tell us with his little eyeless figurines? By defining art as an 'absurd activity', as 'research of the impossible and a hopeless attempt to grasp the flicker, the psyche, the essence of life,' Giacometti partially answers that question. Every man is alone by himself, and everyone treads their own path in this seeking, in this 'impossible activity'. Therefore, the protest of the audience against an 'incomprehensible' song, painting, or figure is mainly the result of misunderstanding the very essence of art. That is how creation proves itself to be the original goal of art, while the work of art is its 'unfinished symbol'. Art is whole during creation; joy is undisturbed, but there is only part of it in the work of art, which is often the source of the artist's suffering. Sometimes we have a hard time grasping the true meaning of one portrait or sculpture because the work of art is separated from the artist and from the act of creation that is its essence. Visits to galleries might leave us indifferent because no 'eternal flame' burns in them. 'Those used to be paintings, but not anymore', says Jean Dubuffet. A work of art is the result of fire that used to burn in one soul, but itself is not that fire. It is the ash remaining after a fire.

STYLE AND FUNCTION

The contrast between artist and artwork, between subjective and objective principles, can be observed once again, this time in the artwork itself, in the light of the age-old debate regarding the primacy of either style or function. Style and function relate to one another as man and object. Style is personal, individual; function is faceless, objective. Style is created, while function is analysed, studied, and construed. Style can be dignified, monumental, breezy, sincere, or experienced. Style is unfathomable and inexplicable, while function is reasonable. Style is human (Buffon), function is a fact, 'objective reality'.[88]

We distinguish between two independent and separate activities: aesthetic shaping and technical perfecting. The first aims to please humanity's inexplicable aspiration for beauty and form; the other keeps in mind function as an expression of human need. The first tends towards diversity and individualisation, while the second pulls toward uniformity and standardisation. What is particularly interesting here, from the standpoint of ideas presented in the second part of this book, is how both of these tendencies, when prolonged and separated from one another, lead to a lifeless result. Of course, it is

88 It is difficult to provide a satisfactory definition of style. Here is an interesting one, originating from Werner Niels: 'Between the system of forms and the spiritual currents of an era, there is a causal connection. Each form is a superstructure of the prevailing spiritual and emotional currents, a materialisation of societal needs and ideals. Styles are the manuscripts of humanity. To the informed observer, they tell more than any precise historical analysis.' Werner Niels, *The End of the Functionalist Era*)

possible to observe them most clearly in the case of architecture due to its mixed nature. Aesthetic shaping alone, developing form without connection to function, quickly turns into degenerated decor and creates a structure that looks artificial and empty, like a backdrop. Conversely, technical perfecting alone, bearing in mind only naked function, results in a cold and faceless object, with a tendency towards equalisation and monotony. 'If we build honestly', says Mies van der Rohe, one of the proponents of functionalism, 'a church must not differ from a factory'.

All of the fundamental duality of the world is repeated once more in the contrast between style and function.

ART AND CRITICISM (THE FAILURE OF CRITICISM)

The stated facts can explain the failure and limitations of criticism. Criticism tries to explain a work of art, when in fact, it is precisely a priori incapable of that, due to its rationalist method. That is why it is said that 'criticism murders works of art'. It wants to 'think up' something that is not even a fruit of thought in its basis.[89]

For an artist, it is a completely inner vision moved by suffering and experiencing. It is not a result of analysis and logical reasoning, but 'a daughter of sadness and pain' (Picasso). That is why critics more often blur the approach to a work of art than they illuminate it. After he read a piece by Kafka, Einstein— in a letter to Thomas Mann—complained, 'I could not read it. Human spirit is not complicated enough to understand it.' But critics managed to 'surpass' even Kafka himself. Alfred Kazin wrote that it is easier to read Kafka than most of his interpreters. 'Kafka would name their books as yet another example of his alienation from humanity.' Dostoevsky contrasted the opinions of common readers to the articles of his critics and educated interpreters. We can read in one of the notes from his diary from 1876, 'I always had

89 "A painter is not an intellectual. In painting, intelligence leads to nothing. What is needed is light in the soul." (Andre Marchand) "Painting is something that speaks to human emotions. One must always return to the sources. They are the purest and truest. But our civilisation is intellectual, and the intellectual does not understand visual art in the least."(Roger Bissiere)

the support of readers, but not critics.' Art seeks an uncritical audience. For an observer that is too critical, an artwork will dissolve itself to a series of information or morals, but the true intent will remain foreign. Therefore, it is very possible to assume that a certain amount of average observers will be closer to the real message of the artwork than the erudite critics, simply because the former will manage to experience it by not trying to 'understand' it. Very often, complete disagreement of audience and critics in their evaluation of an art piece or a song can originate from these two completely different approaches.

For the same reasons that criticism is impossible in art, theology is impossible in religion. (William Faulkner famously compared critics with priests). There can be no science about religion. True religious and ethical questions can be adequately expressed by drama, theatre, and novels. The Gospel and Qur'an are not theological writings. This is another point of congruency or even dependency of religion and art. Christianity can truly exist only as a history of Christ, and not as theology. Jesus and Gospel are one thing; Paul and Church are something else.

In conclusion to this contemplation about points of contact between religion and art, we must say that art becomes a seeking for God through seeking for man, and that the fact that some of the artists are nominally atheists does not change a thing because 'art is a way of acting, not a way of thinking' (Alain). There are non-religious paintings, sculptures, songs, but there is no non-religious art. The phenomenon of an atheist artist—which is generally very rare—can be ascribed to inevitable human contradictions and relative independence of human conscious logic from spontaneous but inasmuch authentic general endeavour that represents human response to total pressure of 'heaven and earth'. If there is no religious truth, there is no artistic truth either!

CHAPTER 4

MORALITY

DUTY AND INTEREST

The contours of two different orders that comprise the entirety of reality are not yet completely clear. On one side is creation with its freedom, spontaneity, consciousness, and personality; on the other side is evolution with its causality, entropy, inertia, and anonymity (homogeneity). Two further elements in these chains are duty and interest. The former is central to morality, the latter to politics.

Duty and interest represent two different motivators of human action that typically cannot be compared: duty is always selfless, and interest has no connection to morality. Morality is neither functional nor rational. If I risk my life entering a burning house to save my neighbour's child and return carrying a dead child, can we say that my actions have no value because the outcome was unsuccessful? Morality is precisely what assigns value to this seemingly futile sacrifice or attempt made in vain, just as architecture is 'what makes the ruins beautiful' (Auguste Perret). The sight of defeated justice, which nonetheless captures our hearts, appears as something 'out of this world', because how could we find earthly, logical, scientific, and generally rational reasons to justify the act of a hero who falls because he chose justice and virtue? If only this world exists, confined by space and time, and only nature that is indifferent to justice and injustice, then the sacrifice of the hero who loses in this world due to his commitment to justice would seem meaningless. Conversely, it is precisely because we refuse to see his act as meaningless that it serves as a proclamation of God, announcing another world with entirely different meanings and laws, opposite to this world of nature with its rules and interests. We approve this 'irrational' act and stand behind it with all our being, not knowing or even seeking any explanation—it is either intuitively understood or not at all. The greatness of a heroic act does not lie in its utility, as it is often useless, nor in its practicality, as it often lacks sense. The drama experienced and endured remains the brightest trace of the divine in this world, containing eternal and universal value and significance for humanity as a whole. The reality of another world becomes increasingly evident to us because we cannot regard tragic heroes who fought and lost in this world as defeated but rather as victors. Victors? But in which world are they victors? How can those who lost peace, freedom, or even their lives be considered victors? Evidently, not in this world—thus, they must be victors in another world, fundamentally different from ours. These martyrs become the genuine heralds of that other world, more than all prophets and preachers. Their lives constantly present us with a dilemma: either human existence possesses an additional, completely different meaning from this temporary, relative, and limited one, or these heroes, whom we cannot cease admiring, were simply 'lost causes'. But if we accept the latter assumption, an entire world begins to crumble.

It is precisely because the moral phenomenon—although a real aspect of human life— cannot be rationally explained, that it serves as the first and perhaps the only practical evidence of religion. Moral behaviour is either madness or it has meaning because God exists—no third option is available. We must either reject morality entirely as mere prejudice or introduce into the equation a term we could call 'the term of eternity'. Only if life is eternal—meaning only if God and a world beyond the natural one exist—does human moral behaviour have meaning, whether it involves sacrificing minor personal interests or one's life.

The number of people who consistently act according to the laws of virtue is small, yet this infinitesimally small minority represents the pride of humanity and every human being. There are few moments in our lives when we act purely out of duty. Nevertheless, these rare moments—when we transcend ourselves, disregarding self-interest and practical advantage—represent an indestructible value in our lives. A person is never morally 'neutral'; they are always either sincerely or insincerely moral, often both simultaneously. Throughout different eras, people's actions and behaviours varied, but discussions about justice, truth, equality, and freedom have consistently maintained striking similarities. Wise individuals and heroes have spoken sincerely and in the name of truth, whereas politicians and demagogues have spoken hypocritically, driven by self-interest.

Yet, even this false morality promoted by demagogues and hypocrites is instructive regarding the issue at hand. Feigned morality, moral insolence, and the centuries-old rhetorical exploitation of justice, equality, and humanity confirm the reality of genuine morality as compellingly as the exalted martyrdom of heroes and saints. Political history, particularly recent events, is replete with examples of freedom's enemies supporting not only systems of repression and surveillance but also systems whose proponents loudly advocate freedom and justice. These proponents present the agendas of limited interest groups seeking power as a struggle for freedom, democracy, and justice. Even Ivan the Terrible (Ivan Grozny), infamous for monstrous crimes and labelled a royal executioner, sought moral justification when he prepared to execute 400 boyars and princes. Whether he personally needed this illusion or he did so to please his people (for demagogic purposes), the unavoidable necessity of appealing to moral justification is clear in both cases.

Hypocrisy, as a false form of morality, underscores the genuine value of true morality, much as counterfeit money derives its temporary worth from the existence of authentic currency. Hypocrisy thus demonstrates that everyone implicitly expects or demands moral behaviour from others.

INTENTION AND DEED

Things exist objectively within the realm of nature. The Earth revolves around the Sun—not the other way around—regardless of whether we know or like this fact. We might even resent it, but we cannot change it. Facts hold no significance from a moral standpoint; they carry no moral attributes and thus are morally non-existent. Conversely, in our inner, human world, things do not exist objectively—indeed, they do not exist at all in the natural sense. Here, we are direct participants, and the appearance of that inner world depends entirely upon us. Any part of this inner world not created by our striving does not exist at all; this is the domain of human freedom. Unlike in the external world—where actions are dictated by necessity, and distinctions like wealth and poverty, intelligence and ignorance, education and primitiveness, strength and weakness are independent of our will and do not express our authentic self—in the inner world, there exists complete freedom and equal opportunity. This freedom is absolute, unhindered by material or natural constraints, as everything is determined by intention and aspiration. Every person may not be capable of doing good, but every person can aspire towards and love the good. Many people might never have the opportunity to actively right a wrong, yet each person can inwardly condemn and hate injustice, both within themselves and in others. This inward condemnation constitutes repentance.

Morality, therefore, is not primarily about the act itself but rather about striving to live righteously, demonstrating willpower, and engaging in a personal struggle for salvation. Being perfect or sinless is not inherently human; to sin and repent is more authentically human. Consider Alyosha and Mitya Karamazov: Alyosha is admirable, almost flawless, whereas Mitya, fully human, is passionate and sinful. Yet, could we confidently declare which of them is closer to Divine mercy? We perform many unintended actions, and equally, we intend or aspire to many things that we never accomplish. These distinctions create two separate worlds: the heart and nature. Even if an intention remains unrealised, it fully manifests in the world of the heart—it is a complete reality. Conversely, an unintended action, although fully realised in nature, does not occur at all in our inner world if it lacks intention.

This contrast between aspiration and deed reflects the fundamental divide between humanity and the external world, appearing similarly in ethics, art, and religion. Intention, artistic aspiration, and piety all belong to one another internally and relate in the same manner to their external, worldly expressions: behaviour, artwork, and religious ritual. The former are experiences of the soul, whereas the latter are experiences of the external world.

Deeds are judged according to intentions; Deeds are judged according to consequences. The first is the message of every religion; the second is the message of every political system and revolution. These represent two conflicting logics. One implies the negation of the world, the other the negation of the individual. Science and materialism inevitably lead to questioning the authenticity of intention in human behaviour. It has been proposed that intention is neither primal nor original, but rather a consequence to be interpreted, not a cause. According to this view, human actions result not from intention but from something beyond consciousness, existing within the realm of general determinism.

In contrast, religion proposes an inner centre in every human being, fundamentally distinct from the external world—this is the core of each being: their soul. Intention signifies an internal step towards one's deepest self, an inward verification or affirmation of an action. Whether or not the action is outwardly executed, it is forever enacted internally. Without this inner consultation, a person's action is merely mechanical or coincidental, occurring within the transient, external world.

A person is not defined by their actions but primarily by their desires and aspirations. A writer does not merely recount actions but delves into the hidden motives within the soul of their hero. Without this exploration, their writing is merely a chronicle rather than true literature. The Dutch ethicist Arnold Geulincx expressed the significance of intention in ethics clearly. According to him, our true being consists only of knowledge and free will; we have no real power to act outside our consciousness. Acting is largely beyond our control, resting entirely in God's hands. Morality, therefore, is found exclusively in righteous intention, not in righteous action.

Hume develops a similar idea:

> It is evident that when we praise any actions, we regard only the motives that produced them, and consider the actions as signs or indications of certain principles in the mind and temper. The external performance has no merit. We must look within to find the moral quality. This we cannot do directly; and therefore fix our attention on actions, as on external signs. But these actions are still considered as signs; and the ultimate object of our praise and approbation is the motive that produced them. (David Hume, *A Treatise on Human Nature*)

When we decide to perform a deed, we have already performed it in eternity. Its external execution is part of the earthly realm; it is therefore conditioned, inadequate, inauthentic, circumstantial, and even meaningless, if you wish. Aspiration and intention are free, while execution is subject to limitations, laws, and conditions. Intention is entirely ours, whereas execution involves external and circumstantial elements. Morality resides in aspiration, not in behaviour. If this were not the case, a eunuch would be considered a chaste man and a gastric patient would serve as a role model of moderation—yet clearly, this is not so. A person is good if he desires good according to his own understanding, even if that same good is perceived as evil by others. Similarly, a person is evil if he desires evil based on his own perception, despite this possibly being perceived as good by others. It always concerns the individual, his personal understanding, his unique inner world that belongs exclusively to him. Each person is entirely alone and equally free within this purely internal and inherently social relationship. This is the underlying meaning of Sartre's assertion that every individual is 'responsible for everything he does' and that there are no innocent victims or innocent prisoners in hell (J. P. Sartre, *Huis Clos*).

DRESSAGE AND UPBRINGING

The most moving and remarkable aspect that old texts can offer us is their stories of transformation and moral rebirth. An internal movement—free and inexplicable—has turned even the greatest sinners and oppressors into humble ascetics and fighters for justice. This transformation is always instantaneous; it does not involve a process, gradual reformation, or external influences. Instead, it is an event occurring deep within the soul, an inner experience already existing alongside an energy that fundamentally reshapes a person through its intensity. Such transformation is intrinsic to human beings, thus excluding processes, causality, conditioning, or any rational explanation. It is a drama whose essence is freedom and creativity. Good and evil reside within the human soul. External influences, altered circumstances, dressage, laws, or coercion cannot genuinely 'reform' a person; they can only modify his behaviour superficially. Virtue and vice are not 'products like sugar and vitriol', as Hippolyte Taine or Zola believed. Tolstoy demonstrates in *Resurrection* that manipulating people—the essence of prison reform—merely corrupts them further. True rebirth or transformation occurs spontaneously from within, as a result of movements occurring deep within the soul.

From a religious standpoint, any external attempt to eradicate evil is ultimately futile. This truth underpins the Christian and Buddhist principle of 'non-resistance to evil'. Therefore, dressage is largely ineffective in genuinely shaping a person's moral character. While dressage can instil virtues such as endurance, skill, and strength in a soldier, it cannot instil qualities such as honour, dignity, enthusiasm, and bravery, as these latter virtues are attributes of the soul.

It has repeatedly been demonstrated that laws, terror, pressure, violence, and coercion cannot effectively impose genuine beliefs or sincere behaviours. Every educator knows that persistently steering children in one direction often provokes resistance and ultimately ignites desires and inclinations towards something entirely opposite. This phenomenon stems from the inherently human nature of individuals. Dressage is ineffective precisely because humans possess a soul. Its impotence and the inherent uncertainty of upbringing offer tangible proof that a human being is fundamentally an animal endowed with a soul and, thus, freedom.[90]

Consequently, every genuine upbringing is essentially moral upbringing, representing the opposite of dressage. The purpose of authentic upbringing is not to directly alter an individual (which, strictly speaking, is not even possible), but rather to trigger an inner flow of experiences through examples, advice, scenarios, or similar means, thus fostering a genuinely internal decision favouring goodness. Without this internal decision, true transformation does not occur; at best, only behavioural changes result, which may be superficial, feigned, or transient. Behaviour that fails to engage our deepest willpower and remains superficial is not genuine upbringing—it is merely dressage. True upbringing demands our personal participation and effort. Consequently, upbringing outcomes are inherently variable and unpredictable.

Individualists believe in the possibility of internal transformation, or inner rebirth, whereas positivists believe in external

90 Therefore, you will find that materialists believe in the omnipotence of education in the sense of conditioning (e.g. Helvétius in the work *De l'Homme*), whereas Christians claim that it is completely without influence.

reform and behavioural changes. The philosophical foundation behind these beliefs is clear: if wrongdoing results from free choice and malicious intent, external reformation measures have minimal chances of success. Conversely, if wrongdoing is a product of circumstances and poor habits, reforming offenders is achievable by changing their circumstances and fostering new habits. This difference marks the distinction between inner transformation and mere dressage.

Every type of upbringing carried out by officials or authorities—especially by the military or police—is invariably dressage, never genuine upbringing. Upbringing is an intangible, subtle, entirely indirect influence upon the human soul, conveyed through love, personal example, forgiveness, and even punishments that provoke inner reflection and genuine change. Dressage, fundamentally animalistic in nature, comprises systems of measures and actions designed to guide or coerce the human-animal into specific behaviours—so-called 'correct' behaviours. True upbringing is intended for humans, whereas dressage is suitable only for animals.

Law-abiding citizens can indeed be created through dressage, but not because they respect laws genuinely; instead, they comply out of fear or habit. Internally, these citizens may be spiritually lifeless, emotionally drained, yet they avoid breaking laws simply due to conditioning. Literature frequently explores this theme of outwardly upright citizens who are morally hollow, contrasting them with offenders who may be fundamentally noble and virtuous.

Hence, there are two forms of justice: human and Divine. The internal breadth of humanity is immense, almost infinite. Humans possess the capacity for both the gravest crimes and the noblest sacrifices. The greatness of humanity is not primarily in aspiring towards good but in the capacity to choose freely. Any humiliation or degradation of a person reduces or limits this freedom of choice. There is no genuine goodness outside free will, nor can goodness be imposed through force. Freedom is the prerequisite for genuine goodness, and freedom and coercion negate one another. There is no compulsion in religion (Surah al-Baqarah, 2:256), and the same principle applies to ethics. Dressage, even when enforcing correct behaviour, is essentially immoral and inhuman.

MORALITY AND HUMAN MIND

The concept of human freedom is inseparable from ethical thought. Throughout history, despite the many transformations ethical thinking has undergone, freedom has remained its constant foundation. To reject freedom is to reject ethics as an idea. Just as space and quantity are fundamental to physics, freedom is fundamental to ethics.[91] The mind comprehends space and quantity, but it does not comprehend freedom. This is where the divergence between reason and genuine ethics begins.

Freedom is a suprarational category, while the function of the mind is to uncover nature, mechanisms, and calculations in all things—ultimately leading it to discover itself in everything. This creates an inherent circularity, as the mind is unable to perceive anything beyond its mechanical self in nature. This explains why many ethical theories ultimately reduce themselves to paradoxes. After extensive intellectualising, they often arrive at conclusions such as selflessness equals selfishness, or the negation of pleasure is itself pleasure. This tendency led Voltaire to formulate his famous *reductio ad absurdum*: 'Sacrificing one's life in one's own interest?!' The rational, logical analysis of moral phenomena is therefore often reduced—much to the bewilderment of the analyst—to explanations based solely on nature, self-interest, and self-love.

When the mind studies nature, it discovers only its all-encompassing causality. When it studies human beings, it once

91 The essence of spirit is freedom, just as the essence of matter is weight (according to Hegel).

again finds nature: instincts and the rule of the two great masters—pain and pleasure. These, however, are merely reflections of human enslavement, not of freedom. The same intellectual mechanism that reduces God to the 'First Cause' (Unmoved Mover) also reduces the soul to mere psyche, and art to an art piece and a technique. The attempt to rationally establish ethics will never lead beyond so-called social morality—which is, in reality, nothing more than a set of behavioural rules designed to maintain group cohesion. In other words, reason reduces ethics to a form of social discipline. Morality, however, is not a product of reason—neither in principle nor in practice. The mind can examine and establish relationships between things, but it cannot generate true value judgements in the moral sense; it is incapable of producing genuine moral affirmation or rejection.

For instance, the principle that spiritual standardisation of individuals is unacceptable is ethically self-evident to any person with a moral sense. However, it remains rationally indemonstrable. Science cannot objectively substantiate that something is 'wrong' in a moral sense, just as it cannot draw a precise, scientific line between kitsch and art—it cannot mathematically determine the relationship between beauty and the lack thereof.

Neither nature nor the mind makes a distinction between justice and injustice, good and evil. These qualities do not exist in nature. From a purely scientific perspective, what does the uniqueness of an individual truly mean? A scientist must be more than just a scientist—he must be a human being—to grasp the significance of such a question.

This is why the famous ethical maxim that a good man is always happy, while a bad man is always unhappy cannot be rationally understood. Even Christian ethics is not structured as a scientific doctrine; rather, it presents itself as an ethical framework embodied in a single personality—Jesus

Christ. It is not an ethics that is merely taught, but one that is experienced.

The three famous tenets of the French Revolution—equality, freedom, and brotherhood—cannot be deduced from science or proven scientifically. In fact, without the involvement of something beyond science, science itself would be more likely to establish the opposite principles: inequality, absolute social discipline, and the anonymity (alienation) of human beings as mere units within a perfectly organised collective.

Could Jean Valjean (*Les Misérables*) turn to science to resolve the moral dilemma he faced? Was he supposed to sacrifice the interests of a great number of people to save one simple but innocent man? What kind of solution would that be? Would science not, by its own logic, side with the so-called common interest? This question is inherently beyond the scope of science, and any answer it might provide would be fundamentally at odds with the deepest instincts of the human soul.

What Victor Hugo presents so vividly and movingly in 'a storm under one skull' is not merely an internal conflict within the mind of one man, but a battle between his reason and his soul—a crushing clash of arguments belonging to two fundamentally different dimensions of human nature. At its core, this is a dialogue between the mind and the conscience, in which two opposing logical systems, irreconcilable by their very nature, continually take turns. However, this debate is not truly logical or mathematical; it only appears so on the surface. Ultimately, no final conclusion emerges from this internal struggle, because the arguments belong to two distinct realms—they are qualitatively different, incomparable, and cannot be measured, added, or subtracted. They belong to two different worlds: heaven and earth.

In the end, a man can only make a choice in this dramatic dilemma for himself and within himself. Jean Valjean's decision represents a defeat of the mind but a victory for humanity—a victory that cannot be rationally explained or justified, yet one that is silently and unanimously affirmed by all people.

And yet, let us attempt to scientifically analyse and explain this particular—but at the same time intangible and elusive—moral sentiment. Or consider this: we all instinctively accept as self-evident that an involuntary offender should be freed of responsibility. And yet, despite its absolute clarity and sensibility, this position remains scientifically unprovable.

What every human heart instinctively accepts often collides with insurmountable obstacles when subjected to scientific proof and rational explanation. Does this mean we should abandon our duty simply because the mind cannot justify or support the inner voice that compels us? If we refuse to do so, we remain firm in our moral stance, even without fully understanding the rationale, standing against the dictates of reason, relying on a *sui generis* certainty—in other words, we are believing.

What role, then, does the mind play in moral decisions? Hume answers this question with clarity and precision:

> A crime, for the mind, is nothing more than a sequence of motives, thoughts, and actions bound to a particular personality and specific circumstances. We can analyse these connections, trace the origins, and examine the commission of the act—but disapproval only arises once we allow our feelings to speak. It is then that the act becomes marked as moral evil.

And further:

> The mind, at its fullest, can only reveal relations between things. Yet in a value judgement, something entirely new emerges—something not contained within factual judgement and explicable only through the productive strength of feeling.

According to Hutcheson,

> Just as it is directly clear to us that the value of pleasure in art or science is higher than the pleasure in a meal, so we also directly differentiate moral good from all other experiences.[92]

He argues that the ability to distinguish moral good is not contingent upon intelligence or education. Moral judgements, in his view, are not mediated by reason—they are direct.

This fundamental distinction between science and ethics is reflected in all practical matters. Science, for example, accepts artificial insemination, 'test-tube babies', and euthanasia, or 'mercy killing'. These procedures are inconceivable without science—it created them. However, all ethical systems, regardless of their formal or nominal connection to religion, reject these practices as contrary to the fundamental principles upon which life is built

Ethics aligns with religion and art in this stance, though their reasoning differs. For religion, artificial life and artificial (violent) death are unacceptable because life and death are not under human authority, but God's. For humanism, artificial insemination and euthanasia violate human dignity by reducing individuals to objects, opening the door to manipulation and abuse. For an artist, birth and death are sacred mysteries, and they should remain so.[93] Three of Hamlet's most famous monologues are devoted to death.

Yet, in contrast, for science, death is merely a biological event, a banal physical fact—nothing more than a definable moment in the cycle of life. The divide between these perspectives is absolute—they are incommensurable.

---

92 Francis Hutcheson, *A System of Moral Philosophy*, Vol. 1, Article VI.

93 All cultures have created their own forms of mourning. These include Black funeral ceremonies, the Greek *klama* (ritual wailing), and various Jewish funeral customs. Jews remain in the house for seven days after the death of a close relative, and for a full eleven months, sons recite prayers for a deceased parent, etc.

From a scientific standpoint, eugenic sterilisation, human experimentation, artificial insemination, and euthanasia are entirely logical and rational. It is impossible to find any rational or scientific arguments against them. How, then, can science prevent its own abuse?

The French Academy of Moral and Political Sciences declared its opposition to artificial insemination, basing its stance on an entirely unscientific reasoning that: 'Artificial insemination represents a violation of the foundations upon which marriage, family, and society rest.' Similarly, Cuenot, addressing artificial death, argued:

> The feeling of respect toward life and motherhood has nothing in common with logic, and I do not believe that euthanasia, which is almost enforced in certain cases, can ever be legalised. (Lucien Cuénot, *L'Eugénique*, Revue d'Anthropologie, 1935–1936).

Issues such as euthanasia, artificial insemination, sterilisation, organ transplantation, and abortion are scientific only in a technical sense. Their implementation is a moral question, one that science is incapable of resolving.

> The plan to treat people as livestock seems at once revolting and comical; it offends our sense of personal dignity.[94]

Artificial insemination was first developed for veterinary use before being transferred to human medicine. The issue at hand is a conflict between humanism and biologism, individualism and materialism. Once again, man faces a primordial dilemma: should he follow his interests or his spiritual imperatives?

Biology offers the means for 'progress', but in exchange, it demands that man relinquish his soul—his human dignity.

94 Jean Rostand, *La Biologie et l'Avenir humain.*

> Today, humans reject this progress, though it lies within reach, rather than attaining it by means that revolt them. But will they reject it tomorrow? Or forever?[95]

It is natural that Christians, along with poets and artists, recoil from the vision that science unveils. For Christians, it is 'Luciferian naturalism', as Rémy Collin describes *in Plaidoyers pour la Vie Humaine*. For poets, it is a 'mass of programmed brutality', as Andrei Voznesensky calls it in *Oasis*.

Materialists, by contrast, embrace the prospects biology offers, a stance that is logically consistent with their worldview. However, no matter how immense and spectacular scientific progress may be, it can never render morality and religion obsolete. Science does not teach humans how to live; it establishes no judgements of value. The values that elevate biological life to human life would remain incomprehensible without religion.

For religion is the knowledge of a higher world, and morality is the knowledge of its meaning.

95 Jean Rostand, *La Biologie et l'Avenir humain.*

SCIENCE AND SCIENTIST, OR THE TWO CRITIQUES OF KANT

However, there is a 'pure' reason and a 'practical' reason. Thought can deny God, yet humanity and lived experience affirm Him. This distinction explains the frequent discrepancy between a scientist's personal beliefs and science as a method or set of findings. Not everything a scientist says, thinks, or believes can be classified as science. Rather, science constitutes just one aspect of a scientist's total understanding of the world, emerging solely from the mind's critical, comparative, and organisational faculties. In this process, the intellect rejects any explanation that necessitates the supernatural, retaining only what can be explained through natural cause-and-effect chains, experimentation, and verification. Only the conclusions that withstand this rigorous scrutiny qualify as science. Consequently, science inevitably grasps only nature, while everything beyond nature escapes or seeps through its methodological net. These represent the inherent boundaries of scientific inquiry. While science typically halts at these boundaries, the scientist—as a human being—continues to search.

For instance, Oppenheimer did not require Indian philosophy to construct the atomic bomb, although he might have turned to it when grappling with the moral dilemmas surrounding the weapon's use. Nevertheless, towards the end of his life, Oppenheimer entirely abandoned atomic science and fully immersed himself in the study of Indian philosophy. Similarly, Einstein exhibited a lasting, profound interest in Dostoevsky's literary works, especially *The Brothers Karamazov*, which clearly had little to do with mass–energy relationships or the speed of light. Einstein's fascination with Ivan Karamazov's moral struggles was not connected to his role as a scientist but rather to his broader identity as a thinker, a human being, and even as an artist, as every person, to some degree, embodies artistry.

A significant distinction exists between pursuing science and possessing scientific knowledge. The former aims to understand the world, while the latter seeks to utilise it. Hence, science does not hold the same meaning for scientists as it does for everyone else. To the general public, science represents merely an accumulation of results, predominantly quantitative and mechanical in nature. For scientists, however, science is a pursuit filled with personal exploration, continuous effort, dedication, sacrifice—in short, an entire life. More significantly, for the scientist, it encompasses the joy of discovery, an elevated sensation imbued with the highest ethical value. It is in this joy that the human rises beyond the scientist, revealing the thinker and the poet within.

Thus arises an important divergence between what a scientist discovers personally and what they present to the broader world. It is only when science is detached from the scientist's lived experience, when it 'cools down' and becomes a mere aggregate of objective, impersonal knowledge, that it assumes an indifferent and ultimately non-religious role. Through its inherent rejection of metaphysics and its inevitable silence on fundamental existential questions, science inadvertently fosters atheistic attitudes—not necessarily in the scientist, but within the wider audience.

A classic embodiment of this duality—this conflict between thought and life, nature and freedom—appears clearly in Kant's two Critiques. Famously, Kant re-establishes religious notions of God, immortality, and freedom in his *Critique of*

Practical Reason, notions previously dismantled in the *Critique of Pure Reason*. In the *Critique of Pure Reason*, Kant speaks as a logician and scientist, while in the *Critique of Practical Reason*, he expresses himself as a thinker and as a human being. The former encapsulates the inescapable outcomes of logical and analytical thinking, whereas the latter reveals the emotions, experiences, and hopes inherent to human life. The *Critique of Pure Reason* results from a methodical analysis, objectification, and fragmentation of reality, whereas the *Critique of Practical Reason* emerges from an internal discovery and certainty born within the soul, offering answers to the dilemmas of the world when viewed holistically.

These two works do not negate each other; rather, they stand in parallel grandeur, each in its way confirming the fundamental dualism inherent in the human world.

MORALITY AND RELIGION

Morality can be permanently founded only on religion, yet morality and religion are not identical. Morality, as a principle, cannot exist without religion, but as a practice—an individual case of behaviour—it does not necessarily depend on religion. What unites the two is a shared premise: the existence of another, higher world. By being 'another', that world is religious; by being 'higher', it is moral. This relationship illustrates both the interdependence and the autonomy of morality and religion. It follows a certain internal consistency that is neither automatic nor mathematical but practical, with possible deviations, yet it reasserts itself over time: atheism ultimately leads to the negation of morality, while every true moral transformation begins with religious reformation.

Morality is, in essence, a transfused religion—its embodiment in aspirations and rules of conduct. This means that a person's voluntary behaviour or their treatment of others aligns with the recognition of God's existence. The moral imperative to fulfil one's duty, regardless of hardship or risk (which distinguishes morality from actions driven by self-interest), is only justifiable if this world and this life are not the entirety of existence. This is the fundamental point of convergence between morality and religion.

Morality originated from prohibitions and remains fundamentally prohibitive. A prohibition, by its nature and origin, is religious. Of the Ten Commandments, eight are prohibitions. Morality consistently operates as a restrictive principle, opposing the animalistic instincts of human nature. Christian ethics, though not the sole example, is perhaps the most prominent and illustrative of this principle. The history of ancient religions is filled with prohibitions that may appear irrational to us today. However, from an ethical standpoint, no prohibition is entirely meaningless. While some prohibitions may have rational justifications, their primary purpose is not utility.

Morality, therefore, is not simply 'life in accordance with nature', as the Stoics defined it. If we take 'nature' in its true sense, morality is more accurately described as life against nature. Like humanity itself, morality is irrational, unnatural, and ultimately supernatural. There is no such thing as a purely 'natural' human or a 'natural' morality. A human confined within purely natural boundaries is, at best, an animal with a developed brain. Likewise, morality constrained within natural limits ceases to be morality—it becomes a form of selfishness, an intellectualised and enlightened self-interest.[96]

It is not the morally superior but the strongest and most adaptable who prevail in the Darwinian 'struggle for survival'. Biological progress does not lead to human dignity or even morality—if human dignity is indeed a foundation of morality. The Darwinian man may achieve the highest degree of biological perfection, even becoming 'superhuman', yet in doing so, he risks losing his essential human quality, including his dignity. Only God could bestow the latter upon him.

A similar dynamic applies to social progress, which is often considered an 'extension' of biological evolution. English ethicist Bernard Mandeville posed a provocative question: what role does morality play in the progress of society and

---

96 Someone has observed that the word 'nature' is used in 52 different senses. In this exposition, 'nature' denotes the entire reality outside the human essence, and thus also includes the human being in that part where he belongs to the world: his body, desires, instincts, and intelligence.

civilisation? His answer was stark—none at all, or worse, a hindrance when morality is taken seriously. According to Mandeville, the very means typically regarded as wicked are the most powerful drivers of social progress because, as he states, 'what increases man's needs is what advances his progress the most.' He goes further, asserting that 'so-called moral and physical evil in this world is the main driving force that makes us into social beings.'[97]

If all forms of progress—first biological, then technical—are fundamentally based on selection, where the stronger suppress or even eliminate the weaker, then morality must stand in direct opposition to progress. Morality has always insisted on the protection of the weak, the cultivation of compassion and conscience, and, ultimately, the salvation of those who are vulnerable. Here, morality and nature have found themselves on opposing sides, as they have been since their inception. Nietzsche made this conflict explicit: 'Free yourselves from conscience, compassion, and forgiveness—those inner tyrants of humanity. Press down the weak, and rise higher upon their fallen forms...' This is the stark separation of morality from biological determinism.

The division is absolute: exterminate the weak, protect the weak—two opposing imperatives that distinguish biology from spirituality, zoology from humanity, nature from culture, and science from religion. Nietzsche was perhaps the only thinker to apply biological laws to human society with full consistency.[98] The result? A philosophy that rejects love

97 Mandeville, *A Search into the Nature of Society*. The English thinker Henry Buckle, starting from the static nature of moral norms, claimed that morality slows the progress of humanity. Progress is movement, change; whereas morality is static (Henry Thomas Buckle, *History of Civilisation in England*). Compare this with Hegel's notion that 'evil is the form in which the driving force of world development appears.'

98 If Nietzsche was the philosophical continuation of Darwinism, then Hitler and his National Socialism were the political derivative of both doctrines.

and justifies violence. For Nietzsche, Christianity—especially its ethics—was 'the most insidious poison ever introduced into the strong, healthy body of vigorous humanity.'

Plato, in Phaedo, presented a markedly different vision of authentic ethics. Ordinary courage, he argued, is merely a form of cowardice. Ordinary art is a veiled craving for pleasure. This kind of virtue, according to him, is a commercial transaction, a mere shadow of true virtue—a virtue of slaves. The truly moral man, Plato contended, aspires only to move away from the corporeal and closer to the purely spiritual. 'The body is the grave of the soul.' True awareness, in his view, can never be attained in earthly existence; it comes only after death. Therefore, the ethical man is unafraid of death. To philosophise and to live truly means to constantly prepare for death.

Plato saw evil as the ruling force of this world and argued that morality is neither a natural ability of man nor something that can be rationally established. Ethics, understood in this way, could never obtain rational proof for its validity—nor could it even seek such proof. Inevitably, Plato had to resort to metaphysical rather than anthropological evidence, thereby becoming the forerunner of theologically based ethics. This development was unavoidable. As is well known, Plato introduced the doctrine of pre-existence, according to which all knowledge is merely recollection.

A necessary assumption of this doctrine—and similar teachings—is belief in immortality.[99] Plato's reflections on ethics led him directly to a religious worldview.[100]

Two other great ancient ethicists, Epictetus and Seneca, were led by their reflections to a particular religion—Christianity.

99 Among the great Islamic thinkers, Ibn Rushd (Averroes) directly addressed this question. According to him, morality is the essential content of universal religion.

100 Pierre Abélard (11th–12th centuries) considered Plato to be a Christian.

There are strong indications that Epictetus was a Christian, and it is well documented that Seneca corresponded with St Paul. In fact, St Jerome includes Seneca in his *De Viris Illustribus* as part of a list of Church writers.

Christianity serves as an exceptional example of the perfect compatibility, strong mutual affinity, and near unity between a supreme religion and a supreme ethical system. The Renaissance, with its art almost entirely inspired by Christian religious themes, offers a striking illustration of how religion and ethics can be seamlessly interwoven through superb artistic expression.

From a historical perspective, moral thought is one of the oldest exclusively human intellectual pursuits. The only idea preceding it is the idea of the divine, which is as old as humanity itself. These two concepts—the divine and the moral—have remained inextricably linked throughout history, persisting in their close connection to this day. There is virtually no significant ethicist in the history of moral philosophy who has entirely avoided an engagement with religion—whether by affirming the necessity of religion for the establishment of moral principles or, conversely, attempting to disprove this necessity with equal fervour.

Indeed, the entire history of ethics can be seen as a long and complex narrative of the intertwining of religious and ethical thought. Although statistical evidence is not the ultimate measure of truth in such matters, it is worth noting that religious ethicists have consistently outnumbered secular ones, while atheistic ones remain a very rare exception.

The experience of secular ethical movements—those that sought to assert the independence of ethics from religion—offers further insight into this relationship. Such movements emerged in France, England, the USA, Germany, and Italy during the nineteenth and twentieth centuries, under names such as the Societies for Ethical Culture, Ethical Societies, and Settlements. However, their historical trajectory reveals a consistent pattern: every serious engagement with morality, whether in theory or practice, naturally gravitates towards religion or at least draws closer to it over time.

This era in the history of practical ethics is of profound significance to the subject at hand. Even in French state schools, where so-called morality classes were introduced as a substitute for religious instruction, the textbooks of these courses still mirrored the catechism format used in Christian denominations.

Unfortunately, it is impossible to comprehensively trace the development of these ideas, their contradictions and their constant oscillation between religion and science. However, one key observation stands out: despite their persistent efforts to assert an independent position from religion, these moral movements have—often unconsciously—gravitated towards religious principles. This dual tendency—to resist and yet inevitably approach religion—is highly revealing for the phenomenon under examination.

It is entirely possible to imagine a person who is deeply religious yet immoral—just as it is possible to conceive of a moral person who is irreligious. The distinction lies in their respective domains: religion is about knowledge and affirmation, while morality is about life and action in accordance with that knowledge. As in all other aspects of human existence, there is an inherent conflict between knowing what is right and actually living by it.

Religion answers the question: How should I think? What should I believe?

Morality answers the question: How should I act? What should I strive for?

The message of another world, as conveyed by religion, always comes with a demand: to live in accordance with the broader, infinite vision it presents. However, this demand is not identical to the vision itself. A moral system as lofty as Christ's ethics is an extension of an equally profound and clear religious consciousness—but even the inquisitor's religion was sincere, despite the paradox of this claim. The frequent repetition of this phrase—appearing in various forms in over fifty places in the Qur'an—underscores the essential unity of two concepts that are often separated in practice: religion ('believe') and morality ('do righteous deeds'), along with a simultaneous imperative for believers to strive toward both. Moreover, the Qur'an also reveals the reverse relationship—showing how moral action can lead to faith: 'You will never attain righteousness until you spend from that which you love.' (Qur'an, 3:92). This shifts the traditional sequence: it is no longer 'believe, and you will become righteous', but rather: 'be righteous, and you will come to believe.'

Thus, for those asking, 'How do I begin to believe? How do I strengthen my faith?', the answer is clear: 'Do righteous deeds; you will find God through action—perhaps even before you fully understand Him in thought.'

MORAL AND USEFUL: THE SO-CALLED MORALITY OF "COMMON INTEREST"

Another form of negating morality is the rationalist negation, which arises from dissolving the dualism of duty and interest—reducing morality to what is beneficial or pleasant, and thus stripping it of its independent value. This tendency, which can be traced throughout twenty centuries of ethical thought, from Aristotle to Russell, was most clearly articulated by one of the earliest great materialist thinkers of the West, Paul Holbach.

Having established his famous maxim that 'interest is the only motive of human actions', Holbach outlines the following schema:

> All sensations, perceptions, and ideas generated by external objects stimulate the senses, either favourably or painfully, shaping human experience. A person approves of those that bring pleasure, seeking their renewal, while avoiding those that cause pain. In short, a person loves what produces pleasure and detests what produces suffering. Since man lives in society, surrounded by beings who, like him, seek pleasure and fear pain, virtue consists of whatever is truly beneficial—whatever consistently serves the interests of individuals living together. Conversely, vice is whatever is truly harmful—whatever causes enduring injury to human coexistence.

According to Holbach, conscience is merely 'awareness of how our actions affect those around us and, in turn, ourselves', while guilt is 'the fear we feel once we realise that our actions have made us contemptible or hateful in the eyes of others.' (Holbach, *Système de la Nature*)

Similarly, Jeremy Bentham, the leading theorist of utilitarian morality, is equally clear and systematic in his reasoning:

> Nature has placed mankind under the governance of two sovereign masters, pain and pleasure. It is for them alone to point out what we ought to do, as well as to determine what we shall do. (Jeremy Bentham, *Principles of Morality and Law)*

Following the same logic, Helvétius asserts that all human behaviour follows the path of least resistance and that no one acts unless they believe they will gain greater pleasure or reduce suffering through their actions. Just as water cannot flow uphill, man cannot act against this fundamental law of his nature.

From this perspective, all morality is simply refined egoism—a well-calculated form of self-interest. Through intellect and reflection, humans transform their natural desire for pleasure into moral imperatives. The human intellect and memory allow individuals to move beyond immediate self-interest, instead shaping their behaviour according to a 'total eudaimonistic score'.

Through this rational evaluation, humans elevate biological, zoological, 'Darwinian' experiences of pain and pleasure into the abstract moral concepts of good and evil. Good and evil, then, are nothing more than pleasure and pain elevated by intellect, reflection, and calculation. Thus, the morality of utility remains entirely within the bounds of nature and this world. However, at its core, this remains a morality of utility, never transcending the boundaries of self-interest to become authentic morality in the true sense of the word.

Yet, almost all of human experience contradicts the materialist stance outlined above.

People tend to define as morality those behaviours they find uncomfortable or demanding—asceticism, celibacy, material sacrifice, fasting, self-restraint, renunciation, and sacrifice for principles or the well-being of others. However, the morality of utility stands in direct contradiction not only to the ethical understanding of a civilised man but, perhaps even more strikingly, to that of a primitive man.

It was, in fact, the primitive man who first 'invented' an elaborate system of prohibitions, taboos, and obligations—practices whose non-utilitarian nature is particularly evident, as they often lack any rational or pragmatic justification. Morality is not 'useful' in the conventional sense of the word.

Can it truly be said that the motto 'women and children first' (or prioritising the wounded and elderly) is useful from a purely societal perspective? Is ensuring justice or revealing truth always advantageous? Countless situations arise where injustice or falsehood appears more beneficial.

Tolerance—whether religious, political, racial, or national—is not 'useful' in the ordinary sense of the word. Maintaining a stance of permanent tolerance towards potential opponents is rarely done out of interest; rather, it stems from principle, humanity, and a higher moral imperative that is 'purposelessly purposeful'.

Similarly, caring for the elderly, the infirm, the disabled or the terminally ill is not an act dictated by utility. Morality cannot be measured by its usefulness, and the occasional alignment between moral behaviour and utility does not imply that something becomes moral simply because it proves beneficial in a given period of human history. On the contrary, such compatibility is rare and incidental.[101]

101 The people's understanding of this situation is expressed in the well-known words: 'An honest man and a fool are brothers.' It is symptomatic that, although it fully recognises the non-utilitarian nature of morality, folk wisdom nowhere in the world preaches dishonesty and corruption.

The optimistic belief that honesty and self-interest naturally align, or that 'honesty is the best policy', has proven to be naïve—perhaps even harmful. Since people regularly witness the opposite, this notion seems destructive. People must be freed from this obsession with utility. A truly righteous person is only the one who realistically acknowledges the cost of sacrifice and, when facing inevitable temptation, remains loyal to principle over personal gain. Were virtue truly profitable, shrewd scoundrels would hasten to present themselves as its finest examples. But this is not what we see in reality.

The insights of criminologists provide an educative—and sobering—lesson. A 1951 study by the Chicago Police Department revealed that over 90 per cent of burglars and robbers in the city remained unidentified. Similarly, Kiefer's survey in the United States demonstrated that criminals rob hundreds of millions of dollars annually and most enjoy their gains without interruption. Crime pays—criminologists conclude, and they add: 'Especially for those who do not perpetrate it directly'.

This refers to the masterminds behind organised crime—mafia leaders, gang bosses, and financiers—who orchestrate illegal activities while avoiding direct involvement.

'It appears to be a rule: the greater the profit from a murder, the lower the likelihood that its perpetrator will be caught and punished', claims an American criminologist. But what can we say about the profitability of legal crimes—such as the production of pornographic literature, comic strips, or crime novels? A pornographic film, for instance, costs ten times less to produce than a regular film, yet its profits are ten times higher (according to data from a 1976 survey in Paris).

Generally speaking, using crime for entertainment is a massive and highly profitable business—casinos, brothels, and similar enterprises generate immense revenue while generally carrying little to no legal risk. Crimes on a larger scale—aggressive wars, occupations of other countries, and persecutions of minorities—could be examined as a separate chapter. Can it be said that the extermination of Mexican Indians did not pay off for the Spaniards, or that the systematic annihilation of indigenous people in North America did not benefit white settlers, or that the exploitation and pillage of colonised nations did not enrich their colonisers? Thus, the logical conclusion follows: crime pays—unless, of course, there is a God.

It is possible to establish the morality of utility purely through rational analysis, at least as a theoretical model. But it is not possible to establish a morality of selflessness and sacrifice, true morality—without God. Aristotle's inconsistency in Nicomachean Ethics is well known, where he derives philanthropy from self-love ('because philanthropy starts with one's own personality' – Aristotle) and then asserts that:

> ...an ethical person will do many things for his friends and his homeland: he will sacrifice money and possessions, but will never push himself forward; he will gladly leave positions and honours to others. Even more, he will die for others and for his homeland if necessary.

It is evident that these positions are incoherent and do not stem from the same philosophical source. Many have pointed out this contradiction. Schleiermacher criticises Aristotle for merely presenting 'a bunch of virtues', while F. Jodl observes that Aristotle is clearly inconsistent when he attempts to derive even heroic conclusions from the principle of rational ethical self-love, arguing that such conclusions 'certainly cannot be derived from that principle.' When Aristotle claims that 'we do not step outside the realm of self-love, even in heroic acts—for even those who sacrifice their lives for others are choosing something great and noble for themselves', he is engaging in a distortion of selfishness and self-love—extending their meaning far beyond what they represent in the world of an ordinary man, even to the point where they encompass their own negation: selflessness and sacrifice.

If someone jumps into a burning house to rescue a child, can it truly be said that he acts out of selfishness or for his own benefit? Yes, but only in a very special sense—if we define his action as fulfilling a duty, serving the highest good, or acting in the ultimate interest of all, including himself (the hero). In this particular case, sacrifice and interest do not collide because the 'interest' at play is not in the common sense of the word, but in the absolute sense—a moral interest. The distinction between common interest and moral interest (if we allow such an expression) presupposes the differentiation of two worlds—the temporal, finite world and the eternal, transcendent one. Only under the assumption that another, higher world exists can we understand sacrifice as acting in one's own best interest. Without this assumption, the line is clear: life.

We define authentic morality as acting in opposition to personal interest or, at the very least, independently of it. However, there exists another phenomenon that appears similar but is, in essence, fundamentally different: social and societal behaviour. In social behaviour, an individual is not directly guided by immediate personal interest but rather by social interest—which, upon closer examination, is merely indirect personal interest.

Societal behaviour is essentially the same pursuit of need satisfaction, but now extended to a broader, societal framework. Society itself becomes the expression—or the sum—of all personal interests, now structured in a way that allows for their more efficient satisfaction. This new social structure imposes duties on individuals, which superficially resemble moral obligations.

Actions aimed at achieving personal interest are now reframed as societal duties—as collective obligations. Since these duties may sometimes appear disproportionate to individual interest (demanding sacrifices or contributions that exceed personal benefit) or even contradict an individual's immediate desires and preferences, they create the illusion that the individual is acting not out of self-interest, but 'in the name of something greater'—in the name of a higher principle.

In reality, society (the collective) is merely a specific mechanism for fulfilling personal interests. What changes is not the underlying motivation, but only the external form through which individuals act to achieve the same fundamental goal: personal interest. So-called common interest is, in the final analysis, nothing but personal interest expanded—as self-serving and morally neutral as the individual pursuit of gain. The only difference is that personal interest, in this case, is strategically calculated for the long term, protected from accidents and miscalculations, supported by the similar self-interest of a multitude of other individuals within the same group, and insulated from direct losses and conflicting forces.

This transformation of individual self-interest into collective action is facilitated not by heart or soul, but by intelligence. If the calculation is done correctly (excluding errors or manipulations by those who define social action), this would result in the 'greatest personal interest for the greatest number of individuals'—the principle of the Greatest Happiness.[102]

What human intelligence imperfectly achieves in social organisation, nature has perfected through instinct in the animal kingdom. This is evident in the social behaviour of highly evolved Hymenoptera species (such as ants and bees) and pack behaviour in certain mammals. These examples of social coordination in animals, though remarkable, ultimately demonstrate that social behaviour is not moral behaviour in the authentic sense.

---

102 The author of this famous formula is the English materialist writer J. Bentham.

The distinction lies in their very essence: social behaviour is rooted in interest, while moral behaviour opposes interest or remains entirely separate from it. One is motivated by selfishness; the other is guided by duty. The former is based on gain, calculation, wisdom, discipline, and intellect; the latter is possible only in the name of God.

Another key distinction further clarifies this differentiation: moral behaviour is always rooted in self-improvement and aligned with the ideals of goodness, truth, and justice. In contrast, collective behaviour is based on discipline, can be criminal and most often is immoral or amoral.[103] The common good is never the good of all humanity—it always serves the interests of a specific, closed group, whether political, national, or class-based. Tolstoy referred to this as the 'scandal of the state' or the 'scandal of the common good.'[104] The common interest of one group or nation may require the exploitation, colonisation, or even extermination of members of another group or nation. The history of nation-states in the modern era, particularly the history of imperialism, is filled with instances where so-called 'common interest' has taken an openly criminal character.

Recent history provides a particularly striking example of how the logic of 'common good' or 'goal' can lead to mass confusion and delusion with tragic consequences. First, *The Communist Manifesto* declared that proletarians reject morality as a bourgeois hoax. Later, the Second International revised this stance, asserting that it accepted the principle of justice and rejected the notion that the goal justifies the means. However, Lenin practically reinstated the position of the *Manifesto*, asserting that 'only actions that contribute to the victory of the proletari-

103 In every ethical consideration, one cannot overlook Leibniz's famous formula: 'Morally good is that action which is directed towards the perfection of man.' The aspiration to perfection, however, has nothing to do with utility; it is founded on the essence of the human spirit.

104 Tolstoy, *Christian Doctrine*, p. 61.

at are moral.' This statement constitutes a direct negation of morality, reintroducing the principle of justification by goal alone.

By applying Lenin's principle, Stalin reached the following conclusions—all deemed necessary and, therefore, moral in the name of the proletariat's victory, as he defined or chose to define it:

- Establishing concentration camps
- Expanding the state and police apparatus to an unprecedented level
- Eliminating all criticism of authority, from local officials to the highest leaders
- Cultivating the illusion of infallibility, assigning supreme wisdom to leaders
- Creating a culture of fear to suppress any potential resistance at its roots
- Organising periodic mass purges to eliminate undesirable individuals, groups, or even entire nations
- Corrupting the army, police, political elite, and compliant intellectuals through high salaries and exclusive privileges
- Establishing privileged state-run supply networks (such as 'ministerial' warehouses) for the ruling caste
- Executing complete manipulation of the masses
- Monopolising all means of communication—press, radio, and television—to perpetuate propaganda on: democratisation and freedom, humanism and prosperity, the bright future of socialism, the virtues of leaders and party officials
- Maintaining foreign occupations under the guise of 'freely expressed will' from the subjugated nations
- And so on, *ad infinitum.*

The only requirement was to declare these measures as serving the victory of the proletariat—and suddenly, all became not only permissible but moral.[105]

---

105 In a handbook for Soviet citizens, we read that the highest duty is loyalty to the working class. This "highest duty" is therefore defined not ethically, but

While religious morality upholds the principle of non-resistance to evil—the only principle that can be found, either explicitly or implicitly, in all religion-based moral systems—the morality of utility proclaims the opposite principle: mutuality.

Utilitarians explicitly state that if one adheres to morality while others do not, their actions become irrational. This conclusion is entirely logical within a utilitarian framework. However, this fact further confirms that utilitarian morality is not genuine morality—it belongs more to the realm of politics than to ethics. Establishing mutuality as a valid moral principle inherently relativises morality and severs it from the foundation that gives it unconditional authority. The morality of utility is often referred to in English literature as the 'morality of consequences'. In this system, an action is considered moral or immoral based on the assumption that, as a general rule, it tends to produce good or bad outcomes. However, as we have already observed, authentic morality does not concern itself with consequences. In fact, this perspective often goes so far as to negate the act itself as merely an external expression of behaviour.

True morality ultimately focuses on intentions and motives. The role of a human being is to strive and to act—and in doing so, they have fulfilled their ethical duty. The results and consequences of their actions remain in God's hands.

---

politically. However, when a regime declares itself the representative or embodiment of the interests of the working class, it easily follows that loyalty to that very regime becomes the highest duty of every citizen. Stalin's abuses began and were carried out precisely in this manner. Or consider a similar, more recent example: in a textbook on Marxist ethics used in secondary schools in Hungary (an official textbook in 1978), one can find the assertion that a child (son or daughter) "must under no pretext kill their mother, unless she becomes a class traitor." The publication of the textbook provoked fierce controversy, prompting a statement from the authorities that it would be withdrawn.

MORALITY WITHOUT GOD

Practical moral experience frequently provides examples of moral conduct in individuals who are indifferent to religious teachings or even proclaimed atheists. At the same time, there is often a clear discrepancy between a person's declared beliefs and their actual behaviour. Many people identify as devoutly religious—some even preach religious values—yet live as hardened materialists in practice. Conversely, there are many indoctrinated materialists who, in practical life, are the most noble ascetics and fighters for others. A wonderful human comedy—one that brings even the clearest, most honest thinkers into delusion—is born and develops in this mess and inconsistency. There is no automation between our beliefs and our behaviour. Our behaviour, our morality, is not only or primarily a function of a consciously chosen stance and life philosophy. It is more often a result of upbringing and understandings accepted in childhood than of any later, consciously adopted philosophical or political stance. If someone is raised from childhood to respect elders, to keep their word, not to differentiate between people, to love and help those close to them, to speak the truth, hate hypocrisy, and to be a simple and proud person, it is certain that these values will mostly remain the mark of their personality, regardless of their political stance or formally adopted philosophy later in life. This morality that a person possesses—if it is not their own religion—is then a transferred religion.

In such cases, upbringing has succeeded in passing down certain originally religious values regarding human relationships but has failed to reinforce the religious foundation that originally justified those values. However, from abandoning religion to abandoning its moral framework, there is only one step—the step of consistency. Some people never take this step, which allows this contradictory situation to persist.

It is precisely this phenomenon that complicates moral inquiry and creates the paradox of moral atheists and immoral believers.

The question of whether morality without God is truly possible will likely remain a theoretical debate forever, without the possibility of practical examination or historical validation. The reason for this is simple yet profound: throughout all of human history, there has never been a completely irreligious society.

Even communities whose generations are born and raised in complete indifference to, or even hatred towards, religion—based on officially accepted atheist propaganda—cannot serve as a reliable answer to the question of morality without religion; that is, whether a purely atheist culture and society are possible. Such societies, regardless of all their efforts and the walls they build around themselves, cannot exist outside space and time. All the past, which radiates in countless ways, is present here, as is the rest of the world that affects them—whether intentionally or spontaneously.

I boldly assert that the rules of behaviour, legal systems, and social structures of a society whose members have been raised in absolute ignorance of religion would be drastically different from anything we have encountered so far—even in societies commonly described as secular or strongly influenced by atheist ideologies.[106]

106 Even language itself. It could be demonstrated that, as a result of the reduction of human relations to function, language could be reduced to one hundredth of its current vocabulary. This impoverishment of language can already be observed today in the so-called specialist (or functional)

It is possible that many self-proclaimed nonreligious individuals would be deeply unsettled if they were confronted with the ideals and legal frameworks of a truly atheist society or if they were suddenly faced with a vision of a fully realised atheist world.

There may be moral atheists, but there is no moral atheism. Even this morality of the nonreligious man has its source in religion—though in an earlier, bygone religion of which the man is no longer aware, but which continues to influence and radiate in hundreds of ways from everything that surrounds him: family, literature, film, architecture... Even in places where the sun has completely set, all the warmth that radiates by night still comes from the sun. The warmth remains in the room, even though the fire in the hearth has died. Just as coal is 'sun in the basement', so too is morality a bygone religion—a style of behaviour stemming from a vision of the world that we owe to religion.

Only through the complete destruction or total elimination of the spiritual inheritance of past centuries would it be possible to create the psychological conditions necessary for the truly atheist upbringing of a new generation.

For 20,000 years, humanity has lived under the constant influence of religion. It has shaped every aspect of life, including morality, law, social norms, conceptions and even language.

Thus, we are led to a fundamental question: Given all of human history, is it even possible to 'produce' a purely atheist generation? For such an attempt to succeed, it would require complete psychological isolation from the entirety of human cultural and intellectual history.

---

language used in the technical and social sciences. The impoverishment of language is also linked to urbanisation, that is, the disappearance of the village, which has long been a constant source of renewal and enrichment for language—but all of these are interconnected phenomena.

Leaving aside the Bible and the Qur'an, this generation would also need to be shielded from almost all forms of art, music, theatre, and literature. They would never be allowed to hear a symphony or witness a drama—from Sophocles to Beckett. Humanity's greatest architectural achievements would have to be hidden from them, just as almost all major works of world literature. They would have to be raised in complete ignorance about almost everything that we call the fruits or the expressions of human culture.

Even a single exposure to a monologue from Shakespeare's *Hamlet* on death, a glimpse of one of Michelangelo's frescoes, or the knowledge of a fundamental legal principle like *nullum crimen sine lege* might be enough to suddenly reconstruct an entirely different worldview—one that is not purely atheist. This is because the human mind has a predisposition towards religious 'deviation', an innate tendency to seek meaning beyond materialism.

However, the case is not the same when it comes to scientific knowledge.

There would be no risk in introducing future atheists to mathematics, technical sciences, and even certain areas of reductive sociology or political economy.

The Chinese Cultural Revolution (1968–1970) is too recent an event to allow for a full assessment of its long-term effects. However, one of its undeniable goals was the systematic destruction of historical spiritual and cultural legacies because they contradicted the state's official ideology and philosophy.[107] Unlike a political or social revolution, the very concept of a 'cultural revolution' suggests that the problem had already been identified: atheism, in many cases, remains superficial, verbal, and rhetorical—a mere phrase. It was

107 As is well known, this revolution, among other things, banned the works of Tolstoy, Shakespeare, and Beethoven—which is entirely logical.

impossible to achieve a consistently atheist social system because cultural traditions—embedded in art, folklore, laws and literature—continued to radiate a quiet and unassuming religious presence.

It remains uncertain what all of Marx's intellectual and spiritual influences were. However, his early writings reveal a strong humanistic influence drawn from literature and his upbringing.[108] His theory of alienation is almost entirely a moral and humanist theory—unexpected in a materialist thinker.

Yet, as the years passed, Marx himself seemed to become more aware of the 'fallacies' of his youth. The distinction often made between the 'young Marx' and the 'mature Marx' can be felt clearly and it reflects an inner maturation —a process of purging his early idealist inclinations. This was, in essence, a gradual liberation from religious and moral influences and a more rigorous execution of a materialist worldview.

Thus, today's generation—regardless of its declared non-religiousness or even atheism—has not grown up in ignorance of religion but in constant polemic with it.

Refusing to accept Christ's principles of love, brotherhood, and unity in the name of God, this generation has nonetheless been unable to fully discard them. In a peculiar delusion, it has retained these principles—only now in the name of science and society.

This is why we cannot take today's generation and its world as proof that an atheist culture is truly possible.

In reality, this culture—and the generation that sustains it—has been shaped by a continuous, subtle, yet undeniable influence of religion and its profound ethical principles.

108 Marx himself said that Aeschylus, Shakespeare, and Goethe were his favourite poets. Every year, he would reread Aeschylus in Greek. He often recited Homer and Ovid. The Rousseauian roots of Marxism (e.g. ideas on the origin of social inequality and property) are recognisable in this doctrine.

Strictly speaking, the new generation may have adopted a new ideology, but its moral upbringing and ethical framework are inherited from an earlier era.

The builders are the same—only the method of building has changed.

Every system, when put into practice, always ends up resembling the people who implement it more than the ideas and declarations it formally upholds.

If we accept that morality, rather than ideology or political orientation, defines human essence, then we can say that today's world was built by people of an earlier moral tradition who now operate under new ideas.

They introduce idealism and sacrifice into the execution of ideologies that explicitly negate idealism and sacrifice.

Those who claim that today's 'moral incentives' for work in places like China and Russia represent a conscious or unconscious exploitation of deeply ingrained religious values are correct in their observation. Because, from a strictly atheist perspective, what could it possibly mean to reject material rewards in favour of moral incentives? It is only natural to pursue religious goals through idealism and materialist goals through calculation and self-interest. Anything else is an inconsistency.

Thus, the true question of morality without religion is this:

Can what religion demands from humans in the name of God be demanded from humans in the name of humanity?

Materialists, when attempting to construct an ethical system, often invoke this formula—even though it is a prime example of logical inconsistency or selective forgetfulness. When discussing the motivation for moral behaviour, they propose conscience as a substitute for fear of God, and argue that humans should love goodness 'out of awareness, not out of fear.' For instance, an atheist ethicist once declared:

> I would even claim that it is precisely atheism that elevates humanity and human morality. If I, as a free human being, without any external command, find within myself an inner imperative that tells me 'do not steal' or 'do not kill', and if I derive this from nothing absolute—neither societal nor divine—then I do not consider this a degradation of man.
>
> (Belgrade *Dialogue of Atheists and Theologians*, May 1971 – Exposition of Professor Vuk Pavičević)

Yet, given the reality of human experience, we must ask:

Who here is truly redefining terms? Are conscience and moral awareness truly part of the material world? Is emphasising 'man' instead of 'God' not simply a tautology? And is faith in humanity not just a lesser form of religion?

The materialist invocation of moral behaviour in the name of man, rather than God, is particularly paradoxical, considering that Marx himself asserted that faith in humanity as an abstract concept was no less an illusion than religious belief.

In this, Marx was entirely correct—for if there is no God, then there is no true concept of 'man' either (a notion captured in the well-known formula: if there is no God, there is no human). Lenin's assertion that scientific socialism has no connection to morality is well documented, as is the statement in *The Communist Manifesto* that workers reject morality.

Communism does not emerge from ethical or humanitarian concerns, but rather as a historical necessity, dictated by the material development of society. Unlike the pragmatic interpretations of Marxism that circulate today for day-to-day political use, the classical Marxist texts are quite explicit: the law of exploitation operates with the inevitability of a natural law in human relations and society. Every man will exploit another for as long as he is able to, or until he is prevented by force.

This leaves no space for conscience, scruples, ethical considerations, or natural human compassion. Were there room for such moral constraints, some of Marxism's core tenets would be called into question. According to this view, exploitation persists until objective socio-economic conditions eliminate it. It does not depend on the individual will of people, their moral sensibilities, upbringing, personal nature, philosophy, or even their social bonds—whether familial, national, or otherwise. When Marx cites examples of children being exploited by their own hungry mothers in *Capital* (see chapter 'Workday'), he does so deliberately. He highlights an extreme, atypical case precisely to illustrate the absolute and universal nature of the law of exploitation in human society.

It is, therefore, curious that some modern Marxists now attempt to construct a so-called secular ethics before our eyes, invoking 'humanity' and abstract humanist values.[109] Marx was adamant that references to humanity, humanism, and conscience were manifestations of idealism—closely linked to religion. We agree with Marx on this however, it seems that for practical reasons, many of today's Marxists cannot do the same. Unlike Marx, who could comfortably declare that morality does not exist from the confines of his study or the British Library, those who attempted to implement Marx's ideas and build an actual society could not so easily declare that otherwise consistently materialist stance.

In order to construct a Marxist society—and, more importantly, to sustain it—they found themselves demanding from people a level of idealism and self-sacrifice that exceeded even the expectations of religious prophets. Thus, they found themselves in the contradictory position of having to 'forget'

109 Nor did Engels hold a particularly high opinion of ethics 'based on insights into one's own consciousness and conscience': 'In reality, every class, even every profession, has its own morality, and breaks it wherever it can do so with impunity. And love, which ought to unite everything, manifests itself in wars, quarrels, domestic disputes, divorces, and in the greatest possible exploitation of some by others.' (Engels, *Ludwig Feuerbach and the End of Classical German Philosophy*)

certain foundational Marxist doctrines— when circumstances required it.

Thus, the question is not whether an atheist (or materialist) can desire, defend, and build morality and humanity—but whether he can do so while remaining entirely within the framework of materialism.

The philosophical debate surrounding Epicurus' teachings provides a historical example of how harmony between materialism and ethics cannot be sustained for too long.

The renowned Hellenistic philosopher (341–270 BCE), though a materialist in his explanation of the world, remained ambiguous in ethics. He preached that happiness lay in pleasure yet advocated for 'ataraxia'—a state of serene peace and spiritual tranquillity. He himself valued spiritual pleasures more than sensual ones. But his disciples resolved this inconsistency by reducing his ethics to a purely eudaimonic path, and today, Epicureanism has—quite logically—become synonymous with sensual pleasure as a life ideal.

There is an internal consistency between his materialist cosmology—which asserts that the universe is merely a mechanical interaction of material particles in empty space—and eudaimonism. However, no such consistency exists between his materialism and the primacy of spiritual values or ataraxia. Thus, the accusation that Epicurus' followers 'distorted' his philosophy is unfounded. In reality, they simply aligned his teachings with their natural materialist conclusions. Materialism, when followed to its logical end, must ultimately negate ethics.

From this, two conclusions emerge:

First, that there is no morality as a principle or idea without religion—only practical morality sustained by inertia. The further morality drifts from its original religious source, the weaker it becomes.

Second, that no moral order can be built upon atheism—though atheism does not immediately eliminate morality or in any case social discipline, which remains as a lower form of morality. On the contrary, when atheism becomes a practice and attempts to construct a society, it will often seek to preserve existing moral structures to the greatest extent possible. This is evident in the practices of socialist states in the twentieth century.

However, the fact remains that atheism lacks the means to preserve or defend the fundamental principles of morality. It is completely powerless against the rise of purely utilitarian, selfish, or amoral demands once morality is challenged conceptually.

It can only suppress such demands through coercion—not through persuasive ethical arguments. This leads to an inescapable question:

If life is purely material, if we exist only for today and vanish tomorrow, then why should an individual not prioritise their own comfort and self-interest above all else?

Atheism has no logical rebuttal to this stance without contradicting itself.

The spread of pornography and the so-called 'new morality' of sexual freedom—or rather, sexual irresponsibility—was curbed in socialist countries not through moral reasoning, but through censorship and force. Such measures were artificial, as no coherent moral argument existed to counter these trends within an atheist framework.

Where such moral arguments were attempted, they were logically inconsistent, maintained only by the suppression of free and open critique.

In reality, these arguments were remnants of old, inherited moral values still embedded in human consciousness or preserved by the state as a matter of social necessity.

However, these inherited morals—when scrutinised—contradict the official materialist philosophy and logically have no place in such a system. Thus, if we allow ourselves some simplification, we can conclude: morality is simply 'another aggregate state' of religion.

CHAPTER 5

CULTURE AND HISTORY

PRIMARY HUMANISM

Rationalists and materialists are typically characterised by a linear interpretation of history. For them, the development of the world begins at zero, and history as a whole represents continual forward progress, despite occasional deviations or temporary setbacks. Thus, the present is always seen as something more than the past and something less than the future. This perspective becomes clearer when we remember that materialists regard history primarily as the development of the material conditions required for human life—in other words, a history of things rather than a history of humans as active subjects. Consequently, their view encapsulates a history of civilisation rather than one of human culture.

However, the history of humanity and culture neither originates at zero nor progresses linearly; it has a 'prologue in heaven' as its initial act. Early human societies began at only a slightly more favourable position compared to the animal groups from which they had evolved. Yet, these societies expressed distinctly human forms and remarkable ethical values from the outset. Humanity entered its historical epoch carrying significant moral capital—capital it neither derived nor inherited from its animal predecessors. Science has confirmed, but never fully explained, the nature and origins of this genuine and fundamental humanism present within early human communities, especially during those distant times when the boundary between human and animal was still uncertain. By rejecting religious explanations *a priori*, science effectively closed off avenues for fully comprehending this phenomenon.[110]

In his description of the ancient gens—the foundational units of prehistoric societies around the world—Lewis Morgan, in *Ancient Society*, identified the following characteristics as central to the social and moral life of these early communities:[111]

- A gens elects its chief, who can also be replaced; upon replacement, the former chief resumes the role of a common warrior like any other.
- Marital and sexual relations within the gens are strictly forbidden; this prohibition is consciously maintained and rarely violated.
- Members of the gens provide mutual protection and support, extending even to acts of self-sacrifice.
- Warriors demonstrate heroic behaviour and uphold chivalrous treatment of prisoners, who are typically not executed.
- All members of a gens are free individuals, equal in status and connected by a sense of brotherhood.
- The adoption of new members into the gens involves a religious ceremony; religious rituals primarily take the form of dances and games, with idols being notably absent.
- The tribal council comprises representatives from the various gentes (sachems), deciding community matters in a public setting attended by the entire tribe. Decisions must be reached unanimously.

---

110 A vague memory of this era of primordial humanity has been preserved in the legends and fairy tales of almost all peoples as the classic myth of the so-called 'Golden Age' or (in the Bible) as the 'Age of the Patriarchs'. 'The general belief that the past was bad only came with the theory of evolution,' claims Russell (B. Russell, *History of Western Philosophy*, p. 601).

111 Morgan's description refers to the gens of the Iroquois in North America, which is considered the classic form of the primordial gens.

Amazed by this description, Friedrich Engels exclaims:

> That gentile system is astonishing in its naïvety and simplicity! Without soldiers, gendarmes and policemen, without nobility, kings, prefects or judges, without dungeons and litigation, everything runs in an organised flow. Every disagreement or dispute is solved by the community concerned, the gens or tribe, or certain gentes among themselves… There can be no poor or destitute. Communist society and gens know their obligations toward the old, sick and disabled in war. Everyone is equal and free, including women. There are no slaves yet, nor subjugation of other tribes… And the admiration of all white people who came into contact with unspoiled Indians, for the personal dignity, sincerity, strength of character and bravery of these barbarians, confirms the quality of men and women created by such a society. (F. Engels, *Origin of the Family, Private Property and the State* (1884)).

The society that Morgan described was vividly depicted by one of his compatriots, J. Fenimore Cooper, in his novels, and there is no doubt that another American, R. W. Emerson, had Native Americans in mind when he said: 'I saw human nature in all its forms. It is the same everywhere, except the wilder it is, the more virtue it contains.' In his books, Tolstoy considered the society evident in the still unspoiled life of the primitive Russian muzhik as the ideal society. Here, as elsewhere, these moral and human values existed alongside very low levels of material and societal progress.

We also find impressive facts about the cultures of primitive African peoples in the General History of Africa books published by UNESCO (two out of eight books have been published as of now). For example, it has been demonstrated that foreigners, white or black, enjoyed hospitality in black kingdoms and possessed equal rights to those of the native population. In contrast, a foreigner entering ancient Rome or Greece often became a slave. These and similar facts likely prompted Leo Frobenius, the renowned German ethnologist and great expert on Africa, to write: 'Black people are civilised to the bone, and the idea that they are barbarians is a European invention.'[112]

We must question the nature of the values we encounter simultaneously among Native Americans, indigenous African tribes, Tahitian peoples, the primitive Russian muzhik, and even the lowest castes in India. What is their origin? How did they emerge at the very beginning of history, and why are they quantitatively diminishing as historical progress advances? Where did the idea of caring for the elderly and disabled, such as that found among the Iroquois tribe, originate? Does it have an animal origin? The various forms of 'care' observed among animals are always based on utility—thus lacking humanity in the genuine human sense, as actions performed for an idea or principle. Morgan concludes his renowned book with these words:

> Democracy in governance, brotherhood in society, equality and general education will introduce the next higher level of society, to which experience, mind and science are constantly aspiring. They will be the next revival, but in a higher form, of freedom, equality and brotherhood of the old gens.

Morgan anticipates that freedom, equality, and brotherhood in future civilised societies will be derived from three powers: experience, mind, and science. At least two things are clear at this moment: (1) freedom, equality, and brotherhood in ancient communities did not originate from experience, mind, and science; and (2) the century of experience, mind, and science that passed since Morgan's book, *Ancient Society* (1877), did not confirm his predictions at all.

---

112 Of course, it is easy to recognise that Frobenius here understands "civilised" to mean "cultured".

Perhaps we can attribute the widespread prejudice—seeing barbarism and civilisation not only as two opposing poles of social and technical progress but also as contrasts between evil and good—to the fact that history is written by the civilised rather than by barbarians. When someone destroys cultural heritage or commits genocide, we feel justified in calling it a 'barbaric act'. Conversely, if we demand tolerance and humanity, we call upon people to behave 'as a civilised nation'. It is remarkable how stubbornly these perceptions persist, despite countless facts suggesting otherwise. It is precisely the history of the American continent that could lead us to the opposite conclusion. Was it not civilised Spaniards (the conquistadors) who destroyed not only the cultures of the Mayans and Aztecs but also the peoples of these regions in the vilest, most unprecedented ways? Was it not white settlers, always coming from civilised countries, who systematically exterminated indigenous tribes—precisely those astonishing gentes Morgan wrote about—in a way almost unparalleled in recent history? As late as the mid-nineteenth century, the American government paid a set price for every Indian scalp. The shameful Atlantic slave trade lasted over three hundred years alongside the growth of Euro-American civilisation as its integral component, ending only in 1865. During this time, approximately 13 to 15 million free people (exact numbers will never be known) were captured through literal manhunts. Here, too, civilised savagery confronted the free and gentle primitive man. Modern imperialism must also be mentioned in this context, representing the encounter between European civilisation and the so-called backward, uncivilised or less civilised nations. Wherever it appeared, imperialism manifested itself through violence, deception, hypocrisy, subjugation, and destruction of the material, cultural, and moral values of weaker, primitive nations.

Our prejudice concerning the Middle Ages is predominantly of the same nature. Was the Middle Ages genuinely an era of darkness and universal misfortune? The answer depends largely on one's perspective. By the standards of civilisation, it undoubtedly was. Helvétius, one of Europe's earliest materialist philosophers, described the Middle Ages as a period when 'people were turned into animals', and its laws as 'a masterpiece of absurdity'. Inevitably, thinkers such as Berdyaev or the painter J. Harp, both Christians, reached entirely different conclusions about the same period.[113] Typically, we hold a rather simplified and one-dimensional view of the Middle Ages. Although poverty, discomfort, and lack of hygiene predominated, medieval societies possessed more than just a stronger sense of internal cohesion. It was an age characterised by intense ideological life, without which the energies and aspirations of Western humanity cannot be fully comprehended. The Middle Ages produced grand works of art and achieved a synthesis between a remarkable philosophy (Greek philosophy) and remarkable religion (Christianity). 'Gothic architecture is one of the most significant human achievements,' asserts Clark, and it is indeed a product of the Middle Ages. During this period, despite the absence of scientific and technological advancements, a form of qualitative progress was accomplished—what A. N. Whitehead referred to as qualitative, rather than quantitative, advancement (A. N. Whitehead, *The Future of Religion*). If there truly is something Faustian in Western civilisation, it was forged and refined through the immense spiritual and political struggles of the Middle Ages. Without this era, the modern age, at least as we recognise it today, could not exist.

113 J. Harp: 'I am against mechanised things and chemical formulas. I love the Middle Ages, its tapestries and its sculptures.'

ART AND HISTORY

In a certain sense, culture exists outside of time and history. It experiences its rises and falls but does not demonstrate progress or historical development in the general sense of these terms. There is no accumulation of 'knowledge' or experience in art comparable to that in science.[114] From the Palaeolithic era to the present day, we do not observe a progressive increase in the expressive power of art as a function of historical advancement. Civilisation recognises distinct epochs, such as the Stone Age and the Atomic Age, but such a linear trajectory is absent from cultural history. From a civilisational standpoint, the Neolithic represents progress, yet from an artistic perspective, it signifies decline. Palaeolithic art surpasses Neolithic art in its authenticity and expressive power, despite preceding it by thousands of years. Everywhere, poetry emerged before prose; humans sang before they narrated stories. Poetry did not require accumulated experience or external models. A similar independence from temporal progression can also be identified in fundamental moral principles and religious doctrines. Research by Andrew Lang, W. Schmidt, Conrad Preuss, Coppers, and others supports the view that every religion was initially pure and simple, becoming distorted only later through practice (proto-monotheism

114 Everything concerning science – it is the opposite. Science is based on continuity. Where this continuity is lacking and where it is not ensured through tradition or writing – there is no science, and no civilisation either. Progress precisely consists in the ability to remember and to continue.

theory). Consequently, the concept of a 'history of culture' may be considered inherently contradictory. Instead, one might only meaningfully discuss a chronology of cultural phenomena. Jacques Risler notes:

> As soon as they were recently discovered, the true value of ancient Egyptian reliefs and sculptures, found in the Nile Valley and dating back approximately four to five millennia, was recognised. Many contemporary artists draw inspiration for their works from these primeval reliefs, engraved into tomb walls, and from graceful figures fashioned from clay, marble, gold, and alabaster. This art is at times delicate and refined (the era of Thutmose II and Thutmose III), at times monumental and powerful (the era of Khufu), and at other times realistic and less symbolic (the era of Akhenaten).[115]

At the time of its discovery, America was approximately 5–6 thousand years behind the Old World according to the civilisational timeline, not having even reached its Iron Age yet (H. G. Wells). However, such a scale is clearly inapplicable when evaluating American art. Frescoes of extraordinary beauty were discovered in Bonampak (Mexico), a temple housing the oldest paintings found on the American continent. A major exhibition of Mayan sculptures, held in Paris in 1966, vividly illustrated the phenomenon of a sophisticated culture that did not advance into a civilisation.

> This serious, refined art, whose expressive range spans from astonishing simplicity to highly baroque ornamentation, remains mysterious to this day. No one has yet succeeded in explaining how it emerged, already perfected around the 4th century, in the forests of Petén and Chiapas, featuring elaborate ceremonial centres, imposing architectural temples atop pyramids, ornamental sculptures, a hieroglyphic script, and an intricate numeric system revealed by the

115 Jacques Risler, *La Civilisation arabe.*

script itself. The Parisian exhibition of Mayan sculptures displayed several remarkable pieces: bas-reliefs, statues carved from hard stone, and masks crafted from artificial marble, notable for their ghostly whiteness, seemingly intent on conveying messages from centuries long past. Within Mayan sculpture, two almost opposite artistic directions can be observed: one encompassing bas-reliefs and stelae, and the other represented by sculpted heads. The former demonstrates ceremonial art bound by numerous conventions, distinctly contrasting with the extreme simplicity of the sculpted heads, especially those in artificial marble. One such mask goes beyond mere realism, appearing to be an actual portrait. Two other heads, featuring more expressionist elements and executed in the grotesque baroque style, contribute a striking and vivid note to this unique collection of artistic beauty. (Excerpt from a report on the aforementioned Paris exhibition).

According to Nietzsche in *The Birth of Tragedy*, Hellenic drama—particularly tragedy—represents the pinnacle of artistic achievement, illustrating the highest manifestation of human culture within what is termed Hellenic civilisation.[116]

'None of the contemporary poets reaches the greatness of Homer or one of the Greek tragedians' (André Maurois). The mystery is complete: art reaches one of its highest milestones at the dawn of human civilisation. Hegel considers ancient Greece the 'golden age of philosophy', while Roger Cailloit remarks, 'As far as philosophy is concerned, I often come to the conclusion, as many others do, that it did not make any progress at all after Plato. Perhaps it is due to the nature of art that it does not progress: it always seems to be beginning anew.'

116 Marx makes a similar statement when he says that works of ancient art represent "unattainable standards and models". Carried away by enthusiasm, Marx seems not to grasp the full scope of his statement. Is culture not a reflection of civilisation, or a superstructure built upon it? If so, how can there be "unattainable models" already within a slave-owning system?

Cicero's ethical writings (e.g., *De finibus bonorum et malorum or De amicitia*) remain equally relevant today, whereas his works on the organisation of labour or the structure of the state—typical civilisational topics—appear entirely anachronistic. The book by the anonymous Roman author *De rebus bellicis (On Military Matters)*, which, among other things, included intriguing sketches of military devices, now retains only historical interest. The same cannot be said for Seneca's work *On Bliss* or Virgil's poetry from the same period.

The harp, or its immediate predecessor, dates back to the third millennium BCE. *Man'yōshū*, a Japanese poetry anthology from the 7th and 8th centuries containing over 4,000 predominantly lyrical poems, remains among the masterpieces of world poetry. As early as the 10th century—what Russell calls the beginning or 'lowest point of European civilisation'—European architecture suddenly attained a state of perfection, producing works of unprecedented beauty and harmony.[117] 'Towering stone structures rose amid humble clusters of wooden houses, like monumental hills emerging from the earth.' (K. Clark).

The tragedies of Sophocles and Aeschylus can be adapted to every era simply by changing costumes. Euripides wrote *The Trojan Women*. Jean-Paul Sartre wrote a play with the same title. Thus, two creators separated by more than twenty centuries can become co-creators in art (it is often noted as Euripides–Sartre's *The Trojan Women*). Such continuity is impossible in science. What remains today of Aristotle's physics,

117 Historians usually regard the 10th century as almost as dark and barbaric as the seventh. The reason lies in the fact that they view it from the standpoint of political history and the written word. If we read what Ruskin called the "book of art", we will gain an entirely different impression because – contrary to all expectations – the tenth century produced works that were just as brilliant, technically skilled, and even just as beautiful as those of any other century… "The quantity of artistic works is astonishing." (Kenneth Clark, *Civilisation*, p. 34)

Ptolemy's astronomy, or Galen's medicine? Speaking of two of Aristotle's scientific works—*Physics* and *On the Heavens*—Russell remarks that, in light of modern science, 'scarcely a single sentence from either could be accepted today.' For example, in *On the Heavens*, Aristotle proposes a theory according to which things beneath the Moon are subject to birth and destruction, whereas everything above the Moon is uncreated and indestructible. Or consider his explanation of gravity: each body has a 'natural place' and a 'borrowed place'. Thus, when a stone falls, it strives to reach the natural place belonging to all stones—the Earth's surface. How does this 'theory' of gravitation compare to Newton's?

Art flows from the undeveloped world to the developed one, moving from east to west or south to north. Science, however, travels in the opposite direction, much like things naturally move from areas of higher charge to those of lower charge. Eastern melodies, Indian folk music, songs and dances from Africa, and the art of Oceania have penetrated the West. Exotic wooden sculptures created by illiterate villagers from Tanzania's Makonde tribe are captivating audiences worldwide.[118]

The art of Oceania, one of the most undeveloped regions globally, is displayed in galleries across Europe and America, considered equal to works from so-called cultured regions. Western civilisation has proved itself receptive to this wave of authentic art. The discovery of African art significantly

118 'In recent times, the world's most renowned art galleries have begun to include among their notable exhibits imaginative compositions carved from ebony wood, spontaneously created by young men and elders from the Makonde tribe beneath the thatched roofs of their modest homes along the roads near Dar es Salaam… With unprecedented ingenuity, these artists, in their ebony figures, evoke the struggle between good and evil, the intimate connection between birth and death, joy and sorrow, conflict and harmony… Other Tanzanians hold them in high regard both for their marvellous art and for the widespread belief that the Makonde people possess the terrifying skill and power of ancient shamans.' (from a travelogue through Black Africa).

influenced the trajectory of modern Euro-American art and has partly fuelled revolutionary artistic movements in the West. (At the same time, it is hardly possible to make a serious comparison between European and, for example, African science, economy, technology, or social organisation.) Elie Faure asserts that a black mask from the Ivory Coast and a fresco from the Sistine Chapel generate an equal level of 'sensible excitement' (*L'Esprit des formes – History of Art*).

The International Festival of Black Art in Dakar in 1966 was a cultural event of the highest order, featuring ensembles and groups from 39 countries. By contrast, an industrial or commercial fair showcasing nations from the African continent might go largely unnoticed. Although the black world remains undeveloped scientifically and technologically, this is not the case artistically, as art does not acknowledge the distinctions of 'developed' and 'undeveloped'. Black Africa is genuinely a cultural superpower, excelling in folklore, music, songs, and especially dance. The inner jungle regions of Irian represent perhaps the most authentic living museum of prehistoric human culture, where civilisation has not progressed beyond the Stone Age. Yet, what about culture? The missionary Dipera, who spent over 20 years there, provides an answer:

> The aesthetic sensibility is highly developed among the primitive populations, and their artistic objects exhibit astonishing qualities. Although there is some literature on the subject, it hardly captures all the variations and the richness of ideas and forms. Their remarkable sculptures of stone and wood, paintings, engravings, and beautifully crafted statuettes, alongside their intricate choreographed dances resembling ballets, performed in spectacular costumes, constitute incredible spectacles.

Scientists belong exclusively to their own era; poets belong to all times.

ETHICS AND HISTORY

Culture is a static exploration of why I live; civilisation is a constant progression of how I live and satisfy my needs. One concerns the meaning of life, while the other relates to the manner of living. Civilisation advances continuously, from the discovery of fire, watermills, and steel, through the invention of the alphabet and machines, to atomic energy and space exploration. Conversely, culture involves seeking, returning, and repeatedly beginning anew.

Humanity as the subject of culture, with its characteristic flaws, virtues, doubts, and illusions—the entirety of its inner nature—displays remarkable durability and is nearly unchangeable. All current ethical dilemmas and questions were already familiar two thousand years ago. From Confucius, Socrates, Jesus Christ, Muhammad (pbuh), Kant, Tolstoy, Gandhi, to Martin Buber—spanning from the 6th century BCE to the present day (Martin Buber died in 1965)—the great moral teachers of humanity have fundamentally preached the same ethics.

Unlike rules for social organisation or methods of production, moral truths are eternal.[119] The essential ethical puzzle originates with Creation itself, in the 'prologue in heaven', an act preceding all human history. Intelligence, education, or experience alone cannot help us draw closer to or better understand these figures. Jesus proclaimed profound truths

119 In the "real" world, everything is the opposite: "Change is the law of economic life." (J. K. Galbraith).

even as a newborn, and he was merely thirty-three years old when sentenced to death. He required neither knowledge nor extensive experience to articulate fundamental truths about God and humanity, because such truths cannot be grasped through knowledge or experience alone.

Are these truths not indeed 'hidden from the wise and learned, and revealed to little children'? (*Gospel of Luke*, 10:21).

Fundamental moral demands are unaffected by time, place, or social circumstances. Despite vast differences in social and political organisation, varying degrees of development, and the diversity of beliefs and religious symbols, a surprising consistency and unity emerge in moral foundations.[120] Epictetus and Marcus Aurelius, a slave and an emperor, taught the same moral philosophy using strikingly similar language. Upon closer examination, differences in understanding good and evil or permissible and impermissible actions relate only to minor issues. Examples frequently cited to illustrate how moral norms vary according to historical or other contexts never truly concern fundamental moral principles but rather issues of formal morality or behaviour. On the contrary, remarkable consistency and immutability in core ethical standards can be observed throughout history.[121]

120 'Although people sometimes speak differently about what God is, they always understand equally what God requires of them.' (Tolstoy)

121 Here are some of those principles: tell the truth; overcome hatred; be a simple and modest person; regard other people as equals; show solidarity; strive for freedom; defend your own rights and the rights of others; earn your own bread; respect the labour of others; respect parents and elders; fulfil promises and obligations; protect the weak; socialise with people; do not rejoice in the misfortune and failure of others; do not envy their happiness and success; do not be conceited or walk with arrogance; be patient in enduring pain; do not flatter the powerful, do not oppress the weak; do not judge people by skin colour, wealth, or origin; have an independent opinion; be moderate in pleasures; do not be selfish, etc. Can one really say that these values are relative and change 'depending on circumstances or the economic structure'?

Let us consider Kant's famous 'categorical imperative'. This principle, first formulated by Kant in *Groundwork of the Metaphysics of Morals* as 'Act only according to the maxim whereby you can at the same time will that it should become a universal law,' and in *Critique of Practical Reason* as 'Act so that the maxim of your will can always simultaneously hold as a principle of universal legislation,' can be traced back even to the earliest philosophers. When asked how one might live most righteously, Thales, one of the seven wise men (born in 624 BCE), responded: 'If we ourselves do not do what we rebuke in others' (*Diogenes Laërtius*, I, 36). Pittacus of Mytilene, another of the seven sages, expressed the same principle: 'Do not do yourself what you reprimand in your close ones,' while Marcus Tullius Cicero similarly advised, 'Everything that you rebuke in others, you should yourself avoid to the utmost.'

The Jewish sage Hillel, who lived around the same period as Christ in Palestine, offered the following concise summary of faith to a polytheist who had requested a brief explanation: 'What you do not wish for yourself, do not do to others. The entire Torah is contained in this; everything else is mere explanation' (*Babylonian Talmud*, Tractate *Shabbat*). Confucius, a contemporary of Buddha and Pythagoras, taught the same principle in China (*Lun Yu,* or *Analects of Confucius*). Naturally, this concept was articulated most distinctly by Jesus in his renowned words: 'So in everything, do to others what you would have them do to you' (*Gospel of Matthew*, 7:12; *Gospel of Luke*, 6:31).

This brief overview of the categorical imperative indicates that this fundamental ethical principle does not, in fact, possess a history in the conventional sense. Its forms may vary slightly, but the essence remains unchanged. India, described as a land of 'high culture and low civilisation', seems to exist outside time and history. Monuments visible at every turn testify to intense activity—but an internal, static form of life, devoid of historical progression. Meditation allows for discovering spiritual secrets, but it does not grant power over nature nor does it alter the external world. Hinduism is an ethical rather than a social system, focused exclusively on personal, inner, moral improvement. Since the era of the *Upanishads*, India has been preoccupied solely with the individual's position in the cosmos (Mircea Eliade). The Indian caste system—petrified like its massive pyramidal temples, which reflect monstrous size and endurance—contains within it a denial of time, society, homogeneity, and history. Any social or historical effort would swiftly topple this imposing structure, which can only remain standing in a world turned inward or directed toward the heavens, indifferent to external events occurring in the real (in this context: ephemeral) world.

ARTIST AND EXPERIENCE

As there is no evolution in the life of art, so there is none in the life of an artist. Every artist starts anew and works as if no one before him had ever created anything. The artist simply does not utilise others' experiences—only their own. In science, the usage, continuity, and accumulation of others' experiences is an essential precondition. In art, however, using the experiences of others constitutes imitation, repetition, and academism, and thus leads to the death of art.

Picasso painted for 70 years, and during this period he passed through his cubist, neo-cubist, impressionist, surrealist, and neo-realist phases. Yet this was no evolution—no progress from worse to better, or from less perfect to more perfect. As with the entirety of culture, it was merely a drama of continual searching and finding.

There are other quite interesting facts regarding this creative, extra-experiential (or extra-historical), purely human character of art. For example, there is science for adults and science for children. The understanding of science—and subsequently its reproduction, application, and the drawing of practical conclusions—depends, among other things, on education, age, and experience. In contrast, there is no distinct music for adults or music for children. Tests involving the works of Bach, Mozart, Beethoven, Debussy, and Chopin have demonstrated that children understand (or fail to understand) classical music at the same level as adults. Beethoven's famous cycle of 32 sonatas—the best of its kind in the history of music—is simultaneously pedagogical literature for young students and repertoire for the most seasoned pianists. Picasso began painting at the age of two, before he had even learned to speak. Ovid started speaking in hexameters at an age when other children were just beginning to talk. Mozart gave concerts at the age of six.

Art is not knowledge, even though it is discovery; but it is discovery not through the mind and education, but through the heart, love, and simplicity of the soul. 'Many a villager, once they finish their work, takes a piece of wood and starts creating a sculpture. They do not require ten years of academy for that. All I want to say is that art is available to everyone, and it does not require any special talent or education. Everybody is an artist,' said Jean Dubuffet, the French painter. This is reminiscent of Tolstoy and his school in Yasnaya Polyana, where he exclusively discussed the deepest religious and ethical truths with children.[122]

Understanding art, religion, and ethics is not intellectual and logical; it is an internal understanding. Here, it is not mind addressing the mind, but heart and soul speaking to heart and soul alike. The facts presented here fundamentally challenge our conventional understanding of 'progress' in human culture. Culture has no history, and humanity remains the constant within world development.

---

122 'Together with a group of children from Yasnaya Polyana, Lev Nikolayevich discussed the most important questions of human life, which, after being reworked with these young collaborators, became unusually clear to everyone. Each idea was jointly examined, developed, explained, and simplified in expression, and in that form, Lev Nikolayevich would write it down. In such a form, it was accessible to the mind of every person.' (Petrov, *Tolstoy*)

CHAPTER 6

DRAMA AND UTOPIA

IDEAL SOCIETY

Does evil originate within, from the dark depths of the human soul, or does it come from outside, from the objective conditions of human life? This question divides all people into two distinct camps: believers and materialists. For believers, all good and evil reside within the human being. Consequently, violence must be renounced because external violence represents a struggle against imagined, non-existent evil. Violence can only be justified when it is self-directed, inwardly, through penance and asceticism. On the other hand, to assert that evil exists externally—that humans are evil solely due to their adverse living conditions, and that changing these conditions will transform humans—is the most godless and, simultaneously, the most inhuman idea ever conceived by the human mind. This notion reduces a human being to an object, a helpless vessel controlled by external, mechanical, unconscious forces. 'Evil resides within the human being' and 'evil resides within the social environment' are two contradictory statements that logically exclude each other. This contrast gives rise to two equally contradictory and irreconcilable phenomena: drama and utopia.[123]

Drama is an experience of the human soul, while utopia is an occurrence within human society. Drama represents the highest possible form of existence in our universe, whereas

123 The concept of utopia is used here in its original sense: as a vision of an ideal organisation of human society modelled on perfect animal collectives – the beehive, the swarm, the anthill.

utopia is merely a dream or a vision of paradise on Earth. There can be no utopia within drama, just as there can be no drama within utopia. This tension illustrates the fundamental conflict between the individual and the world, or between personality and society.

We find an exploration of these themes in Plato's *State*, the earliest known text addressing this issue explicitly. It reads as follows:

> Let us imagine the foundations of the state. Those foundations will be our needs... How can the state satisfy all those needs? Does not someone need to be a farmer, another a builder, and a third a weaver? Must each person not perform the work for others that only they know how to do? Warriors must be fierce towards enemies yet gentle towards friends. To possess these two virtues—fierceness and gentleness—they must also be philosophers, as they must distinguish between friends and enemies. To ensure such warriors become good guardians of the state, they must be carefully educated... The beginning of upbringing is most crucial. It begins by telling fairy tales, which is why the state must censor the writers who create them. Rulers may lie in the interests of the state, but others may not... Since subordinates must obey their superiors, any contrary statements in books must be removed, and gods and heroes must be portrayed as noble... Sad, soft, and lazy melodies should be forbidden; only heroic and martial music should be permitted... Intoxication is prohibited... A citizen must not spend life in sickness and healing, as this harms the state. He must either fulfil his duty or die... Therefore, it is preferable to kill someone likely to suffer prolonged illness or produce sick offspring... Rulers and warriors should be selected through upbringing; however, if their sons do not exhibit equal ability, they should be returned to the class of producers. By maintaining such an education system, each future generation will surpass the previous one, just as it is achieved when cultivating plant or animal species...

The mechanism of utopia is inhuman but perfect. If the essence of drama is freedom, the essence of utopia consists of two opposite principles: order and uniformity. At the beginning of the sixteenth century, Thomas More published his short but epochal book, *Utopia* (1516), about the ideal state located on the island of Utopia. The second part of this book is of greater interest here, thus its key points will be outlined briefly. The island of Utopia is crescent-shaped, consisting of fifty-four large cities, as uniform as possible in appearance and way of life. Each city is surrounded by agricultural land, complete with houses and farming equipment. The rural population is organised into cooperatives of forty members, each with a designated host and hostess. Every thirty cooperatives are overseen by a leader known as a phylarch. Each cooperative is allocated two slaves. After spending two years in the countryside, twenty cooperative members return to the city, replaced by twenty new city members, who will also spend two years in the village. Thus, there are no permanent farmers. They produce chickens without hens by employing a type of incubator. They strive to generate a surplus to share with other cities. A large number of citizens participate in the harvest to ensure its swift completion.

The capital city, Amarot, lies on a river near the sea; it is equipped with a water system and is fortified. Houses are impeccably clean, neatly arranged on both sides of streets, which are uniformly thirty feet wide. Doors are never locked, as there is no private property; houses are reassigned every ten years through a draw using cubes. Citizens carefully tend their gardens, and blocks of streets compete among themselves for excellence. Every citizen, regardless of gender, learns a trade. The primary trades are masonry, blacksmithing, woodworking, and the processing of wool and flax. Each family produces their own clothes, which are identical across the entire island, varying only according to age, season, sex, or marital status. Every citizen inherits the trade of their father.

The working day lasts six hours: three hours before noon, followed by lunch and a two-hour rest, and then three more hours in the afternoon. Everyone goes to bed at eight o'clock and sleeps for eight hours. A leather suit is worn during work, capable of lasting seven years. Each city consists of 600 families, each family containing ten to sixteen members and headed by the eldest member, the chief. Families manage their numbers carefully, ensuring they remain within established limits. Surplus members from larger families are redistributed to those with fewer members. Every group of thirty families has one large communal residence where the phylarch lives, and at the sound of a trumpet, all members assemble for a shared meal. Eating at home is permitted but viewed as dishonourable and a waste of time spent preparing food. Citizens of Utopia can travel within Utopia only with permission from the authorities, and so on.

Associations with trends and phenomena in certain contemporary societies arise spontaneously: limitation of freedom 'in the interest of society', cult of leaders, societal discipline, dissolution of familial and parental relationships, art serving the state, Darwinian selection, euthanasia, social (rather than familial) upbringing, the primacy of the state over the individual, openness to technological progress, gender equality in societal division of labour, property levelling, mobilised labour, competitions, collectivism, uniformity, censorship, and so forth.

Drama deals with the individual, whereas utopia deals with the world. In utopia, the vast inner world of the human being is reduced to an imaginary reference point. Given the assumption inherent to every utopia—that humans lack souls—there can be no genuinely human or moral problems. People function rather than live within utopia. They do not live because they do not possess freedom. In such an environment, individuals have no character; instead, they have a 'psychology' defined solely by their function in the societal division of labour and reproduction of their lives. Concepts of 'good' and 'evil' lose all meaning. Every utopia, including so-called scientific socialism, is inherently devoid of value judgements; it is entirely schematic, existing, in principle, beyond good and evil.

According to Marx, the ultimate result of history is the communist state—an abundance of goods for all, total material satisfaction. Conversely, according to Hegel, the meaning of human history is the triumph of the idea of freedom—therefore, drama. Socialism is essentially a projection of the laws governing the material world onto human and social life. Communist visions of eternal peace (or a classless society) reflect a vision of the material world's distant future in a state of entropy. A classless society is thus Clausius's law of entropy projected onto social life. Religion, by contrast, sees at the end of everything only the Final Judgement; instead of universal levelling and equilibrium, it anticipates drama. For this reason, drama represents a principled and historical continuation of religion, whereas utopia is essentially a form of science. Quetelet authored a sociology book aptly titled *Social Physics*. Every theory about society represents an extension of physics or zoology.

There are political utopias, beginning with Plato's and continuing through Thomas More, Campanella, Fourier, Saint-Simon, Robert Owen, and ultimately Marx. Additionally, technological and science-fiction utopias, starting with Bacon's *Nova Atlantis*, must be considered. Day by day, technology and so-called progress are constructing a monstrous scientific–technological mechanism within which human beings inevitably lose their individuality, becoming mere components. Aldous Huxley envisages the future human as an artificial creation, a product of technology crafted by humanity itself. Owing to advances in genetics (genetic engineering), human embryos will eventually be processed in vast laboratories according to precise recipes. Scientifically produced, fully identical human beings—copies with 'optimal qualities' but no personalities—will result from these procedures.

Dr David Klein, Director of the Institute for Medical Genetics at Geneva University, conducts experiments involving the removal of nuclei from frog egg cells and replacing them with nuclei from other frogs, thereby producing organisms with the desired genetic characteristics. Once perfected—an achievement Dr Klein believes may require forty to fifty years—this process could make it possible to produce animals, and consequently humans, with predetermined qualities. These ideal specimens might even be identical to one another, 'like one egg to another.' Aldous Huxley pushes this perspective of technological utopia to its logical absurdity:

> In the year 2500, a brave new world will reign on Earth, guided by the principles of Equality, Uniformity, Stability. The central science of that world will be biology, the techniques of which will facilitate the creation of standardised humans, thousands of twins working at identical machines, performing identical functions.

In this 'brave new world', there will be no sinful individuals, no defective beings—individuals will not be held responsible and punished, but merely removed from the mechanism. There will be no good or evil, no aspirations, dilemmas, doubts, or rebellions. Drama will be eliminated, and utopia established.

UTOPIA AND MORALITY

Contrary to general opinion, man does not incline towards a functional but rather towards a non-functional world. The widely accepted definition of man as a social animal is of highly questionable validity. Sociality—if understood as the tendency to live in a herd, swarm, flock, or hive—is more zoological and biological than truly human. What can genuinely compare to the social life of bees or ants, or the 'sociality' of a cell in an organism living in perfect harmony, simultaneously for itself and for others? The materialist Hobbes bitterly claims, 'Man is antisocial by nature'. Indeed, in a certain sense, man is an incorrigible individualist who often exhibits a distaste for, or even an inability to, conform to herd life. It is only those who are less human among humans, the less successful examples of humanity, who champion functionality, order, regularity, uniformity, and the primacy of society over the individual. Precisely because this type of person is most efficient in these terms, they have managed to impose their perspective as dominant. Corporals are always more efficient than poets—a tragic fact that speaks volumes about the strength and weakness of everything human and humane.

A soldier in a barracks has all basic needs fulfilled: housing, food, clothing, and employment. Order, security, discipline, hygiene, and even a form of equality or levelling prevail. Nevertheless, most would readily agree that a barracks, despite all these supposed benefits, represents the worst imaginable societal model. Some contemporary societies are, in fact, nothing more than large barracks—or are well on their way to becoming such. Beautiful slogans adorning them change little or nothing of their fundamental essence. Humanism and morality are intrinsically linked to the name and vocation of humanity. A member of society or a citizen of utopia is not authentically human; rather, they are 'social animals' or 'animals gifted with reason'. A true human possesses morality—or immorality—but a mere member of society has only a function.

Morality always presupposes norms. If our actions are not conscious and voluntary, if we only behave as we must—as is the case in utopia—then every norm, and consequently morality itself, becomes meaningless. Even the most humane behaviour in communism would not be moral. This is precisely the meaning behind the Marxist claim that there is no morality in communism and that morality cannot exist therein. Morality is abolished in communism because individuals relate to one another directly, without mediation by any norm. The fact that every ant in an anthill performs its task perfectly has nothing to do with morality; ants simply cannot behave otherwise. Likewise, when bees expel sick or worn-out honeybees from the hive, their actions are neither immoral nor moral. Neither the bee's 'sacrifice' for the hive nor its 'honest work' is moral; it is merely the operation of social mechanisms.

This is the true meaning of Lenin's statement that scientific socialism does not contain 'a single grain of morality', a claim that generated considerable misunderstanding and confusion but represents the most far-reaching recognition of the connection between communism and utopia.[124] Marxism is a uto-

124 Compare the following text by the well-known Soviet legal theorist Y. Pashukanis: 'If the connection between the individual and the class is truly so vivid and strong that the boundaries are virtually erased, and the advantage of the class genuinely becomes identical with personal advantage,

pia precisely because of its scientific nature—particularly in its claim to scientific foundations. Every utopia is essentially utopian precisely because it views human life as a strictly external phenomenon—a matter of production, consumption, and distribution—and holds that it can be ordered through science and the application of scientific methods: schemes, relations, balances, pressures, resistances, factors, averages, institutions, laws, prisons, and measurements, believing that human life is entirely resolved through these means.[125]

Materialist conclusions, when applied to society, lead towards socialism or communism. However, these same conclusions, consistently applied in the life of an individual, result in what we commonly refer to as epicureanism. An Epicurean is, therefore, a practical materialist. Because man is only conditionally and theoretically a part of society, whereas in real life he remains an independent individual, a separate entity naturally more inclined towards personal rather than social existence, Epicureanism emerges as the practical, and socialism as the theoretical, outcome of materialist philosophy. 'If I only have one life, then it belongs solely to me'—this stance is more logical than any kind of self-sacrifice for present or future generations. Within society, man constantly strives to live, think, and behave as an independent individual. Moreover, he exhibits a continual tendency to breach societal norms and laws. Any system that neglects the individuality of man and insists on perceiving him solely as a member of society, by force and regardless of these opposing facts, is inevitably built on a flawed assumption.

---

then there is no longer any sense in speaking of the fulfilment of moral duty; then the phenomenon of morality does not exist at all.' (Yevgeny Pashukanis, *Allgemeine Rechtslehre und Marxismus*, (1929) p. 141)

125 The ultimate slogan of both socialism and communism is framed in terms of production and consumption: 'Produce according to ability, consume according to work (according to needs).' Or the well-known Leninist formula: Communism = Marx + electrification.

It is futile to hold up examples such as bees or ants to man. If a bee could think, it would not submit itself unquestioningly to instinct; rather, it would attempt to avoid work, consuming instead the honey produced by others. A termite does not willingly sacrifice itself for the survival of its colony; if given a choice, it would almost certainly opt for life over death. With humans, it frequently happens that a person verbally supports and promotes common interests (yet acts otherwise). Indeed, many practical problems faced by socialist systems revolve precisely around this contradiction—the widely recognised issue of responsibility or, rather, irresponsibility within such systems. Animal collectives, as we understand them, cannot experience this distortion because animals, at crucial moments, have no choice to act selfishly, ignoring collective interests. Humans, however, do possess such choice, and this fact cannot be overlooked.

Therefore, societies face a critical decision: either to design a social system compatible with beings capable of choice or to destroy that ability through coercion and conditioning. Humanity is currently moving along one of these two paths. Socialist thinkers have always recognised that individual psychology—the inherent human desire for individuality and freedom—is the greatest obstacle to realising their vision of collective, social paradise. Thus, they consistently discuss society, production, distribution, masses, and classes, consciously avoiding the problem of the human being as a personality. They contrast 'rights of nations' with individual human rights, emphasising social rights over personal rights. In realistic, human conditions, each commitment to a less favourable alternative, every surrender of personal interest for social benefit, involves an inner struggle of motives, thereby becoming a matter of morality.

Faced with this reality, materialists increasingly refer to 'conscience', defining it as social conscience—the individual's awareness of belonging to a collective, and realising their life fully as a member of that collective. Yet 'conscience' is merely another term for 'morality', which leads materialists to introduce a foreign element, entirely absent from the inventory of materialism. If man truly were, or even could become, solely a member of society, socialism would be achievable. However, such an image of man is one-sided and thus untrue. Conversely, because man is fundamentally an independent individual, a being capable of making choices, a moral entity capable of both right and wrong behaviour—in short, because he is human—socialism, in its consistent and pure form, remains impossible.

SERVANTS AND HERETICS

There is a certain kind of people who admire strong government, who prefer being under strict control, and who adore external order, the kind that prevails in the army, 'where it is clear who commands and who obeys.' The newly built parts of cities—uniform houses arranged in neat rows with identical façades—appeal more to their tastes. They enjoy the brass music, uniforms, spectacles, parades, and other illusions that 'embellish' life and make it easier. Above all, they appreciate that 'everything is according to the law'. These are people with a servant mentality. They genuinely love being servants; they value security, order, establishment, and enjoy being praised by their superiors. They delight in being 'in favour'. Such individuals are typically honourable, calm, loyal—in short, proper citizens. Servants relish authority, and those in power relish having servants; they complete one another as two parts of a single whole. If authority does not exist, servants will invent it.

On the other hand, there is another unfortunate, cursed, or damned kind of people who constantly rebel and always seek something new. They speak less about bread and more about freedom, less about order and peace and more about human personality. They refuse to acknowledge that the emperor pays their salaries, asserting instead that it is they who feed the emperor—'Authorities do not sustain us; we sustain authorities'. These eternal heretics generally neither love the government nor does the government love them. If religious, servants adore people, authorities, idols, and totems; freedom fighters and rebels celebrate only one God. For while slavery and submission accommodate idolatry, true faith aligns naturally with freedom.

SOCIETY AND COMMUNITY

One should distinguish between society—understood as an external aggregate of units bound together by interests—and a community, defined as a group of people internally connected through a sense of belonging. Society is based on material needs—on shared interests. Community, however, emerges from spiritual needs and collective aspirations. Humans are anonymous members within a society, linked or separated by interests. Within a community, humans are brothers, bound together by shared ideals, mutual trust, or simply by a profound sense of unity. Society exists because living within it makes acquiring goods or securing survival easier. A child cannot survive without the assistance of others, and adults cannot thrive without associating with others—this external necessity forms the origin of society and sociality. Therefore, the human tendency towards social life does not arise from one's true nature, but rather from necessity. As Hobbes asserts, one does not seek society for its own sake but for the benefits it provides.

Laws based on strength, subjugation, exploitation, or at best, a balance of interests, govern society. Only community recognises justice, mutual assistance, solidarity, and brotherhood. Many misunderstandings arise from confusing these two concepts.[126] When Jesus speaks of love among people, he is right.

126 As an illustration of the opposition, I am referring to here (society–community), I would like to draw the reader's attention to an interesting phenomenon in the United States, which is of recent origin and therefore not yet sufficiently known or studied. It concerns a strong wave of ethnicity and cultural pluralism that has swept through contemporary America.

When Hobbes speaks of the war of all against all, or Marx about eternal exploitation, they, too, are correct. However, Jesus has a community in mind, while Hobbes and Marx refer to society. Adam Smith identified sympathy and the drive for revenge as forces regulating interpersonal relationships, but sympathy and revenge belong to the domain of community rather than society. Through the creation of society, civilisation dismantles personal, direct relationships among individuals, replacing them with external, anonymous, and indirect relations. The former were embodied in familial and kinship ties, in shared rites of birth, marriage, and death, and in direct, mutual care—person to person. In place of these bonds, which most evidently make a man human, civilisation establishes institutions of care and delegates responsibility to appointed officials. Thus, contrasting with family or a spiritual community (e.g., Islamic *jamāʿah*), there arise production collectives and the state, along with its institutions, as expressions of the objective interests of its members.

The deepest impulse behind this wave, as Victor Turner explains, is the search for community and the need for spontaneous togetherness – *communitas. Communitas*, says Turner, is a spontaneous and self-generating community. It is an "anti-structure" and fundamentally opposes the social framework, 'just as hypothetical antimatter opposes matter.' 'Togetherness lies at the heart of religion, literature, drama, and the visual arts, and its traces, deeply imprinted, can be found in law, ethics, and even in economics.' (Turner) And Dillon Ripley, Secretary of the Smithsonian Institution, explains: 'There is no effective antidote to the standardisation of mass culture, but festivals of folk life help preserve the fabric of cultural pluralism and radiant diversity. They reveal and revitalise communities that are a powerful bulwark protecting individuals from the world of the mega-state and mega-corporations.' It seems that society had to develop to the level reached in America for people to begin to understand some essential differences between society and community – especially that the development of society does not lead to community but rather distances itself from it. This mass movement towards the exploration of roots (Halley, *Roots*) and the revival of tradition, which arose entirely spontaneously in the 1960s in America, received a strong boost when its protagonists succeeded in pushing for the adoption of a special law to promote ethnicity (Ethnic Encouragement Act).

The so-called 'collective spirit' is often mentioned, but no such phenomenon truly exists. Civilisation cannot impart to a collective something it inherently lacks. In fact, a collective is merely the sum of its individual members, who typically do not know one another and remain strangers to each other. They are connected solely through external factors—such as the manufacturing process, the factory building, or the agricultural land they work upon. Within such a collective, there is no genuine sense of 'me' or 'you', only 'them'. This reality may explain the paradox of people feeling lonely in large, densely populated cities. Human closeness is fundamentally a spiritual rather than a spatial category, as exemplified starkly by modern skyscrapers. Within a skyscraper, residents feel as isolated as if they were in a desert, despite living beneath the same roof.

Collectives exist, but genuine communities—*communitas* do not. Religious ceremonies, in which people pray or dance together, have historically brought people closer; by contrast, political or production gatherings—so-called 'collective meetings'—often have the opposite effect, distancing participants from one another. According to court records from a large city (Belgrade, 1972), one-third of criminal trials for insult and defamation originated precisely from such meetings. True community among people can only be based on sympathy, love, compassion, and selflessness—feelings inherently tied to religion. Strictly speaking, justice is not essential for society's survival, yet it is a necessary condition for maintaining a community; indeed, it is fundamental to the very existence of a community. It is conceivable that a strong and organised society could be built entirely upon inequality and injustice, as Plato envisioned in *The Republic*. The independence of society from moral ideas is evident in the fact that all societies, by their very nature, behave immorally, because a society is a structural entity governed primarily not by moral but by physical conditions of stability.

This law is absolute, provided man is merely an animal—even the most advanced one.

However, the more a man transcends animal existence and fully embodies human characteristics, the less this law applies. Ultimately, society and its rules vanish to the extent that individuals become true personalities; precisely at this point of humanisation, community emerges and begins to exist. Nevertheless, the law described here reflects only a theoretical perspective. Pure society and pure community exist exclusively as principles. In real life, every society—because it consists of human beings—gradually acquires the characteristics of a community, proportionate to the extent that its members are authentically human. Instead of remaining merely a society or utopia, it begins to exhibit human dimensions, partially evolving into a community. The opposite is equally true. Early Christian communities offer perhaps the best example of spiritual communities, yet even they organised shared meals, known as *agape*, which gave them a certain social dimension. Such facts led some to interpret original Christianity as a social movement and Christian equality as a form of communism. This interpretation, however, is mistaken, reflecting a fundamental misunderstanding of the true essence of these phenomena.

PERSONALITY AND "MEMBER OF SOCIETY"

The tragedy of Christianity as a historical phenomenon is manifested in two facts: the Inquisition and the emergence of the first European utopia, which has Christian origins.[127] Campanella's *The City of the Sun* represents a typical anti-Christian vision because it advocates for an earthly kingdom rather than a heavenly one, and consequently, it addresses society rather than the individual. *The City of the Sun* marks a renunciation of Christianity's essential goals, initiating an era dominated by economic and social theories in Europe and across the world. The objective of religion is not to bring order to the external world; it represents aspiration and obligation, rather than comfort or a path toward a better, cosier life. Christ was not a social reformer, nor are the French Revolution and scientific progress pathways towards achieving the Christian ideals of peace and love, as Ernest Renan naïvely believed and wrote. Jesus was preoccupied with the destiny of the human soul and its salvation, while utopia is merely a naïve human dream of an ideal society characterised by eternal harmony and peace. Religion, as the history of human martyrdom, shares nothing with utopia and its illusory 'success'. One is the Kingdom of Heaven, the other the Kingdom of the Sun—*Civitas Dei* and *Civitas Solis*. These two kingdoms do not belong to the same order of things. Drama is unfamiliar with the concept of 'social security', just as utopia

127 Friar Tommaso Campanella, *Civitas solis (The City of the Sun).*

is oblivious to human dignity. That is why Marx speaks of the exploited, whereas Dostoevsky speaks of the humiliated and insulted. 'Social utopia sought human happiness and natural law—human dignity. Social utopia envisioned relationships in which people would cease to be abused and oppressed, while natural law constructed relationships where there are no longer humiliated and insulted.'[128]

When Campanella was writing his vision of an ideal society, he was undoubtedly inspired by the Christian principle of love for one's neighbour. However, in his compassion, the poor monk failed to notice that in his vision there were no longer neighbours, neither close nor distant. The neighbour disappeared, lost amidst the relations of production, consumption, and division of labour. His neighbour neither loves nor hates, is neither good nor evil, has no soul; instead, he is merely an anonymous yet perfect unit, assigned his place in the schematic arrangement of *The City of the Sun*, performing his function unfailingly from birth until death. Viewed in this manner, utopia is the vision of an alien reality, just as drama is a story about the other side. Shakespeare or Dostoevsky may serve as an illustration of this other perspective, one that perceives the world as drama. The human soul, in all its terrifying enormity, emerges vividly before us when reading Dostoevsky's novels. The inner struggles and inner events are so immense that the entire external world, with all its wealth and poverty, states and courts, successes and failures, appears unreal and irrelevant by comparison.

The visions of the world seen from the perspective of drama and from that of utopia essentially have nothing in common. They occupy two entirely opposite ends, relating to each other as quality relates to quantity, man to society, and freedom to necessity. In utopia, you see the world clearly, yet the human being is merely an auxiliary point, enabling you to

128 Ernst Bloch, *Natural Law and Human Dignity*, (Belgrade, 1977), p. 7.

perceive the broader sketch or scheme. Conversely, in drama, man eclipses the whole world by his magnitude, reducing the external world to mere backdrop, apparition, almost an illusion.[129] *Utopia* is as truthful as the statement that man is simply an animal gifted with a brain. It is the product precisely of these two worldly facts: human needs and human intelligence, meaning man's aspiration as an intelligent being to satisfy his (always natural) needs. Since he has needs, man must strive to live in society; since he is intelligent, he seeks the best-organised society, one in which the 'war of all against all' is eliminated. Thus, an ideal society does not hold freedom and individuality as its principles, but rather order and uniformity.[130]

This clearly indicates a direct connection between utopia and evolutionist theories about human origins. The renowned naturalist Rudolf Virchow explicitly pointed out this fact—Darwin's theories, in a certain way, created the conditions for all subsequent socialist movements. To become suitable for various socialist experiments or to be a good citizen of any utopia, man must be 'tailored' according to Darwin. However, a true and real man is inherently too individualistic and irredeemably romantic to comfortably fit into the functioning of any utopia or to become an ideal member of society. Eliminating everything specifically human, especially individuality and freedom, has proven to be an essential precondition for utopia. Therefore, utopia is a religion for atheists, not for believers. Yet this religion is an illusion if man is indeed a personality and not merely a 'perfect animal'. It could be said that the alternative to the so-called ideal society became impossible from the primordial moment of Creation—the moment of 'humanisation of the human'. Since that moment, humanity

129 All religions retained the kind of astronomy that recognised the Earth (and man) as the centre of the world. Hence the Church's bitter resistance to Copernicus.

130 Let us recall that Epicurus' social ideal was not freedom but security.

faces eternal dissatisfaction, restlessness, conflict, and drama. ('Go away as enemies to each other forever', Qur'an, 2:36).

An ideal society consists of a uniform and endless procession of depersonalised generations who are born, produce, consume, and die in monotonous repetition, stretching on indefinitely into a 'rusty' infinity. The fact of Creation—the involvement of God in human existence—rendered this mechanical existence impossible, exposing it as an illusion. This realisation is the root of the fanatical resistance of all utopias against God and religion. While prophets of the ideal societal organisation declared society and all its interests as the supreme law, God ordained that the supreme law would instead be the human being. He granted freedom so that the world would serve as a trial, affirming man and his soul as the highest values. Thus, believing in the possibility of utopia equates to cultivating a naïve optimism based on the negation of the human soul. Only someone who does not believe in the human soul and personality can believe it is possible to 'appease' and 'tame' a human being, transforming him into a compliant member of society, accepting his role as part of a mechanism.[131] Conversely, believing in the human soul means practically believing in an indomitable sea of insubordination, doubt, fear, and rebellion. It means believing that the human being is an incorrigible individualist who will refuse to be standardised, subdued, or 'appeased', and that even if he is provided comfort and abundance, one day he will reject it all with contempt and seek to reclaim his freedom, his human right—because 'man is an animal that refuses to be so.' Herein lies the direct connection between atheism and all ideas about the ideal organisation of human society. Atheism is the necessary precondition for believing that such a society, in its fully consistent form, is even possible.

131 Otherwise, it will prove true in practice that societies which have not undergone the schooling of monotheism are more suited to utopia. In such societies, it is easier to impose standards of submission, uniformity, manipulation, leader cult, and conditioning — without which a human utopia is impossible.

UTOPIA AND FAMILY

The family is not the basic cell of society, as some older constitutions claim.[132] The family and society are disparate, mutually opposed concepts. Sympathy or feeling is the binding principle in a family, whereas interest or intellect—or both together—form the basis of society. Any advancement of society involves, to the same extent, a withdrawal from family. If the societal principle is carried to its ultimate consequence, achieving a state of utopia, the concept of family itself disappears entirely. The family, as the centre of intimate and romantic interpersonal relationships, stands in fundamental opposition to all assumptions underlying utopia. Engels recognised this fact in his own way and with different intentions in mind:

> The development of the family throughout history is about the constant narrowing of the circle that once primarily encompassed the entire tribe—a circle dominated by marital unions between the two sexes. By continuously excluding firstly closer and then increasingly distant cousins, and eventually relatives by marriage as well, every form of group marriage becomes practically impossible; in the end, only a couple of loosely connected molecules remain, and when they dissolve, marriage completely ends.[133]

---

132 In the new *Constitution of the USSR* (1977), it is now the 'labour collective'.

133 F. Engels, *The Origin of the Family, Private Property and the State* (New York, 1942) p. 41.

As with everything else in utopia, childbirth is devoid of all sentimentality, becoming merely a kind of function or mode of production. In Plato's *Republic*, we read:

> Women between twenty and forty should be confined to special rooms with men between twenty-five and fifty-five, and the children born from these relations should be raised in state institutions without knowing their mother or father. Intercourse is allowed for women under twenty and men over fifty-five, but the fruits of these unions should be removed, or the newborns placed in a special location where they will die of hunger. Family life and love are out of the question.[134]

Engels expresses this idea even more clearly:

> According to materialist understandings, the decisive factor in the final instance of history is the production and reproduction of immediate life. Yet production itself has two sides: on the one hand, there is the production of means of living—food, clothing, habitation, and the tools required; on the other hand, there is the production of human beings themselves, the continuation of the species.'[135]

He continues:

> It will be shown that the first condition for the liberation of women is the introduction of the entire female population into public working life, and this requires the abolition of

---

134 Utopias reject love because it is a personal rather than a 'social' relationship between people. Among the goals of the Chinese Cultural Revolution—the most far-reaching practical attempt to realise a utopia to date—was the education of young people in the rejection of love as a 'bourgeois tendency'. Love could exist only as love for the homeland, socialism, and Chairman Mao, while in its natural sense it was seen as a 'poisonous weed' of the old society that had to be eradicated. Even in literature, love between a man and a woman was long a taboo subject, and books dealing with it disappeared not only from bookshops but also from libraries. However, after the death of Mao Zedong, when Tolstoy's *Anna Karenina* appeared for sale, queues of buyers reportedly stretched at times to over 100 metres.

135 F. Engels, *ibid.*, Preface to the 1884 edition.

> the nuclear family as the socioeconomic unit. By transferring means of production into communal ownership, the nuclear family ceases to exist as an economic unit of society. The private household stops being the economic unit and transforms into a social industry. Childcare and upbringing become public work; society cares equally for all children, whether they are born within or outside marriage.[136]

According to Marx, the disappearance ('dying out') of the family represents the socialisation of humans, their transformation into 'completely social beings'. All the basics of human existence—social, material, and moral—transfer from the family to society. French author Simone de Beauvoir, a distinguished activist of the feminist movement in France and worldwide, is categorical: 'As long as the myth of family, of motherhood and mother's instinct is not destroyed, women will continue to be oppressed.'[137]

Civilisation does not remove the family only in principle but practically as well. 'First, the man exits the family, then the wife, and finally the kids.' The destruction of the family takes many forms: the decreasing number of marriages concluded, increasing divorce rates, a steadily rising number of employed women, an increase in children born out of wedlock, and the growing number of single-person households.[138] To these should be added a large number of widow households consisting of relatively young people, resulting from frequent car accidents and the increasing prevalence of coronary and malignant diseases, which are also closely tied to some civilisational aspects. In California in 1960, there was one divorce

136 F. Engels, *ibid.*, p. 67.

137 In an interview to a New York based magazine Saturday Review, September 1975.

138 By the number of marriages concluded (around five marriages per 1,000 inhabitants), Switzerland and Sweden are at the bottom of the global ranking.

per marriage concluded. Other centres of the highly civilised world are rapidly approaching this 'Californian ratio'. The ratio of divorces to marriages concluded is experiencing a constant and sharp increase. In the USA, there were 26 divorces per 100 marriages in 1960; by 1975, this number had increased to 48. In the USSR, the percentage of divorces relative to the total number of marriages concluded was just over 10 per cent in 1960, climbing to 27 per cent by 1973. The number of divorces in Switzerland doubled in the past ten years[139], quadrupled in Poland over the past twenty years, and tripled in three decades (1945–1975) in Czechoslovakia. Today, every third marriage in Prague ends in divorce. In a survey conducted among French high school girls, the desire for independence and a pleasant life took first place, while family was placed last (taken from the report of B. Jazzo at the International Congress in Bonn, 1960). The Institute for Sociological Research in Stockholm published the results of a survey (1972) indicating that women engaged in prostitution are usually well-to-do and participate only out of a desire for the 'sweet life'.

According to data from the Economic and Social Council of the UN (ECOSOC), women's entry into active economic life over the past twenty-five years has occurred twice as rapidly as predicted. Today (1975), women constitute 35 per cent of the global workforce. Relatively, the highest number of employed women is in the USSR (82 out of every 100 women able to work), followed by East Germany (80 per cent), Bulgaria (74 per cent), Hungary (73 per cent), Romania (73 per cent), and Poland (63 per cent). France, Sweden, Czechoslovakia, Denmark, and Japan follow these countries. In the group consisting of England, Switzerland, Austria, the USA, and West Germany, approximately half of the total number of

139 With 14.1 divorces per 10,000 inhabitants, Switzerland ranks near the top of the European divorce list (according to data from the Government Statistical Office for 1976).

women are working (49–52 per cent). The primacy of socialist countries, which are not even the most developed among those mentioned, clearly points to the influence of ideological factors. This relates to the ideological stance towards family and women's employment. Another similar fact cannot be explained by technological progress alone: the USSR and the USA have the same (and highest) percentage of children born out of wedlock (10 per cent). The USSR has 'caught up' with the most developed country in the world in this respect, as the general civilisational trend in this regard was reinforced by the negative ideological attitude towards marriage and family. The phenomenon of separated families in China, Korea, and now Cambodia also has the same underlying causes. Millions of Chinese families live separately: fathers on one side of the country, mothers and children on the other, seeing each other only once a year. The stated reasoning for this arrangement is the needs of the state economy—so-called common interest. The family does not represent this interest. On the contrary!

According to one survey, the number of runaway children in America doubled over the past five years, reaching two million in 1976. In this situation, it is the elderly who fare the worst. In truth, the world belongs both to the young and the old, yet civilisation—devoid of moral and religious scruples and governed solely by rational motives—increasingly shapes itself to the tastes and standards of the young. 'The hedonistic era grants the most space to the most active members of society, and those are the young and vigorous,' observed a Yugoslav psychiatrist. Indeed, a worldview that places sex at the top of its value system is bound to heap praise upon youth and ridicule old age. It inevitably deems reverence for elders one of our greatest prejudices. Religion (and culture) has taught the exact opposite across all civilisations.

If the human spirit does not exist, then the old man is the most redundant being in the world. Neither religion nor civilisation can hold a different view—it is, ultimately, a matter of scale of values.

All religions advocate for the family, elevating it as the human nest and the mother as the first and irreplaceable educator. Conversely, all utopias excitedly speak of social upbringing—kindergartens, nurseries, dormitories. Regardless of their names, these institutions share one common feature: the absence of the mother and the handing over of children to paid labour. Plato was the first to present a utopia (*The Republic*), and also the first to systematically articulate the idea of social upbringing. Naturally, this idea culminates in the socialist writings of the nineteenth and twentieth centuries. This phenomenon is entirely logical. If man is indeed a 'social animal' (which he is, in one part of his being), then dressage, social upbringing, kindergarten, and the so-called ideal society are the right solutions, while parental love, family, artistic and religious upbringing, individuality, and freedom are mere superfluous romanticism with no basis in any truth about humanity.

In an ideal society, everyone performs their function perfectly and flawlessly, which means they function impeccably. The mother and family can only spoil this perfect order and disrupt this 'idyll', based on complete levelling and homogeneity. The mother gives birth to and raises a human being, whereas the kindergarten raises a member of society, a future citizen of utopia. A kindergarten is a factory, an upbringing machine. Soviet academician and long-time Soviet government official Stanislav Gustavovič Strumilin (1887–1974) wrote the following in the 1960s:

> By giving social forms of upbringing absolute advantage over everything else, we will very soon have to keep expanding these forms at a pace that will make them available to all citizens from the cradle to the maturity exam within the next fifteen to twenty years.

The erudite academician then elaborates a terrifying vision, not without pride:

> Every Soviet citizen, upon leaving the maternity hospital, will be forwarded to a nursery, then to a kindergarten with all-day stay or dormitory, then a boarding school, and from there, with permission, to independent life—production or further education.

Neither mother nor family appear anywhere in this plan, nor can they, since they simply do not exist within it. We are faced with a technological process instead of raising and nurturing a human being, as if it were a matter of producing chickens. The peak of this 'civilisational' attitude towards the family is perhaps reflected in that famous sentence by Marx (in *Capital*): 'It is from their own parents that children—regardless of sex—often need the greatest protection.'

There are many signs that the USSR is revising this attitude towards family because it is lifeless, but this is a deviation. From a principled standpoint, the essence of the question is not whether Engels' (or Strumilin's) anathematising of the family is right or wrong, but above all, whether Engels could have held a different attitude towards the family. Engels discovered the final conclusions of a consistent civilisation (or utopia, which amounts to the same thing), and civilisation will never be fully realised until man as a personality is destroyed, as that type of man cannot fit into its mechanisms, structures, institutions, collectives, so-called common interests, state justice, discipline, etc. There will always be a secret or open war between man and this 'programmed brutality' (A. Voznesenski).

We take a stance on marriage, family, upbringing, parents, and elders based on what we see in man and our philosophy about man. At one extreme, there is marriage as a contract (the 'new Swedish marriage'), and at the other, marriage as a sacrament, a holy mystery ('Catholic marriage'). Leaving aside the question of which of these two concepts is the correct one, we insist that rationalist philosophy had to see marriage as a contract, whereas Christian philosophy had to see it as a sacrament. Therefore, Engels was not mistaken when he announced the dying out of the family; rather, those Soviet sociologists (e.g. Dr Urlanis) who want to re-establish the 'good old family' are mistaken, at least from the standpoint of official philosophy. Because if man is merely a perfected animal, then the ideological prescription of academician Strumilin is the only correct solution. We do not know what the inner value of human individuals produced by such an industry might be, but it is certain today that quantity is in continuous decline and has reached troubling levels. A woman will not give birth to a child only to lose it immediately thereafter.

There is evident stagnation or decline in birthrates in all civilised countries, partly due to the position of the mother and partly due to the desire for an easy life without obligations (which is itself a direct result of the destruction of religious and cultural values). Pierre Chaunu, a professor at the Sorbonne, claims that the white race is under threat of extinction. According to him, the German nation might practically disappear in the next century as a consequence of declining birthrates. Demographic calculations show that the population of France will decrease from the current 52 million to 17 million citizens. These predictions might seem exaggerated, but the data do point to such or similar conclusions. A series of European countries has recorded a negative rate of demographic growth for years in a row. The population of West Germany decreased in 1976 by 0.33 per cent compared to 1975 (over 200,000 people), and in 1975 by 0.56 per cent compared to 1974. This decrease was 1.7 per cent in West Berlin (data from the Federal Statistics Institute in Wiesbaden).

The Swedish parliament was forced to place the issue of a sudden increase in mentally ill people onto its agenda. This is occurring in a country that has the lowest childhood mortality, the longest average lifespan, where education is free at all levels, where peace has lasted for more than 150 years, which has no issues of overpopulation, the highest labour productivity rates in the world, and one of the highest per capita incomes. Doctor Hans Loman, a famous psychiatrist entrusted by the Swedish parliament to examine the causes of this issue, has so far limited his observations to noting that most married women in Sweden are working and that this fact seriously disrupts such a vital area of life as the family. Over 50 per cent of mothers with children up to age three are employed in Sweden, and over 70 per cent of mothers with children up to 17 years old. 'We have managed to construct for our children an extremely cold, anti-childish society', states one of Loman's reports.

A statistical yearbook for 1976 in Sweden records that almost every child in Sweden is an only child in the family (Czechoslovakia is experiencing a similar situation). Married couples in this country consider families with three or more children 'a luxury' and 'irrational'. Given this state of affairs, demographic experts predict that Sweden will not be able to ensure even the 'simple reproduction' of its population as early as 1990.

Civilisation has turned women into objects for admiration or usage, but it has deprived women of their personality, which alone can carry value and respect. We encounter this situation increasingly, but it is most obvious in various 'miss' competitions and specifically female jobs such as runway and photo models. A woman here is no longer a personality; she is scarcely human, at best only slightly more than a 'beautiful animal'. Civilisation has particularly debased motherhood. Without a moment's hesitation, it placed the calling of a saleswoman, a model, an educator of others' children, a secretary, a cleaning lady, or a cloakroom attendant above that of a mother. Civilisation declared motherhood to be slavery and promised women salvation from it. It boasts about the number of women it has separated (in its own terms—liberated) from family and children and transformed into employees. Conversely, all culture, from time immemorial until today, has been characterised by the celebration of mothers. It transformed the mother into a symbol, a mystery, a sanctity. Culture has devoted its most beautiful verses, most touching melodies, loveliest paintings, and sculptures to the mother. While an agony for mothers is unfolding in the world of civilisation, Picasso paints his marvellous painting *Motherhood*, and with this beautiful hymn to the mother, he announces that Mother is still alive for culture.

Nursing homes go hand in hand with kindergartens. They belong to the same order of things and are essentially two phases of the same solution. Kindergartens and nursing homes evoke artificial birth and death. The presence of comfort but the absence of love and warmth is characteristic of both. Both stand in opposition to the family and represent the result of the changed role of women in human life. Their mutual prerequisite is the gradual elimination of parental relationships: children are without parents in kindergarten; parents are without children in nursing homes. Both are 'wonderful' creations of civilisation and an ideal of every utopia. A family with a mother belongs to the religious view of things, just as a kindergarten with its workers belongs to the opposite one.

PART TWO

ISLAM - BIPOLAR UNITY

CHAPTER 7

MOSES - JESUS - MUHAMMAD (PEACE BE UPON THEM)

HERE AND NOW

There are two histories of Islam: one before and one after Muhammad (pbuh) . The history of Islam after Muhammad (pbuh) (in the narrow sense) cannot be fully understood without the prehistory of Islam, especially its final part, which includes the period of Judaism and Christianity.

The role of these three religions of revelation is immense. Through them, humanity became the centre of history and learned how to observe the world—that is, humanity—as a whole. Under their guidance, humanity recognised the magnitude of external and internal life, external and internal progress, their mutual relationship, and their boundaries. The historical successes and defeats of Judaism and Christianity represent decisive Islamic experiences of humankind. Moses, Jesus, and Muhammad (pbuh) embody three primordial aspirations that ultimately constitute the very human essence.

Judaism represents the worldly, 'left tendency' among religions. All later theories of the Jewish spirit that preach a vision of earthly paradise originate from this tendency. The Book of Job is a dream of justice that should be realised already here on earth—not in eternity, but here and now.

The teaching of immortality was never completely accepted by Jews. The Sadducees[1] still rejected it in the time of Christ.

---

1 A Jewish politico-religious party from the final period of Jewish national independence (2nd and 1st centuries BCE), which relied exclusively on the Mosaic Law, formed the core of the priestly aristocracy.

Maimonides, the greatest Jewish thinker of the Middle Ages, claims that immortality is faceless (which is scarcely less than negating the very idea of immortality). Another great Jew, Baruch Spinoza, goes further, claiming that the Old Testament does not say anything about immortality. Renan, and later Berdyaev, rightly noticed that Jews could not accept the idea of immortality because it is inherently incompatible with their vision of the world, which is always an image of this side. Hasdaj Kreskas teaches that matter is the body of God. 'The Jewish people were unfamiliar with the idea of individual freedom and individual guilt,' Berdyaev writes.

In Spinoza's case, we can easily trace the birth of materialist philosophy within Judaism or from the sources of Jewish tradition—a tradition in which the religious essence remains very thin and shallow compared to the national, political, and worldly content—a situation completely opposite to Christianity. Spinoza establishes an indomitable necessity in the world. The term 'God' can be replaced by 'nature' everywhere in his theological writings, and he himself explicitly gives directions about this. He brings these two concepts closer to each other by removing everything personal, individual, voluntary, and even conscious from the concept of God. Despite excommunication, Spinoza is an authentic Jew.[2]

The kingdom of God announced by the Jews before Christ appeared was expected to occur on Earth, not in heaven, as Christians anticipated. The Messiah—a revenger and executor of justice—is celebrated in apocalyptic Jewish literature. Jews did not expect a prophet who suffers and dies in the Messiah, but rather a national hero and earthly king who would establish the rule of the chosen people. The world in which righteous people are unhappy is pointless. This is the basic stance of Jewish justice and every 'social' justice. The

2 The Amsterdam magistrate banishes Spinoza on the charge that his teachings are contrary to Christianity. This anathema is understandable.

idea of paradise here on Earth is essentially a Jewish idea—not only by its nature but by its origins as well. 'The Jewish mould for history, past and future, consists in a powerful call to the oppressed and less fortunate of all times; St Augustine is the one who adapted this mould to Christianity and Marx to socialism' (B. Russell, *History of Western Philosophy*). All revolutions, utopias, socialisms, and other ideas that advocate a 'heaven on Earth' essentially originate from the Old Testament and Judaism.

The Freemason idea of the ethical rebirth of humanity on a scientific basis is positivist and Jewish on a scientific basis. It would be interesting to examine inner and outer connections between positivism, Freemasonry, and Judaism. One would find not only spiritual but very concrete connections and influences.

The history of Judaism is the history of global economic (commercial) progress. Werner Sombart devoted a significant book to this.[3] Atomic science was called 'Jewish science' in its beginnings. We might call political economy by the same name and be equally correct. In any case, the fact that the biggest names in atomic physics, political economy, and socialist ideas were predominantly Jews is by no means accidental. Jews might not always participate in culture, but they always participate in civilisation. Their appearance can be traced as emigrating from a dying civilisation to an emerging one. This is a phenomenon that keeps repeating itself in the history of the West.

'Throughout the whole Middle Ages, Jews had practically no influence on the culture of Christian countries,' states Russell.[4] But at the point in a culture when the city finally overtakes the village, Jews appear. They can only live and think

3 W. Sombart, *The Jews and Economic Life* (Les Juifs dans la vie economique).

4 B. Russell, *A History of Western Philosophy*, Belgrade, p. 320.

within the concept of cities. Every city of importance was familiar with Jewish colonies: Tyre, Sidon, Antioch, Jerusalem, Alexandria, Carthage, and Rome in ancient times; Córdoba, Granada, Toledo, and Seville in Muslim Spain; Amsterdam, Venice, and Marseille at the beginning of the new era; and today, all large world centres, especially American ones—that is the history of Judaism. There is something symbolic in the fact that Jews were precisely the ones who financed Columbus's voyage, even taking direct participation in the discovery of a world that started developing civilisation from its very beginning. (There is a well-substantiated claim that Columbus himself was a Jew.) Likewise, the forefather of the latest 'atomic age' is also a Jew—Einstein. Jews have been the carriers of external progress, just as Christians were carriers of internal progress.

PURE RELIGION

Jewish materialism (or positivism) turned human awareness toward the world and stimulated interest in external reality throughout history. Christianity turned the human spirit inward, toward itself. The overstated realism of the Old Testament could only be overcome by the equally overstated idealism of the New Testament. The merging of these two demands into one would be achieved by Islam and Muhammad (pbuh), but this would happen sometime later.

According to Christianity, human aspirations and energies should not be split between two opposing directions: toward heaven and earth.

> No man can serve two masters: for either he will hate the one and love the other; or else he will hold to the one, and despise the other. Ye cannot serve God and mammon (money).
>
> (Gospel of Matthew, 6:24)

Tolstoy expands on this thought:

> One cannot at the same time take care of one's soul and of worldly goods. If you desire worldly goods, give up on your soul; if you want to save your soul, give up worldly goods. Otherwise, you will only be torn apart and will not have either one.

And further:

> People want to reach freedom by securing themselves and their bodies from everything that might trap the body and prevent it from doing whatever it pleases. The things people do to secure their bodies—wealth, high position, good reputation—do not give the desired freedom; on the contrary, they trap them even more. To gain more freedom, people build a dungeon out of their sins, offences, and superstitions and close themselves into it.

All the great Church authorities have noted and emphasised a significant difference between the spirit of the Old and the New Testaments. According to some authors, the Gospel of Marcion—which served as a model for Mark—presented Jesus as having abolished the Law of Moses, contrasting the God of love, creator of the invisible world, with Jehovah, the God of justice and saviour of the visible world. According to Couchoud, this Gospel expressed the principles of asceticism, non-violence, and non-resistance to evil even more clearly than the canonical texts. Thus, religion renounces in advance the idea of organising or perfecting the external world. Religion naturally views any human belief that outward transformation can lead to true goodness as an offence—an act of self-deceit. For, religion answers the question: 'How do I live within myself and before myself?'—not 'How do I live in the world and before others?' Religion is a temple on the mountaintop, a refuge to which one ascends to leave behind the vanities of an incorrigible world ruled by Lucifer. That is pure religion.

> Therefore I say unto you, take no thought for your life, what ye shall eat, or what ye shall drink; nor yet for your body, what ye shall put on. (Matthew 6:25, King John Version (KJV))
>
> And if thy right eye offend thee, pluck it out, and cast it from thee....
>
> And if thy right hand offend thee, cut it off, and cast it from thee.... (Matthew 5:29–30,KJV)

> For whosoever will save his life shall lose it: and whosoever will lose his life for my sake shall find it. (Matthew 16:25, KJV)
>
> But I say unto you, that whosoever looketh on a woman to lust after her hath committed adultery with her already in his heart. (Matthew 5:28, KJV)
>
> *(all quotes from the Gospel)*
>
> For it is written: 'I will destroy the wisdom of the wise and bring to nothing the understanding of the prudent.' Where is the wise? Where is the scribe? Where is the disputer of this age? Has not God made foolish the wisdom of this world? (Corinthians, 1:19–20, KJV)
>
> 'And the people asked him, saying, What shall we do then? He answereth and saith unto them, He that hath two coats, let him impart to him that hath none; and he that hath meat, let him do likewise.' (Luke, 3:10–11, KJV)

The similarity to certain socialist principles is entirely illusory, for this is not about society and its structures, but about man and his soul. Religion calls for giving; revolution calls for taking. While the external outcomes may occasionally appear similar, the internal consequences are profoundly different. Yet this path is arduous, and it is meant only for the devoted. When Allah says in the Qur'an, 'Allah does not require of any soul more than what it can afford' (Qur'an 2:286), He clearly had Christianity in mind.

All pure religions, therefore, recognised two paths, two programmes. In Buddhism, there is Mahayana—the 'great path', strict and demanding, for the spiritual elite—and Hinayana—the 'lesser path', more accessible and lenient, for the common folk. These are moral, not social distinctions, for the issue is one of obligation, not privilege. A similar moral division is found in Christianity: the clergy and monastic orders, for example, take vows of celibacy, while marriage is permitted to the laity. Celibacy is seen as the ideal; marriage, evidently, a concession. This intense inner discipline is marked by extraordinary renunciation—entirely personal and deliberately disengaged from any form of social activism.

As they are fundamentally opposed to the use of force, Christianity and religion in general have proven incapable of effecting direct change to the social condition of humanity. Hence the accusation—objectively valid though morally unfair—that religion serves to preserve the social status quo, a state of affairs which, despite all psychological resistance, ultimately favours the rulers.

Christianity is not a practice in the conventional sense, and it should not be judged as one. It is a 'gospel' (as the Qur'an names it—and 'gospel' means Good News), a proclamation of the deepest truths of human life. 'Love your neighbour as yourself', 'Love your enemy and do good to the one who hates you', 'Do not resist evil'—these mottos are so radically opposed to the practical logic of human existence that they compel us to search for a different meaning, one that reveals their true essence. They genuinely speak of another world. ('My kingdom is not of this world', said Jesus.)

The revelation of the Gospel's crystal-clear and uncompromising attitudes marked a turning point in history. With them, humanity attained full awareness of the intrinsic value of the human being for the first time, and in doing so, achieved not primarily a historical, but a qualitative leap. The appearance of Jesus Christ thus stands as a cornerstone in world history ('a sign for all people', Qur'an, 21:91), and the visions and hopes he unveiled have become embedded in all subsequent human striving.

The entirety of Western civilisation—despite all its deviations, delusions, and dilemmas—bears the imprint of Christ's teaching. In the fundamental and primordial conflict—between society and man, bread and freedom, civilisation and culture—the West has ultimately remained on the side of the latter, essentially rooted in its Christian heritage.

ACCEPTING AND REJECTING CHRIST

But religion can only influence the world when it becomes 'worldly'—that is, secular, of this world—when it becomes politics in the broadest sense of the word. Islam is secularised Christianity, turned toward the world. This is the key to both the similarities and the differences between Islam and Christianity.

Islam contains a distinctly Jewish element, but just as many elements that are thoroughly non Jewish. In his classification of religions, Hegel viewed Muhammad's (pbuh) Islam as a direct continuation of Judaism—a position likely shaped by his Christian perspective. Similarly, Spengler referred to the Book of Job as an Islamic book. Mircea Eliade, in his *History of Beliefs and Religious Ideas*, places Muhammad (pbuh) at the border between the second and third (final) stages of the spiritual development of humanity. The third period, still ongoing today, begins with Muhammad (pbuh). According to Eliade, the history of the human spirit is one of gradual laicisation and secularisation. In this framework, Muhammad (pbuh) stands at the threshold between the triumph of religion (Christianity) and the dawn of the secular age. He represents a historical balance point.

Even if Eliade's vision is somewhat one-dimensional—an issue this book cannot accept—it is nonetheless telling that various approaches, regardless of their perspective, tend to position Islam and Muhammad (pbuh) as occupying a 'middle ground'. This impression recurs, regardless of various approaches and explanations across different lines of analysis. Jesus avoided Jerusalem because, like all cities, it was a city of Pharisees, scribes, scholars, infidels—or believers in appearance only. Socialism, speaks not to the villagers but to the citizens of great cities. Muhammad (pbuh) retreated to the cave of Hira, but he returned to the godless city of Mecca to begin his mission. Yet what emerged in Mecca was not yet Islam. Islam truly began in Medina.

In the cave of Hira, Muhammad (pbuh) was a hermit, an ascetic, a mystic—a hanif. In Mecca, he was the messenger of religious thought. In Medina, he became the messenger of Islamic thought. The message Muhammad (pbuh) carried reached its full realisation and awareness in Medina.[5] It was here—not in Mecca—that 'the embryo and source of the entire Islamic social and legal order' was formed.[6]

Muhammad (pbuh) had to return from the cave. Had he remained there, he would have remained a hanif. But by returning, he became the Prophet of Islam. This return marks the meeting of the inner and the outer worlds—of mysticism and reason, meditation and action. Islam began as mysticism and culminated in political and state thought. Religion embraced the world of facts and became Islam.

Man and his soul—that is the relationship between Muhammad (pbuh) and Jesus. 'There is likeness in nature between Holy Scripture and soul… They hide the same mystery in its essence… Soul and Holy Scripture, that symbolically represent each other, thus shed a light on each other…'[7] While Islam is, in a sense, a repetition of man. Like man, it contains a

5 'Today I have perfected your religion for you, completed My favour upon you, and have chosen for you Islam as your religion,' says the final revealed verse from the Medinan period (Qur'an, 5:4).

6 Stefano Bianco, *Polyvalence and Flexibility in the Structure of the Islamic City*, Werk, Switzerland, no. 9/1976.

7 Henry de Lubac, *Introduction à Origène.*

'divine spark', but it also speaks to shadows and the prose of daily life. There are elements in Islam that poets and romantics might find difficult to embrace. The Qur'an is a realistic, even anti-heroic book. Islam is incomprehensible—or, more precisely, non-existent—in its fullest sense without the human being who lives and applies it.

Plato's ideas, Leibniz's monads, and Christian angels all represent the same archetype: a timeless, perfect, absolute, and immovable kingdom of the world. Islam does not idealise such a realm. When the angels bowed to man— 'who was taught the names of all things' by God (Qur'an, 2:30–34)—the Qur'an affirmed the supremacy of life, humanity, and drama over a world of immovable, eternal perfection.

Christianity never reached a full awareness of one, indivisible God. Strictly speaking, Christianity preserves a vivid idea of divinity, but not a clear concept of God. The mission of Muhammad (pbuh) was to bring the Gospel's perception of God as a personality closer to human reason and clarity. In the Gospel, God is a father. In the Qur'an, God is Lord. In the Gospel, God is loved. In the Qur'an, He is primarily respected and feared. This feature of the Christian idea of God eventually devolved into a series of complex and contradictory concepts that compromise Christianity's original monotheism—such as the Trinity, the veneration of the Virgin Mary, and the saints. Such theological developments are not possible in Islam. Despite all historical crises, Islam has remained, in the words of Le Bon, the 'clearest monotheistic religion'. For the human soul recognises only divinity—and this divinity, through the aid of reason, becomes in human consciousness the one and only God: Allah.

Christianity proclaimed a God who reigns over the inner, individual world—of souls and conscience—while Lucifer holds dominion over the material realm (numerous Christian legends portray the near-omnipotence of Lucifer). This is why

Christian faith in God demands inner freedom, while Islamic faith in Allah entails a call for outer freedom as well. The two core dogmas of Islam— 'Allahu Akbar' (God is greatest) and famous Al-Aqida, 'ilaha ill Allah' (there is no deity but God)—are simultaneously its most revolutionary declarations.

Seyyid Qutb rightly notes that these affirmations represent 'a revolution against secular rule that appropriates the fundamental prerogatives of divinity', and that they signify 'removing all authority from clergy, tribal chiefs, princes, and rulers, and assigning it solely to God'. Hence, concludes Qutb, 'La ilaha ill Allah" is the call most hated by rulers in every age.[8]

For this same reason, Christianity could not accept the premise of a perfect man who remained only a man. Christians had to draw a conclusion about the God-man, about Jesus as the Son of God, from the very spirit of Jesus's teaching. Conversely, Muhammad (pbuh) had to remain only human—otherwise, he would become superfluous. While Muhammad (pbuh) appears manly and soldierly, Jesus leaves the impression of an angel. The same is true for women who—unlike Martha and Mary in the Gospel—appear exclusively in the Qur'an as wives and mothers, that is, in their natural function. Thus, the Christian attack on Muhammad's (pbuh) 'overly human nature' is, in fact, a misunderstanding. The Qur'an itself explicitly points out that Muhammad (pbuh) is just a man (Qur'an, 17:93; 18:111; 40:6, etc.), and it even paraphrases future attacks on him: 'And they say [mockingly], "What kind of messenger is this who eats food and goes about in market-places [for a living]?"' (Qur'an, 25:7).

Even the mere comparison of the language of the Gospel and the Qur'an yields insightful conclusions. Words such as:

---

8 The miraculous power of this call was recently put to the test during the Islamic Revolution in Iran, when an unarmed populace overthrew the heavily armed regime of Shah Reza Pahlavi. The most powerful weapon in this struggle was the slogan *Allahu Akbar* ('God is the Greatest').

blessed, holy, angel, eternal life, heaven, Pharisee, sin, love, neighbour, repentance, forgiveness, secret, body (as the carrier of sin), soul, cleansing, and salvation are frequent and central in the Gospel. These same expressions are found in the Qur'an as well, forming the foundation of one worldview—yet they serve as a backdrop for a different set of concepts that come to the foreground in sharp relief: reason, health, purity, strength, purchase, contract, collateral, letter, weapon, battle position, force, battle, trade, fruit, decisiveness, caution, punishment, justice, benefit, retaliation, hunt, cure, interest, and so on.

Islam is not familiar with a special 'church literature' in the European sense of the word, just as there is no purely secular literature in Islam either. Every Islamic thinker is a theologian,[9] just as every true Islamic movement is, by its very nature, a political movement. A comparison between mosque and church leads to similar insights. A mosque is a place for people, while a church is a 'temple of God'. The mosque embodies an ambience of rationality, while the church expresses a mystic one. A mosque is always found at the centre of communal life, beside the marketplace and in the heart of the settlement.[10] A church seeks out elevated locations. Church architecture aims to evoke solemnity, silence, darkness, height, and otherworldliness. 'The truth is that people leave their worldly troubles outside upon entering a Gothic cathedral, as if they are stepping into another world', says Kenneth Clark. Meanwhile, people gather after prayer in the mosque to discuss some very worldly matters. That is the difference.

---

9 And Ernst Bloch adds the characteristic remark that almost all Arab theologians were also physicians. (E. B., *Natural Law and Human Dignity* (Belgrade, 1977) p. 58. One can discern a thread linking philosophy, theology, law, and medicine.

10 St Bernard demanded that churches and monasteries be built as far away from settlements as possible.

Compare the Christian doctrine of papal infallibility with the Islamic infallibility of *ijma* (consensus) ('My people cannot agree upon delusion' (Muhammad (pbuh)). The Gospel addresses man, while the Qur'an addresses men (in plural). Here the principle of nation, entirety, and community emerges. This is not accidental. The first case is entirely in the spirit of Christian elitism and the hierarchical principle of saints and monks (the situation is similar in Buddhism). The second carries a certain secular tone and signifies the qualification of the people as an expression of higher, common reason, forming the basis of all democracy. Islam does not recognise an elite in the form of friars, monks, or saints, nor does it have two different programmes—one for the chosen and another for common folk. This suggests a democratic principle.[11]

Both the Gospel and the Qur'an proclaim the principle of spiritual community, in contrast to the Old Testament (Judaism is a nation).[12] However, while the Gospel remains categorical in this regard, Islam acknowledges nationalities, constituting itself as a new dimension above them—the supranationality of Muslims (*ummah*).[13] Moreover, the Qur'an cautiously reaffirms the principle of kinship and blood relations that Jesus had completely rejected.[14]

The circumstances under which Islam appeared also help us better understand it as a doctrine that unites religion and politics. The Arabs of that era were a powerful people whose strength had not yet been exhausted, equally engaged in merchant and warrior traditions, as well as religious and metaphysical pursuits. Their Ka'bah had not only been a religious centre

11 It is well known that the proposal submitted at the Second Vatican Council to replace the singular institution of the papacy with collective leadership failed—an idea fundamentally opposed to the very nature of Christianity.

12 Compare Qur'an 49:10 and the Gospel (Matthew) 12:47, 48, 49.

13 Qur'an, 49:13.

14 Qur'an, 4:1 and 33:6.

but also a trading hub for centuries. The environment in which they lived did not permit underestimating the importance of economic factors in the struggle for survival. Unlike wealthy Galilee, the cradle of Christianity, where a person could sustain themselves with little effort, life in Arabia required utmost exertion (long merchant journeys, struggles over every square metre of fertile land or every litre of water). Yet, simultaneously, the desert inspired and fostered profound religiousness. These two contrasting facts, under whose continual influence the spirit and instincts of the Arab people developed, made them predestined for Islam—a teaching of both heaven and earth. While the Gospel could say, 'Live as lilies in the field', the Qur'an had to say, 'God gifted you with daylight to spread out and seek food and God's blessings for yourselves.'

According to the Qur'an, not the Gospel, 'God made man to be His deputy on Earth' (Qur'an, 2:30). Man could achieve authority over nature and the world only through knowledge and work—that is, science and action. Through this principle, as well as its attention to law and legislation, Islam demonstrated its aspiration towards not only culture but civilisation as well.[15]

The relationship of Islam toward civilisation is also reflected in its attitude towards the alphabet, one of the most powerful levers of civilisation. Historically first Qur'anic surah mentions the skill of writing (Qur'an, 96:1). Principally speaking, the alphabet is intrinsically foreign to religion. The Gospel remained an oral narrative for a long time, and, as far as we know, it was written down an entire century after Jesus. Muhammad (pbuh) would dictate parts of the Qur'an immediately to his scribe—a practice entirely foreign to Jesus and more akin to the customs of the despised 'writers'.[16]

15 Islam is the only religion to have developed its own integral legal system.

16 Moses also wrote, which is entirely in keeping with his role and mission in history (Numbers 33:2, Epistle to the Romans 10:5).

Even the Qur'anic affirmation of the right to fight evil and resist violence (Qur'an, 42:39) is not strictly religious. The principle of non-violence and non-resistance makes more sense from a religious perspective. This principle appears in almost identical form in Christ's teaching and Indian religious thought. (A direct continuation of the Indian variant is Gandhi's *satyagraha*, the method of struggle through non-violence and civil disobedience.) When the Qur'an approves or even prescribes fighting instead of suffering, submitting, and repeatedly enduring (Qur'an, 2:216, 22:39, 60:2, 60:8–9, 61:10–11 etc.), this represents not a religious-moral but a socio-political code. Muhammad (pbuh) was a fighter. One meticulous chronicler recorded that he had nine swords, three spears, three bows, seven armours, three shields, etc. Muhammad (pbuh) strongly reminds us of Moses, the 'fighting prophet'.[17]

The prohibition of alcohol in Islam is essentially a social prohibition, as alcohol is primarily a 'social evil'. No religion can have anything inherently against alcohol (some religions even used artificial stimulants to induce ecstasy to a certain degree: the darkness of cathedrals and the aroma of incense fall into this category). It is well known that some dervish orders (the Islamic equivalent of monasticism) did not reject alcoholic beverages.

But a dervish represents a degradation of a Muslim. Islam signifies progress from Jesus to Muhammad (pbuh), and a dervish is a return from Muhammad (pbuh) to Jesus. The prohibition of alcohol and drugs does not make much sense in the dervish–Christian feeling and vision of the world. Christians

17 We will find many parallels between Moses and Muhammad (pbuh), and between Judaism and Islam. Such parallels do not exist between Judaism and Christianity. In a certain sense, these two teachings stand in a relationship of thesis and antithesis. This circumstance could explain the phenomenon of antisemitism, which is a distinctly Christian occurrence, entirely unknown among Muslim peoples.

did not feel it inappropriate to say that 'wine is the blood of Christ' (Eucharist). In that, we cannot even see traces of the future Islamic rejection of wine as a grave sin, a *haram*. When Islam rejects alcohol, it does not function as a religion but as a science. However, this blend that we call Islam is not a 'stable compound'. An emphasis on its religious component creates a latent possibility of internal separation: Islam naturally seeks to degrade into religion and mysticism. As soon as awareness and activity weaken, as soon as we forget 'our share in this world' and stop working accordingly—contrary to the Qur'anic imperative—the Islamic state becomes a state like any other, and religion in Islam starts to act like any other religion: the state becomes naked power that only serves itself, while religion drags society into passivity and backwardness. The hereditary caliphate, emperors, emirs, godless scientists, clergy, dervish orders, mystical teachings, and intoxicated poets—all of that is merely an external expression of an internal schism akin to the Christian one: '(Render) unto Caesar the things that are Caesar's, and unto God the things that are God's'—this slogan is Christian but not Islamic. Dervish orders and mystical philosophy at their core are certainly the most characteristic forms of this deviation, which might be called the Christianisation of Islam, a reversion of Islam from Muhammad (pbuh) back to Jesus.

There is also another, opposite danger, yet it is a general impression that the 'materialism' of Islam, its natural and social content, makes the Islamic world resistant to the extreme materialist teachings that constantly flow in from Europe. Don Quixote-like Christianity in pre-revolutionary Russia could not represent any kind of obstacle to the realism of leftist teachings. The absence or failure of Marxist revolutions in Muslim countries is no coincidence. Islam has its own Marxism. The Qur'an retained some of the sharp realism of the Old Testament, and Marxism in Europe is a replacement or compensation for the Jewish, Old-Testament component, which Catholicism and Orthodox Christianity have completely suppressed.[18] Rationalist Protestantism has proven itself significantly more resistant to revolutionary challenges. In this regard, the Protestant form of Christianity is closer to Islam than Catholicism.

It is often the case that, due to historical reasons and political confrontations between Christianity and Islam, their kinship is completely overlooked. The crucial fact that Islam recognises the Bible as a holy book and Jesus as God's prophet is frequently neglected—a fact that would steer the relationship between these two great world religions in a completely different direction in the future if all necessary conclusions were to be drawn from it.[19]

18 The greatest number of points of contact between the Old Testament and the Qur'an can be found in their sharp condemnations of unworthy holders of power and wealth, which are frequent in both books. The Qur'an thunders against the 'arrogant leaders' (7:74), 'sinful elite' (6:123), 'notables' (7:59), 'godless magnates' (11:27), 'profligate wealthy' (34:34), and so on. This is undoubtedly an expression of the social engagement characteristic of both Judaism and Islam.

19 'And say: "We believe in what was revealed to us and what was revealed to you. Our God and your God is one and the same, and to Him we submit."' (Qur'an, 29:46) Or: 'Say: "O People of the Book, come to a word that is common between us and you..."', etc. (Qur'an, 3:64)

CHAPTER 8

ISLAM AND RELIGION

DUALISM OF FIVE PILLARS OF ISLAM

Salah, the Islamic prayer, is not only an expression of the Islamic understanding of the world but also of the way Islam seeks to organise that world. Salah announces two things: 1. There is not only one but two iconic human aspirations; and 2. those aspirations, although logically separate, can be united in human life—prayer will not exist without hygiene, nor will spiritual effort exist without simultaneous physical and social efforts. Salah is the most perfect expression of what we call the 'bipolar unity' of Islam. With its simplicity, salah abstracts this relationship, turning it into a formula, almost like a symbol.

Salah cannot be performed without wudu, the cleansing, yet prayer alone can accompany an 'impurity vow',—a vow we encounter in certain monastic orders within Christianity and Hinduism. According to the sentiment of these orders—a sentiment that is authentically religious—neglecting bodily care and actively disregarding the body even emphasises the spiritual component of prayer. It was believed that true prayer, by its foundational principle, would become more genuine the more it was 'cleansed' of physical 'impurities'. The more pronounced the anti-bodily attitude in prayer, the stronger the emphasis on the spiritual attitude.[20]

---

20 Among the church authorities who particularly emphasised this aspect of prayer, the most resolute was certainly the Apostle James. The extent of this deliberate bodily neglect can be seen from the following lines: 'Cleanliness was regarded with horror.... Saints, both male and female, boasted that water had never touched their feet, except when they had to cross rivers.' (B. Russell, *History of Western Philosophy*, p. 370)

The rational elements of salah are reflected in cleansing (wudu) and the movements during salah. Because of these, salah is not only prayer but also discipline (or hygiene); it is not only mysticism but also sobriety. There is indeed something soldierly about freshening up with cold water in the morning and then praying together in tight ranks. When a Persian lookout saw Muslim soldiers performing the morning prayer together from afar before the battle of Al-Qadisiyyah, he reported to his commander: 'The Muslim army is having a military practice class.'[21] The movements in salah are simple and rigid, appearing like gymnastics from the outside. Five daily prayers, evenly spread throughout the day, accompanied by washing the most exposed body parts (or taking a bath)—the first performed before sunrise and the last deep into the night—represent a powerful, almost brutal, confrontation with comfort and relaxation.

If we now closely examine this 'rational' side of salah, we see that it is not unambiguous. The duality repeats: wudu is hygiene, but hygiene 'is not only knowledge, but virtue too' (Rousseau, *Emile*). Islam had to recognise hygiene as something inherently its own, something 'methodologically' Islamic. The result: Islam elevates hygiene to the level of an idea, tying it organically to prayer. Unexpectedly (only unexpected from the standpoint of pure religion), the Qur'an proclaims: 'Surely Allah loves those who always turn to Him in repentance and those who purify themselves' (Qur'an, 2:222). The expression 'cleanliness is a form of faith' could only appear in Islam; otherwise, in every known religion, the body remains 'out of favour'.[22]

One prayer tied to the Ramadan fast, *taraweeh*, has a clearly medicinal, health-related purpose. This is only possible in

21 Cited by J. Risler in *La Civilisation Arabe*, p. 35.

22 Let us note how the public baths and thermae built by Roman civilisation disappeared with the rise of Christianity. And not only that—the Church would close down the baths and establish monasteries instead. None of this was by chance.

Islam. Contrary to religious reasoning, Islam has connected prayer to nature and its movements by linking prayers to specific times of day and a particular geographical direction (facing the Ka'bah). The timings of salah, as well as those of fasting and *Hajj*, are defined as functions of certain astronomical facts. Perhaps this Qur'anic sentence was more religious: 'Righteousness is not in turning your faces towards the east or the west...' (Qur'an, 2:177), yet the Islamic concept of prayer—which equally includes physical (natural) elements—ultimately prevailed in Islam. Thus, salah became a phenomenon of our world, grounded in space and time. The necessity of precisely determining orientation in space and time significantly influenced the rapid development of astronomy in the early centuries of Islam, and perhaps even conditioned it. We have many reasons to believe this was its goal.

This worldly, pragmatic, and natural meaning of salah acquires another dimension, a social one, through congregational prayer (*salat al-jama'ah*), which is strongly encouraged. Through the mosque and *jama'ah*, we are drawn into the public sphere. Congregational prayer is a gathering for communal prayer but also for direct, personal contact, and as such, it explicitly opposes negative individuality and isolation. Life separates people; the mosque continually brings them back together and mixes them. It serves as a daily school of harmony, equality, togetherness, and goodwill. This 'social' tendency of salah (the process of socialising prayer) reaches completion in the *Jumu'ah* prayer. This prayer is explicitly urban and 'political'. It is performed on a holiday in a central mosque and led by a state official. A vital component of this prayer is the *khutbah*, which is primarily a political message. Christians might argue that prayer has been reduced to its negation through Jumu'ah, a completely understandable conclusion from a Christian perspective, yet unjustified from an Islamic viewpoint.

***

This metamorphosis of religion into Islam can equally clearly be observed in the case of zakat. At the beginning, in the Meccan period of Muhammad's (pbuh) prophecy, zakat was initially a voluntary form of giving to the poor; therefore, it represented charity. As the community in Medina took shape—a historical moment marking the transformation of a purely spiritual community into a state—Muhammad (pbuh) began treating zakat as a legal obligation, a tax levied on the wealthy for the benefit of the poor (the first tax benefiting the poor in history, as far as we know). By adding an element of compulsion to the Christian institution of alms, Islam created zakat, or 'obligatory charity', as J. Risler humorously termed it in his work, *La civilisation arabe*. The same contradictory logic that transformed prayer into salah now turned charity into zakat, and ultimately, religion into Islam.

By proclaiming zakat, Islam primarily stepped forward as a social movement, rather than solely a religion. Zakat gained its true significance only through the creation of the community in Madinah. An indication of the social character of this institution is the fact that the imperative of zakat was mentioned eight times in the chapters of the Qur'an revealed in Mecca and 22 times in the chapters revealed in Madinah.

Zakat is an answer to a phenomenon that itself is not unambiguous, because poverty is not only a social issue. Its cause is not merely scarcity but also evil. Scarcity is its external aspect, while sin represents its internal dimension. How else can we explain the existence of poverty in affluent countries? A third of humanity was chronically malnourished in the second half of the twentieth century. Is this truly due to a shortage of material goods, or rather, to a shortage of compassion? Any genuine solution to poverty must include a confession of guilt; it must essentially be an act of repentance. Every social solution must also be human; thus, it must not only alter social relationships but also relationships between individuals. It must simultaneously address equitable distribution and nurture moral upbringing. It must be both a socio-political measure and an expression of love and compassion.

Misery is a problem, but it is also a sin. It can be solved by changing ownership over material goods but also by fostering personal aspiration, effort, and goodwill. Nothing is truly achieved if ownership over the world's goods changes hands, yet hatred and a tendency toward exploitation and subjugation persist within human souls. This is the essence behind the failures of both Christian and socialist revolutions. 'The amount of evil in the world has not decreased for over 2,000 years. No empire, neither divine nor revolutionary, has come through', writes A. Camus. Religious revolutions were excessively religious, socialist ones excessively socialist. Religion mistakenly believed it would become more authentic by rejecting politics and force, whereas socialism viewed its primary task as persuading humanity that violence is the only way, and mercy a delusion.

Our socialism must also be a religion. Humanity needs a religion that is simultaneously political, and politics that is simultaneously ethical—a form of charity that can become a social obligation, a tax. Thus, we arrive at the definition of zakat. People are reflected through zakat; it is up to them whether it will become more a tax or a voluntary deed from one human to another. Zakat demands that treasure chests be opened, but also human hearts. Zakat is a vast river of goods flowing downward, but simultaneously a spirit of compassion and solidarity connecting heart to heart, person to person. Zakat eliminates not only the misery of the poor but also the indifference of the wealthy. It alleviates material inequalities between people while bringing them spiritually closer.[23]

23 Of course, direct social intervention (that is, not 'from person to person', but through society or the state) may appear to be a more efficient path to social justice. However, social institutions, through their impersonal relations and the spread of general indifference, undermine the very foundations upon which a healthy community rests.

The goal of Islam is not to abolish wealth, but rather to abolish poverty. What is poverty? It is a lack of the goods necessary for a normal life—possessing less than the essential minimum. The minimum standard of living is a natural (and historical) category representing the sum of goods sufficient to satisfy the physical and cultural needs of individuals and their families, in accordance with the level of societal development and wealth. Consequently, society's task is not to perform a levelling but, above all, to guarantee that essential minimum for everyone. The social measures of Islam are therefore limited to eliminating poverty, whose moral and economic justifications are, at best, doubtful.

Every organised society is influenced not only by moral and humane imperatives but also by the imperative of sustaining itself. To be genuinely Islamic, society must simultaneously be maximally humane and maximally efficient. It ceases to be Islamic if humanitarian scruples endanger its stability; conversely, it is equally un-Islamic if an excessive emphasis on efficiency and power leads to violations of essential principles of freedom, law, and humanism. The ideology of an Islamic society is determined precisely by the intersection of these two inherently opposing tendencies and demands.

Theological discussions about zakat usually limit themselves to determining exactly how much to give and from what. However, the principle of solidarity established by zakat is more important than mere percentages and numbers. What truly matters is the principle that the wealthier part of society has an obligation toward the poorer. There should be no doubt that a genuine Islamic order, once achieved, would strive to fulfil this very principle, paying less attention to percentages meticulously debated by learned theologians. The principle's purpose can only be realised if the richer segment of society begins to provide for the poorer according to the latter's actual needs. 'If zakat is the right of the poor

(Qur'an, 70:24–25), then it will be ensured by force if needed, just like any other right.'[24]

Thanks to the educational emphasis on giving, which Islam preaches and practises (according to some authors, the obligation or recommendation to give is mentioned in eighty-two places in Qur'an), a silent revolution took place in Muslim societies through the institution of *waqf*. This institution is unparalleled in significance and scale compared to those in other civilisations. There is hardly a Muslim country in which vast material goods have not been endowed to waqf, no longer serving personal but general welfare. Although waqf is not explicitly mentioned in the Qur'an, its emergence is by no means accidental. It arose spontaneously as a fruit of the spirit of mutual assistance and as a consequence of the educational role of zakat. This humane institution gives hope that important social goals can be achieved without violence. As material goods placed in service of ethical goals, waqf demonstrates that significant economic changes can occur without mediation by material interest. Hence, this institution contradicts so-called natural economic laws. From the perspective of political economy, it is an anomaly, but precisely through its duality— 'an economic category with a soul'—it represents a typically Islamic institution.

Will zakat negatively impact people's motivation to improve their condition through personal effort, as some object? First of all, there are countless misfortunes that no amount of personal effort can overcome (natural defects, disabilities, natural

24 Let us mention here—by way of comparison—an interesting idea proposed by the American economist Milton Friedman, recipient of the 1976 Nobel Prize in Economic Sciences. According to this idea, financial departments would pay a 'negative tax' to all those who earn insufficient income. 'Poverty in America would have long disappeared if public funds were given only to those who truly need them, instead of being spent on inefficient and tremendously costly social services', Friedman stated. Zakat remains what it is, but Friedman's negative tax irresistibly reminds us of zakat.

catastrophes, etc.). Besides, in this sense, zakat is no different from other kinds of subsidies and aid familiar to all civilised—and in some forms, uncivilised—societies. For example, in the 1965 budget, the USA allocated one billion dollars' worth of aid to impoverished Americans.[25] No one was concerned that this substantial sum would negatively affect entrepreneurship in the most entrepreneurial nation in the world.[26]

* * *

This detailed analysis of salah and zakat, two of the most prominent Islamic observances, has illustrated their internal duality. However, when observed externally, their differing positions within the framework of Islam become apparent. Salah then appears as a spiritual component, and zakat as a social one. Salah is directed towards the human, zakat towards the world; salah has a personal character, zakat a social one; salah pursues a subjective goal, zakat an objective one; salah serves as an instrument of upbringing, while zakat is a component of societal order. Nearly all Islamic authorities agree on a certain unity between salah as an individual prayer and zakat as social behaviour in harmony with salah—an attitude that, according to the unanimous opinion of the majority of scholars, goes so far as to claim that salah is worthless if not

---

25 The category of American citizens with an annual income below 2,000 dollars. It is estimated that during those years this category comprised around thirty-five million Americans.

26 Professor Lester Thurow from the Massachusetts Institute of Technology argues quite the opposite. This distinguished economist claims that there is no conflict between social benefits and economic efficiency, and that social programmes can be as economically productive as they are socially just. Rejecting the notion that generous social benefits would undermine a country's economic flow by 'making the people lazy and spoiled', Professor Thurow even asserts that countries which reduce the gap between the richest and the poorest and implement programmes with a strong social emphasis are, one by one, surpassing the United States: Sweden, Switzerland, Denmark, Norway, and soon West Germany. Here too, the 'third' combined path proves to be the closest to humanity—and therefore the most successful.

accompanied by strict adherence to zakat. The Qur'an affirms the unity of salah and zakat through repeated mention of their connection. Abdullah Ibn Mas'ud claims that Muhammad (pbuh) said, 'You have been ordered to pray salah and give zakat; whoever among you fails to give zakat has no benefit from his salah either.' This position can only be explained as a prohibition of separating faith from action, the human from the world—a prohibition explicitly Islamic in its essence. Guided by the same reasoning, Abu Bakr, the first caliph, chose to use force against a tribe that refused to pay zakat. It is reported that he then said, 'By God, I will fight everyone who differentiates between salah and zakat.'

This formula, 'Pray salah and give zakat', is a specific form of another, more fundamental and general 'bipolar' formula—'believe and do good'—which can be considered the foundational form of the Qur'anic religious, moral, and social imperative.[27] It articulates two indispensable pillars upon which all of Islam rests; thus, it is right to regard it as the first and highest Islamic law.

Islam as a whole is characterised by this 'bipolar' unity. *Shahada*—the declaration of joining Islam—is performed before witnesses, reflecting the dual significance of this act. By declaring shahada, an individual joins a spiritual community, for which no witnesses are required, but also enters a socio-political community, imparting legal, not merely moral, significance. No witnesses are necessary to accept religion, as it is a relationship between the individual and God. Indeed, an internal decision or intention alone is sufficient in that case. Declaring it before others is a public element, unnecessary from the perspective of any purely religious viewpoint.

27 A well-known verse from the Qur'an points to this connection: 'Indeed, those who believe and do good deeds, establish prayer, and give zakat will have their reward with their Lord. They will have no fear, nor will they grieve.' (Qur'an, 2:277)

A similar societal component can undoubtedly be found in Islamic fasting. Muslim communities have always perceived it as a manifestation of unity, and people's strong reactions to public violations of this obligation can thus be understood. It was considered (or rather, felt) that such actions harmed internal social cohesion.

Therefore, fasting in Islam is not strictly a religious matter, nor merely a private individual concern; it is instead a social obligation. Such treatment of a religious norm is inconceivable in any other religion. Islamic fasting, a union of asceticism and joy—at times even pleasure—is the most natural and radical educational measure ever practically carried out in the world. You will encounter it both in a royal court and a villager's cottage, in the home of a philosopher as well as that of a worker. Its greatest strength lies precisely in the fact that it is practised.

What is Hajj—the pilgrimage to the Kaaba in Mecca, known as the fifth basic Islamic duty? Is it a religious ritual, a trade fair, a political gathering, or perhaps all of the above? It is clearly a religious ritual, but in the distinctly Islamic sense, meaning it indeed encompasses all these aspects.

The duality of Islam manifests itself in countless other ways. Consider the following ayah from the Qur'an:

> Allah will not impose blame upon you for what is meaningless in your oaths, but He will impose blame upon you for [breaking] what you intended of oaths. So, its expiation is the feeding of ten needy people from the average of that which you feed your [own] families or clothing them or the freeing of a slave. But whoever cannot find [or afford it] – then a fast of three days [is required]. That is the expiation for oaths when you have sworn. But guard your oaths. Thus does Allah make clear to you His verses that you may be grateful.(Qur'an, 5: 89) [28]

28 This saying is attributed to Muhammad (pbuh: 'If you see something wrong, remove it with your hand; if you cannot, then denounce it with your words,

Useful social deeds in the external world are given priority, and only if these are impossible is a purely spiritual act offered as an alternative. (Here, fasting appears as such a spiritual act of repentance, penance, and prayer.)

Or, as another example: the Old Testament prescribes retaliation, while the New Testament teaches forgiveness. Observe how the Qur'an synthesises these two principles, creating a unified 'molecule' from these 'atoms': 'And the retribution for an evil act is an evil one like it, but whoever pardons and makes reconciliation - his reward is [due] from Allah. Indeed, He does not like wrongdoers.' (Qur'an, 42:40)

The synthesis is presented almost literally mechanically in another instance:

> And We ordained for them therein [Torah] a life for a life, an eye for an eye, a nose for a nose, an ear for an ear, a tooth for a tooth, and for wounds is legal retribution. But whoever gives [up his right as] charity, it is an expiation for him. And whoever does not judge by what Allah has revealed – then it is those who are the wrongdoers. (Qur'an, 5:45)

Or: 'O you who have believed, do not prohibit the good things which Allah has made lawful to you and do not transgress. Indeed, Allah does not like transgressors.' (Qur'an, 5:87)

Thus, Islam is not a religion that forbids earthly fruits or one that 'constantly teaches that there are more and more forbidden things'. Islam does not anathematise the Earth. On the contrary, if water is unavailable, earth itself can purify you. The symbolism of *tayammum*—symbolic purification by touching clean earth with one's hands and then wiping the face and forearms—can only hold this meaning.

---

or at the very least with your thoughts—but this last one is the weakest form of faith.' – I am not certain of the authenticity of this saying, but its correspondence with the quoted verse from the Qur'an is clearly evident.

Certain Islamic institutions are religious in their name, form, or origin alone. In fact, one could say they are Islamic in the truest sense of the word. Such institutions include the imperative of hygiene or the prohibition of alcohol. These and similar injunctions do not have their origin or foundation purely in religion, simply because they stem from concern for external, physical, or social life. They are not even integral elements of culture, achieving their fullest significance only within the framework of civilisation. Many populous cities today are unimaginable without a certain level of personal and public hygiene, and alcoholism has proven to be one of the most significant issues precisely in our era of technology and urbanisation.

Following this logic further, it leads us to a well-founded conclusion that Islam naturally tends towards the integration of art and technology. This synthesis is most consistently achieved in architecture. Indeed, Islam views architecture most favourably of all arts, perhaps precisely because it is the least 'pure art', or because it is a 'general art', as Kenneth Clark puts it.[29]

Art overly emphasises the individual, spiritual, and otherworldly aspect of humanity, placing it in opposition to the concept of balance that Islam insists upon. Architecture, however, is inherently pragmatic, functional, and responsive to human needs. (Music certainly occupies the other extreme, being 'the most incorporeal of all arts', according to Schopenhauer.) It is precisely this 'dual' nature of architecture that predestines it to be a characteristically Islamic art form. Like Islam itself, architecture possesses both a soul and a body.[30]

---

29 Kenneth Clark refers to art as a 'social art... that enables people to live fuller lives.' (K. Clark, *Civilisation*, pg. 242)

30 The duality is also reflected in the name itself: architecture signifies something more than *tecture*, a mere building for purely practical purposes—whether by its dimensions, style, or the nobility of its purpose. This is why absolutely functional architecture is not possible—such a notion would be a contradiction in terms, since architecture cannot be reduced to bare

Thus, the extraordinary achievements of Islam in architecture are not coincidental but rather reflect a kind of natural law.

The sources of Islam are also marked by this inevitable duality. Above all, these are the two fundamental sources: the Qur'an and the hadith, each embodying inspiration and experience, eternity and time, thought and practice, or idea and life. Islam is less a way of thinking and more a way of living. All commentaries on the Qur'an illustrate that it is incomprehensible without the hadith, that is, without reference to a life. It is only through the interpretation of one life—the life of Muhammad (pbuh)—that Islam manifests itself as a practical philosophy, a comprehensive life direction. If we include the third source of Islam—ijma—we find ourselves again at the same conclusion. Ijma is the consensus of scholarly opinion on a particular legal (*shari'ah*) issue (unanimous according to Imam Shafi, and majority according to Tabari and al Razi). Islam would not be what it is if it had not introduced number, a quantitative dimension, into what might otherwise have remained an elitist principle. Ijma simultaneously embodies a qualitative (aristocratic or elitist) principle and a quantitative (democratic) principle.

In this framework of duality, the city of Mecca and the cave of Hira have their place as representatives of the contrast between the external and internal worlds, action and meditation at the very emergence of Islam. In the second phase of Islam's development, this duality is embodied in Mecca and Madinah, two distinct periods whose differing spirit and

---

function without ceasing to be architecture. On the other hand, so-called 'pure architecture', architecture without function, does not exist. In this regard, it is telling that nearly all of the great architects of the Renaissance were artists (painters or sculptors), while on the other hand, for example, the great English architect Christopher Wren was originally a mathematician and astronomer. 'Wren's buildings show us that mathematics, measurement, observation—all that constitutes science—was not in hostile opposition to architecture.' (Kenneth Clark, *Civilisation*, p. 212)

significance are noted by every history of Islam. Here, again, is the same contrast (and unity), but now expressed as faith and politics, religious community and political unity.

Finally, the highest tragic figure in Islam is the *shahid* (martyr), and the shahid is described as a 'fighter on God's path'—a saint and a warrior unified in a single personality. What in European Christianity was split into monastic and knightly principles is here merged within the character of the shahid. It is the unity of spirit and blood, two principles which typically belong to distinct orders of existence.

RELIGION ORIENTED TOWARDS NATURE

The Qur'an continuously reiterates its dual demands, constantly reshaping their form: at times urging the combination of meditation with observation. The former belongs to religion, while the latter pertains to science, or rather, the beginnings or the promise of a science. The Qur'an neither contains nor ought to contain ready-made scientific truths. Instead, it holds an important scientific attitude—an uncommon relationship towards the external world for a religion. It draws attention to numerous phenomena within nature, inviting humans to explain and understand them. Here, the call for science (for 'reading'—Qur'an) emerges not in opposition to God but explicitly in His name. ('Read, 'O Prophet', in the Name of your Lord Who created'(Qur'an, 96:1)

The human being, therefore, observes and examines not merely creative nature, but a world that is God's masterpiece. Such observation is thus not objective, indifferent, or 'desireless'; it is instead a blend of scientific curiosity and religious awe. The poetic depictions of nature to which the Qur'an continually returns illustrate this inclination clearly. Let us consider some of these descriptions:

> Have they not then looked at the sky above them: how We built it and adorned it 'with stars', leaving it flawless? As for the earth, We spread it out and placed upon it firm mountains and produced in it every type of pleasant plant—'all as' an insight and a reminder to every servant who turns 'to

Allah'. And We send down blessed rain from the sky, bringing forth gardens and grains for harvest, and towering palm trees 'loaded' with clustered fruit, as' a provision for 'Our' servants. And with this 'rain' We revive a lifeless land. Similar is the emergence 'from the graves'. (Qur'an, 50: 6–11)

He is the One Who sends down rain from the sky, from which you drink and by which plants grow for your cattle to graze. With it He produces for you 'various' crops, olives, palm trees, grapevines, and every type of fruit. Surely in this is a sign for those who reflect. (Qur'an, 10–11)

And He is the One Who has subjected the sea, so from it you may eat tender seafood and extract ornaments to wear. And you see the ships ploughing their way through it, so you may seek His bounty and give thanks 'to Him'. (Qur'an, 16:14)

And Allah sends down rain from the sky, giving life to the earth after its death. Surely in this is a sign for those who listen. And there is certainly a lesson for you in cattle: We give you to drink of what is in their bellies, from between digested food and blood: pure milk, pleasant to drink.1And from the fruits of palm trees and grapevines you derive intoxicants1 as well as wholesome provision. Surely in this is a sign for those who understand. And your Lord inspired the bees: 'Make 'your' homes in the mountains, the trees, and in what people construct, and feed from 'the flower of' any fruit 'you please' and follow the ways your Lord has made easy for you.' From their bellies comes forth liquid of varying colours, in which there is healing for people. Surely in this is a sign for those who reflect.... (Qur'an,16:65-69)

Indeed, Allah is the One Who causes seeds and fruit stones to sprout. He brings forth the living from the dead and the dead from the living. That is Allah! How can you then be deluded 'from the truth'? He causes the dawn to break and has made the night for rest and 'made' the sun and the moon 'to travel' with precision. That is the design of the Almighty, All-Knowing. And He is the One Who has made the stars as your guide through the darkness of land and sea. We have already made the signs clear for people who know. And He is the One Who originated you all from a single soul,1 then assigned you a place to live and another to 'be laid to' rest. We have already made the signs clear for people who comprehend. And He is the One Who sends down rain from the sky—causing all kinds of plants to grow—producing green stalks from which We bring forth clustered grain. And from palm trees come clusters of dates hanging within reach. 'There are' also gardens of grapevines, olives, and pomegranates, similar 'in shape' but dissimilar 'in taste'. Look at their fruit as it yields and ripens! Indeed, in these are signs for people who believe. (Qur'an, 6:95-99)

Have they failed to look at the earth, 'to see' how many types of fine plants We have caused to grow in it? (Qur'an, 26:7)

And He is the One Who created the day and the night, the sun and the moon—each travelling in an orbit. (Qur'an, 21:33)

Indeed, in the creation of the heavens and the earth; the alternation of the day and the night; the ships that sail the sea for the benefit of humanity; the rain sent down by Allah from the skies, reviving the earth after its death; the scattering of all kinds of creatures throughout; the shifting of the winds; and the clouds drifting between the heavens and the earth—'in all of this' are surely signs for people of understanding. (Qur'an, 2:164)

Many are the societies We have destroyed for persisting in wrongdoing, leaving them in total ruin. 'Many are' also the abandoned wells and lofty palaces! Have they not travelled throughout the land so their hearts may reason, and their ears may listen? Indeed, it is not the eyes that are blind, but it is the hearts in the chests that grow blind. (Qur'an, 22:45-46)

> Have they not travelled throughout the land to see what was the end of those 'destroyed' before them? They were far superior in might; they cultivated the land and developed it more than these 'Meccans' ever have. Their messengers came to them with clear proofs. Allah would have never wronged them, but it was they who wronged themselves. (Qur'an, 30:9)

> Do they not ever reflect on camels—how they were 'masterfully' created; and the sky—how it was raised 'high'; and the mountains—how they were firmly set up; and the earth—how it was levelled out? (Qur'an, 17:20)

> Have you considered what you sow? (Qur'an, 56:63)

> Have you considered the water you drink? (Qur'an, 56:68)

> Have you considered the fire you kindle? (Qur'an, 56:71) etc.

An acceptance of the world and the absence of any conflict with nature can be distinctly felt in these expressions, which fully orient themselves towards nature. Within Islam, matter readily lends itself to many beautiful and noble purposes (the body during salah, wealth for zakat). The material world is not portrayed as Satan's dominion, nor is the body perceived as the seat of sin. Indeed, the Qur'an does not hesitate even to portray the hereafter—the object of humanity's highest hopes—in earthly tones. Consequently, Christians have accused it of a sensuality unworthy of religion. Yet, this very fact highlights that Islam is not inherently detached from the material world and does not share Christianity's instinctive rejection of worldly life. Certain verses of the Qur'an spark intellectual curiosity and inspire a spirit of inquiry.

> And We created from water every living thing. (Qur'an, 21:30)

Or

> And on the earth there are 'different' neighbouring tracts, gardens of grapevines, 'various' crops, palm trees—some stemming from the same root, others standing alone.

They are all irrigated with the same water, yet We make some taste better than others. Surely in this are signs for those who understand. (Qur'an, 13:4)

This last sentence is particularly intellectually stimulating, as it highlights an issue lying at the foundation of the entire science of chemistry. As a result, it was precisely the Muslims who ended numerous debates on substantial questions, which had occupied Christianity, and turned instead to chemistry (*al-chemia*). This represented a transition from mystical philosophy to rational science.

A common element across all quoted Qur'anic sentences is the requirement for human activity, which forms the basis of humanity's power over the natural world. Upon exploring the roots of Western power, one finds that it lies not in the strength of armies or economies—these represent only the superficial appearance but fundamentally in the experimental method of thinking, cultivated by Western civilisation since Francis Bacon.[31] Jean Fourastié writes,

> Observation of nature, society, people, is the first stage of primary education that all children in the Western world are receiving.' Interest in the external world contrasts sharply with the orientation of Brahminic and Buddhist philosophers, who turn inwardly towards the inner self... It is futile to indulge the idea that any nation could align itself on the path of progress without adopting the principles of experimental thought introduced by Galileo, Pascal, Newton, and Claude Bernard. Indeed, the prerequisite for any economic and social advancement is a shift in intellectual attitude—a transition from abstract to concrete, rational to experimental, and stagnation to innovation.[32]

Islam cannot be practised correctly at a primitive level of awareness. To perform salah properly, one must possess

31 And Bacon from the Arabs – see Chapter XI of this book.

32 Jean Fourastié, *The Civilisation of Tomorrow*, (Zagreb) pp. 47–48.

accurate orientation in space and time; during prayer, people face Mecca, thus orienting themselves spatially, while prayers must be conducted at precise times defined by astronomical facts. Similarly, fasting occurs at a specific time of year, corresponding to a precise position of the Earth on its orbit around the Sun. Zakat necessitates accurate statistics, record-keeping, and calculation, while the pilgrimage (Hajj) involves travel and the acquisition of extensive knowledge that only long journeys can impart. In short, even if nothing else were considered, the Muslim community must attain at least a minimal level of civilisation merely by adhering strictly to these four fundamental Islamic observances. It cannot simultaneously be genuinely Islamic and remain barbaric.

This tendency is neither accidental nor unintentional; a reasoned history of Islamic science would demonstrate that the development of almost all scientific fields in the first century of Islam originated from the effort to apply Islamic regulations as rigorously and consistently as possible. Only later was scientific inquiry separated from religion, but even then, never completely.

This was first and most powerfully demonstrated in astronomy. Günther's *History of Natural Sciences* includes facts confirming the exceptionally vivid astronomical awareness in the Islamic cultural milieu, an awareness non-existent among the Greeks due to the immutability of their singular worldview. Islam encountered highly developed astrology in the Euphrates valley, almost three-thousand years old, which had accumulated substantial knowledge about celestial phenomena. Yet the belief in a connection between the stars and human destiny was foreign to Islam; its inherent monotheism and rationalism had to transform this astrology into astronomy. Discussing the so-called Baghdad astronomical school, which formed around the renowned observatory of the same name, Sédillot confirms this:

> The characteristic of the Baghdad astronomy school, from its very beginning, is its scientific spirit: proceeding from the known to the unknown and never accepting anything as proven that could not also be verified through direct observation (control).

Abdul-Wafa discovered the third lunar variation six-hundred years before Tycho Brahe. Khayyam's calendar was even more accurate than the Gregorian one we use today. Ibrahim Al-Zarqali (Ibn Zarqala) was the principal contributor to the Toledan Tables, astronomical tables detailing planetary movements, which served as the foundation of European astronomy for a considerable period. Al-Biruni (Abu Rayhan al-Biruni) proposed the hypothesis that the Earth, rather than the sky, revolves around its axis. Ibn Bajja (Avempace) even suggested the possibility of planetary orbits being elliptical rather than circular, among other things.

Astronomy subsequently significantly advanced all other fields of science. ('Modern science is the daughter of astronomy' – Bergson.) This was a direct outcome of the Qur'an. A religion oriented towards nature thus opened a remarkable new chapter in the development of science—one of the most luminous in human history.

***

This tendency towards integrating science and religion—an Islamic tendency in the best sense of the word—found practical expression through the simultaneous construction of mosques and schools.[33] This practice took a literal form in a phenomenon unique to the Islamic cultural milieu: the so-called mosque–school, an architectural structure with a dual function that cannot easily be named in European languages

---

33 Stefano Bianco writes on the same issue in the journal *Werk*, Switzerland, no. 9/1976. The phenomenon in question is referred to by the author as the polyvalence of Islamic spaces (article title: 'Polyvalence and Flexibility in the Structure of the Islamic City').

(in French, the mechanically coined term is *mosquéecole*). This distinctive building is a materialisation, or technical equivalent, of the original Islamic demand for the unity of religion and science, as articulated in the very first words revealed in the Qur'an: 'Read in the Name of your Lord...' (Qur'an, 96:1).[34] The same concept manifested itself in the curricula of these schools, ranging from basic education up to the highest levels. The renowned *Nizamiyya* in Baghdad served as the prototype of the Islamic school for a long time. Although perceived by Europeans as a 'religious college', its curriculum was in fact evenly split between what today we might call theology—such as *tafsir*, *hadith*, *ahlaq*, and *aqa'id*—and secular subjects including law, philosophy, literature, mathematics, astronomy, music, and basic medical knowledge. Moreover, these two areas were integral to, and inseparable from, each other (see: J. Risler, *Ibid.*). By becoming the model for many similar institutions, Nizamiyya became the predominant school type found across all major cities of the Islamic world.

It is a nearly universal rule that schools in the Muslim world cannot be categorised according to European criteria as either secular or spiritual. Particularly noteworthy is that this was a natural state, or spontaneous understanding, for everyone involved, resulting directly from the Islamic spirit as the prevailing perception or sentiment of the world. This understanding has largely been preserved even today, and wherever it has changed, foreign influences can be identified. The original state always aligns with the fundamental Islamic concept of the unity of religion and science. Al-Azhar in Cairo, one of the greatest and oldest Islamic universities in the world—referred to as a mosque by some and as a university by others—has traditionally been a university of a general type. It became

34 There is historical evidence that the first mosque – Al-Masjid an-Nabawi, built by Muhammad (pbuh), also functioned as a school known as Suffah.

purely theological only during its period of deepest decline.[35] Through reforms carried out in 1961, Al-Azhar regained its original, integral character with the establishment of medical and technical faculties. In Pakistan, the state has entrusted the task of mass literacy campaigns to mosque imams—a path fundamentally correct but managed inconsistently and with insufficient enthusiasm. We encounter a similar phenomenon in Iran, where educated military conscripts fulfil their military duty by teaching literacy in villages, using mosques as schools. The mosque-school is one of those symbols to which nothing needs to be added or from which nothing can be subtracted.

* * *

This orientation towards the external world in Islam resulted in a distinctive realism in its understanding of humanity. Accepting nature in general also meant accepting human nature. Rejecting this world, which includes the body, is naturally imposed by every religion. For a religion, embracing this world implies overcoming or surpassing itself. Islam represents the accomplishment of the impossible feat: making a religion like Christianity embrace the reality of the world. Certain Qur'anic verses appear almost incredible, particularly those dealing with pleasure, sexual love, fighting, and hygiene. This represents a most decisive moment in the history of religion, even in the history of human consciousness generally. It marked the emergence of a religion of 'two worlds', an all-encompassing system of human life, and the revelation that humanity does not have to abandon religion for science, nor abandon the struggle for a better life for religion. Islam did not overlook the fundamental fact of suffering, or the struggle against suffering, which constitutes human history; therein lies its epochal significance. While affirming the worth and dignity of humanity in general, Islam remains realistic, even 'antiheroic', regarding individual human beings.

35 The educational institution is over 1,000 years old (founded in 972).

Islam does not attempt to cultivate qualities in humans that are not founded in their nature. It does not aspire to transform us into saints or angels, as such demands are illusory. Rather, it seeks to help us become precisely what we are—human beings. Although it recognises a certain level of asceticism, Islam does not aim to negate life, health, intellect, sociability, or the pursuit of happiness and pleasure. Islamic asceticism exists primarily as a counterweight to instinct, enabling a balance between blood and spirit, between animalistic and ethical aspirations. Islam extends nature's work in shaping humanity through wudu, prayer, fasting, jamaat, activity, observation, and meditation. Nowhere does it oppose nature. Even when its goals differ, continuity with nature always remains.

It is precisely such a stance of a religion that has caused misunderstandings, which persist even today. Islam has been criticised for alleged sensuality, citing certain passages from the Qur'an and examples from Muhammad's (pbuh) life. We need not defend ourselves vigorously against such accusations. Rather, we should state clearly and openly: yes, Islam advocates a natural life rather than asceticism,[36] it favours wealth over poverty and supports human mastery over nature—not only on this planet but, if possible, even among the stars. Yet to truly comprehend Islam means to understand these concepts—nature, wealth, politics, power, knowledge, and joy—somewhat differently from how Westerners typically perceive them.

Islam truly called upon humans to assume full responsibility, and it did not set poverty or martyr-like asceticism as ideals. It did not forbid man to 'taste the salt of the earth and of the great salty sea' (André Gide). It demanded a complete, fulfilled life for humans.[37] This life rests upon coordinates: one

36 'There is no monasticism in Islam'. (Muhammad (pbuh)

37 'O you who have believed, do not prohibit the good things which Allah has made lawful to you and do not transgress. Indeed, Allah does not like transgressors.' (Qur'an, 5:87)

of which is the natural striving for happiness and power; the other an inner moral improvement, the 'continuous creation of oneself'. These tendencies are logically contradictory and mutually exclusive, but in practical life, they interconnect, and their mutual permeation occurs daily in countless ways, either within our own lives or before our eyes. Such a possibility is given only to humans, and through it, this controversial creature can be defined.

The Gospel anathematised instincts and spoke exclusively of the soul. The Qur'an reintroduces them, as instincts, because although not so lofty, they are genuine and real. The Qur'an addresses them with understanding and without judgement. The angelic bow to human beings (Qur'an, 2:34) conveys the stance that the humane is superior to the angelic, just as drama is deeper and more genuine than the doubtful loftiness of an idyll. Humans are not gentle, lovely creatures programmed solely to do good; rather, they are corporeal, crude, contradictory, and torn between aspirations and temptations. In an unnatural desire to transform these people into sinless, infallible beings, we suddenly realise that we have created bloodless, sentimental, and artificial types, as incapable of doing evil as they are of doing good. By separating them from Mother Earth, we separate them from life—and where there is no life and strength, there is no virtue either.

Freud demonstrated that sexuality cannot be destroyed, only repressed, and that repressed sexual urges only bring greater troubles. No matter how lofty the Christian demand for chastity and restraint seems, the Islamic concept of a controlled and moderate sexual life is more suitable for humans, taking into account the real, worldly side of this matter. Islam does not appear here simply as a religion, but as the truth of a complete life. All arguments advocating the benefits of sexual life are rational, worldly, and practical—not religious or ethical, as complete abstinence would indeed be more religious and more moral.

The matter we are examining concerns the harmony of humans with themselves—in fact, the harmony of their ideals with natural human tendencies, whether physical, social, or intellectual. Conflict within this fundamental relationship is the primary significant source of neuroses. Another such source is the conflict between humans and their environment.

The Qur'an addresses the human being less as an individual and more as part of a collective, frequently speaking to people primarily in their capacity as inhabitants. Humans, as members of society, are children of this world; only as personalities are they citizens of heaven. They are social beings by virtue of what they share with other people, rather than through their individual and personal qualities. If the individual on one hand and society on the other are shaped according to separate and independent models and ideals, discord becomes inevitable, and we face the conflict of the individual with their environment, along with all its consequences. By emphasising righteousness rather than Gospel love as the highest demand (Qur'an, 4:135, 5:9, 5:45, 6:152, 7:28, 7:84, etc.), Islam clearly aimed to achieve an identical upbringing of Muslims both as humans and as citizens, since righteousness is simultaneously a personal and a social virtue (Aristotle even calls it a 'political virtue').[38] It is thus realistic to expect that the Muslim, embodying a balance between physical and moral demands, will exist in greater harmony with their environment and with imperatives of survival than those raised according to any other ideal of humanity. Christian teachings, and idealist teachings in general, contribute to feelings of disappointment and insecurity due to their evident contradiction between what they assert about

38 And Thomas Aquinas regards justice as an 'earthly virtue', while love is the 'supreme heavenly virtue' *Summa Theologiae*, II, 191). Love is clearly not quite 'suited' to this world.

human nature and what we actually encounter in real life.[39] Neuroses and psychological deformations commonly observed in the Western world partly arise as a result of the inner tension between the Christian ideal of humanity and the political patterns of society, which develop autonomously and independently from Christian principles. It is a situation where the Church nurtures souls and the state governs bodies according to the principle: 'Render unto Caesar the things that are Caesar's, and unto God the things that are God's.' Western man was taught that he can be Christian privately, while publicly or in business he might even be a Machiavellian. Those unable to solve or endure this conflict become victims of neuroses. Everyone familiar with the Islamic world unanimously shares the impression of extraordinary harmony between individuals and their environment, of the seamless integration of individuals into the social fabric, and of cohesion which is neither artificial, external, political, nor merely legal, but rather internal and organic. This fact persists despite prevailing poverty and stagnation.

The meaning of many of Muhammad's (pbuh) sayings was the condemnation of extreme solutions: 'I am horrified by two things: an ignorant man's piety and a scholar's atheism' (as cited by R. W. Emerson in his book *Life Management*). Muhammad (pbuh) was doubtlessly horrified by many other 'two things': believers who are powerless and potentates who are godless; those with pure souls but dirty bodies; justice without strength, and power without justice. He was not against wealth and abundance, but he was decidedly in favour of richness in virtue and almost certainly against bare virtue devoid of power and protection. He places the struggle for a better life, and the fight against ignorance, sickness, misery, and filth, on an equal footing with moral values. Muslims are

39 See, for example, Karen Horney, *New Ways in Psychoanalysis* (Paris, 1951).

not saints when they pray and fast; rather, they are ordinary people—husbands and wives who dream about love and life's pleasures. If salah and fasting do draw them towards heaven, they still remain humans to their core, participants in real life, to which they invariably return. They do not retreat into caves away from society, neglect their appearance, nor surrender themselves to the enemy's mercy or lack thereof, nor do they 'forbid the good things which Allah has made lawful for you' (Qur'an, 5:87). They do not content themselves with inner freedom alone (since everyone who believes in God is inwardly free); they desire physical freedom as well and refuse to accept slavery. They believe this earthly life is not our only existence, yet they do not wish to forsake or lose it. The Qur'an addresses genuine children of the Earth, who 'walk upon it modestly and joyfully, committing no violence, yet seeking God's bounty and pleasures.'

By defining Islam as the demand to simultaneously live a corporeal and spiritual life, harmonising external and internal worlds—or as the Qur'an says: 'Rather, seek the 'reward' of the Hereafter by means of what Allah has granted you, without forgetting your share of this world' (Qur'an, 28:77)—one can assert that most people, or the vast majority, are Muslims consciously or unconsciously.[40] This is likely the meaning behind the claim (ascribed to Muhammad pbuh) that every child is born a Muslim and only their parents or circumstances convert them into something else. Humans cannot be entirely Christian, because 'Allah does not require of any soul more than what it can afford' (Qur'an, 2:286). But a human also cannot exist merely as a biological fact—a producer and consumer, a citizen of the state, a subject of legal transactions, or simply a member of society—and thus cannot live in an anti-Christ manner either. A human cannot live strictly according to Christ nor completely against him. Rather, one

40 'If that is Islam, then we are living in Islam.' (J. W. Goethe)

must both accept and reject him. Everything we call human destiny on Earth unfolds between these two opposing truths. Islam suits humans precisely because it is shaped according to their inherent nature (Qur'an, 30:30), satisfying the duality of their existence. Every other answer either neglects or favours just one aspect of human life, thereby impairing the human capacity to reach its full potential or causing internal conflict. The human being remains the most compelling argument for Islam.

ISLAM AND LIFE

Dualism is not the highest human philosophy, but it is the highest form of life. Poetry is principally a matter of the heart, yet the greatest poets—Homer, Ferdowsi, Dante, Shakespeare, and Goethe—united both reason and sentiment, science and beauty. Poems concern humans, not society, yet Homer's works contributed to the formation of the Greek nation, and the fiery poetry of John Greenleaf Whittier helped abolish slavery in America. Mathematics is an affair of the mind, yet 'a good mathematician must be somewhat of a poet.' (Weierstrass). All first-class physicists and astronomers were also mystics (Copernicus, Newton, Kepler, Einstein, Oppenheimer). Punishment—despite being repression—can be a powerful moral factor; if just, it has an educational influence both on the perpetrator and others. Fear marks the beginning of morality for humans, just as piety initiates love for God. Sport—although a purely physical activity—clearly has a profound educational function. One of the greatest minds of all time, Plato, received his name from the breadth of his back. Thus, a most noble spirit was nurtured within a strong body. Body and spirit, heart and mind, science and religion, physics and Indian philosophy converge at the point marking life's highest achievements. Pure rationality or pure inspiration always signify degeneration and decline. The secular principle can thus support the sacred; bodily purity can aid spiritual purity, and Salah can represent the highest form of human prayer.

Let us examine some additional phenomena from this perspective.

What is the goal of so-called 'natural upbringing'? Rousseau provides a characteristic answer:

> The goal is one day to achieve what is commonly deemed incompatible, yet what all great individuals have united—namely bodily and spiritual strength, the mind of a wise man, and the strength of an athlete. (J.J. Rousseau, *Emile*).

Discussing a child's upbringing, Montaigne writes: 'To strengthen his spirit, we must strengthen his muscles', and Rousseau observes that despite their many differences, Locke, Fleury, and Krause all agree on this point. Rousseau himself repeatedly returns to this claim in *Emile*:

> The body must have strength if it is to submit to the soul; a good servant must be strong. I know that excess arouses the passions; it also gradually weakens the body. Yet conversely, torturing the body and fasting will often produce similar consequences through opposite means. The weaker the body, the more it commands; the stronger it is, the more obedient it becomes. All sensual passions dwell in softened bodies: the less capable they are of satisfying those passions, the more they suffer under their influence.

In principle, force has nothing to do with morality, yet in real life, there is no justice without force. Justice is thus a unity of the idea of justness and force. Have not political movements removed much injustice that religion and the Church endured for centuries? Égalité, Liberté, Fraternité—these ideals are religious in their essence, but as realities (if indeed they are realities), they resulted from revolution, thus from politics and violence. Religion's inability to realise in practice some of the great ideas it preaches has compromised its demands in the eyes of the oppressed and humiliated. Conversely, violence and politics have gained a certain justification, having provided the means to accomplish ideas which religions discovered and inspired, but of which they could only speak or dream.

Consider human labour as another example. Even at first glance, two aspects can be identified: the activity itself—human and non-utilitarian—and the result of labour, a product motivated by utility and need. Religion focuses on the first aspect; civilisation on the second.

Religion defined human destiny on Earth with the motto: 'In the sweat of thy face shalt thou eat bread', whereas science and materialism promise a kingdom without labour, in which mechanical work increasingly replaces humans and the working day steadily decreases. Religion demands labour for labour's own sake, labour as a moral tool against sin, because 'Idle hands are the devil's workshop; idle lips are his mouthpiece', and because its goal is not 'the production or reproduction of material life'. Conversely, civilisation has precisely the outcome or even the mere product of labour in mind. Addressing this topic, the renowned Marxist writer Henri Lefebvre found it necessary to explicitly clarify that labour, in the Marxist sense, is considered not as a moral but as a production factor (in a lecture at the International Geneva Meetings). The cult of labour in Europe is originally Protestant, not socialist as commonly thought. Religion demands that man himself—me, you, him—engage in labour, showing little concern for the product; civilisation, on the other hand, with its focus solely on results, seeks to circumvent labour as much as possible, whether through the labour of others—slaves in ancient times—or machines in the modern era.

In this discussion, labour is analysed and deconstructed in detail. Taken as a whole, as a useful activity, as a unity, labour serves as much a moral function as an economic one. It is as effective a factor in combating evil thoughts and passions as it is in fighting poverty. In this sense, labour is a distinctly Islamic phenomenon.

This parallelism between usefulness and morality can be clearly traced through a phenomenon that equally belongs to natural and social human life—the prohibition of incest (inbreeding), or the progressive narrowing of permissible familial relations throughout human evolution. This prohibition is at once medically and morally justified—a remarkable instance where the demands of science and ethics converge.

The nearly universal prohibition against marital ties between close relatives, found across various cultures and historical periods, exemplifies what we might term 'natural Islam.' It appears as though life itself has discovered its Islamic path.[41] Yet, is the prohibition of incest purely moral in nature, or is it motivated by biological reasons? A simple answer, excluding either aspect, cannot be given. Biological reasons are unquestionably present. As the renowned Russian biologist Kliment Timiryazev writes:

> There are indeed many facts proving that close kinship between parents adversely affects the health of their children. Today, we hardly need further evidence, as extensive research has demonstrated that this law holds true not only for humans and animals but also for plants. It is a general law for the entire organic world, nowhere more clearly demonstrated than in the plant kingdom.[42]

On the other hand, the antiquity of this prohibition would suggest it was motivated by moral scruples. One may justifiably question whether humans had a clear understanding

---

41 It is interesting how so-called primitive peoples devised simple yet highly effective methods to prevent the unintentional violation of this prohibition. For example, among the Pygmies in Africa and the Indigenous peoples of Australia, each family belongs to a specific totem group, made up of several related families. Several closely connected totem groups form a particular marriage class, symbolised by a plant or animal. When a young man wishes to marry, he may only do so with a girl from a different marriage class. Violations of this rule are almost unheard of.

42 Timiryazev, *The Life of The Plant*, p. 134.

of biological inheritance in those ancient times; thus, we are inclined to perceive the prohibition as primarily moral in character, as many people still do today. Its violation certainly evokes moral condemnation among the general public. In any case, this represents an exemplary alignment between morality and science—a principle at the core of what we term the Islamic approach.

Even some interesting phenomena that have accompanied medicine throughout its historical development point to its 'dual' nature. Medicine has never been purely scientific—not historically, nor today. It has always been wisdom, ethics, and spiritual discipline, and when it has lacked these, it treated only the body, neglecting spirit and strength. In modern times, illnesses have emerged in which even the most thorough examinations could detect no organic changes in the structure of affected organs. The disturbances experienced by patients appear directly connected to their psychological life. Psychosomatic medicine, a new branch that studies the mutual interaction of body and psyche, suggests that stomach ulcers, rheumatoid conditions, certain forms of allergies, bronchial asthma, obesity, diabetes, and migraines are primarily psychological illnesses. Research indicates that psychological conflicts or shocks lie at the root of these and other conditions, with organic changes being secondary, and sometimes entirely absent.

Genuine treatment of people cannot be reduced merely to physical and chemical therapies or surgery and purely mechanical procedures. Modern medicine is gradually embracing the understanding that 'industrialised medicine' and anonymous therapy are fundamentally insufficient—'because there are no diseases, only patients'. Medicine deals not simply with phenomena but with human beings, personalities in a certain respect. The same cause does not always produce the same consequence, nor can two different individuals have precisely the 'same' disease and thus identical treatments. Consequently, we must accept that historical accounts of curing people through relics, prayers, sacrifices, fasting, and faith likely contain a grain of truth. Indeed, all the prophets of ancient times were miracle-workers and healers. Such tendencies persist today. Some hospitals in Paris apply so-called musical therapy—treatment through music—recognising that illness is not merely a physical state, or solely a physico-chemical or physiological disorder.[43] Unlike alchemy and astrology, which evolved into chemistry and astronomy respectively, becoming fully fledged sciences, medicine will always oscillate between two poles in its highest tendencies. For while chemistry and astronomy operate upon matter, medicine has life as its 'subject'—indeed, human life—and as with everything human, it must remain within the realm of integration between science and religion.

If we continue this line of reasoning, we will observe that every art is, at the same time, a craft. No one can deny the distinction between art and craft, yet their unmistakable points of overlap are equally indisputable. Many great artists regarded themselves simply as master craftsmen. A surviving rulebook from a guild of painters and sculptors in Paris, dated 1391, reveals regulations that are indistinguishable from those found in the rulebooks of other trades of the same period. It outlines the rules for learning the craft, the apprenticeship period, the right to open a shop, and so on. We consistently notice two contradictory developments: on the one hand, the separation of art from craft—which did occur and, indeed, had to occur; on the other hand, this separation is never total. Art and craft retain certain shared features. No human endeavour is ever entirely mechanical, yet neither is it ever wholly creative. There is no craft that is not, in part, a creation; and there is

43 The honorary president of the Committee for Music Therapy, based in Paris, is the world-renowned violinist Yehudi Menuhin.

no art that is not, in some respect, a technique. This polarity can also be observed on another plane: on one side stands the painter, on the other the art dealer—a constant reminder that a painting is simultaneously an artwork and a commodity, an economic good with a market value. The publisher stands in the same relation to the writer as the investor (or client) to the architect, or the producer to the film director.

The history of music offers particularly striking examples of the interdependence between technique and inspiration. Titans of music such as Beethoven, Bach, and Mozart all engaged deeply with the technical dimensions of their art and the organisation of orchestras. Beethoven's symphonies—crowning achievements of Western music—would be inconceivable without the technical innovations in musical instrumentation that preceded them. The number of instruments had greatly increased; they were increasingly individualised and grouped into orchestral sections, enabling orchestras to swell to as many as 150 musicians. The symphony, as a form, was unimaginable without orchestra as its external, technical foundation.

* * *

Thus, real life everywhere is the result of the mutual intertwining of two independent factors. In biology, it is the unity of a physical-chemical foundation and a—let us call it—*entelechial* principle. In history, it is the shared agency of a material base and the creative influence of the human, conscious factor—manifested through powerful personalities, dominant ideas, and guiding ideals. The historical state of affairs at any given moment is the result of these two fundamentally independent forces.

The influence of man on the course of history varies, depending on the degree of his will and awareness. The greater the spiritual strength of the people participating in a historical event, the greater their independence from the laws of the external world. This conditionality is in inverse proportion to the awareness and activity of the subject. In principle, the human being is completely free, and external laws hold no power over him. There are instances where people have managed to resist disease and danger by sheer willpower. A man alone among a pride of lions would ordinarily be doomed—but that seemingly natural law does not apply to the lion-tamer. History is an unbroken account of small groups of determined, courageous, and intelligent individuals leaving an indelible mark and altering the flow of events.[44] So-called objective circumstances possess more power the more a human being becomes passive—less a subject and more an object among objects. We gain power over nature, even over history, only when we gain power over ourselves. This is, roughly, the Islamic stance on history.

This essentially Islamic view of historical development not only offers a successful explanation of the flow of events but also defines the real extent of human influence over historical occurrences—clarifying the limits and possibilities of our power, our capacity to shape events, and the distinction between what we wish to do and what we must do as participants in history. Such an understanding explains the possibility of creative intervention by ideas in historical reality and the possibility of transforming that reality through the will and energy of human beings. At the same time, it recognises the role of objective factors and the necessity of grounding action in facts. It rejects historical determinism as firmly as it rejects empty idealism cut off from reality. In this view, facts and ideas, reality and humanity, each hold their rightful place.

44 Qur'an, 2: 249 and 65.

CHAPTER 9

ISLAMIC NATURE OF EVERY LAW

THE DUALISM OF LAW

If the legal system represents human interest protected in the form of rights, as it is commonly defined, then both religion and socialism are inherently ill-suited to the concept of law as a legal system. Religion does not comprehend interest; socialism does not comprehend rights. No right can be founded merely on the basis of interest. It cannot even be legitimately grounded in so-called 'common interest' (or the famous 'reason of state'), because the rationale of common interest and the inalienable rights of individuals are naturally in conflict. If a human being is not recognised as a personality (as is the case in socialism, where he is seen solely as a member of society), then he does not possess any absolute, *a priori*, natural rights. He can only have the 'rights' that the state sees fit to grant him. Outside this framework, the member of society has no other rights.

Rights are inalienable only if they are self-originating—if they are not the product of a monarch's will, a parliamentary decree, or a class decision, but rather a gift of nature or of God; in short, if they are innate and emerge with the human being himself. They are an aspect of human dignity and, as such, transcend time, circumstances, and history, reaching all the way back to Creation. This is the essential link between natural rights and religion—and the clear line of separation between natural rights and materialism.

In *On the Jewish Question* (1844), Marx writes: 'So-called human rights, *droits de l'homme*, unlike *droits du citoyen*, are nothing more than the rights of members of civil society, i.e. the egoistic man, man separated from other men and the community.' Another materialist thinker, Jeremy Bentham, dismissed the concept of human rights with scorn: 'Natural rights is simple nonsense: natural and imprescriptible rights, rhetorical nonsense—nonsense upon stilts.' In one of his texts, Bentham describes the French *Declaration of the Rights of Man* as a 'metaphysical construct'—which, in a way, it is. Georg Jellinek argues that 'The Declaration of Human Rights is an act of the Reformation, not of the Revolution,'[45] and tracing the origins of the tricolour principles—Liberty, Equality, Brotherhood—leads us back to J. J. Rousseau and the American *Declaration of Independence* of 1776, which was itself preceded by the religiously rooted freedom of conscience.

Even Ernst Bloch, who sought reconciliation between Marxism and natural law, was ultimately forced to concede: 'It is not sustainable to claim that humans are born free and equal. There are no inherent rights; all rights are won—or remain to be won—through struggle.'[46]

That is why, from this standpoint, the meaning of history is not a conflict of rights, but a conflict of interests. This is the essence of the so-called 'class struggle'. Whoever prevails in this struggle declares their interest to be a right and expresses their will in the form of law. Hence the Marxist claim: law is the will of the ruling class turned into legislation. In such a view, there is no law and lawlessness, no justice or injustice, no morality or immorality—only interest, which proves stronger in a clash of powers.[47]

---

45 Jellinek, *The Declaration of the Rights of Man* (1904)

46 E. Bloch, *Natural Law and Human Dignity* (Belgrade, 1977) *p. 178.*

47 Here is one such definition of 'law': 'Law is the sum of rules of conduct that express the will of the ruling class... The application of these rules is carried out by the coercive power of the state for the purpose of ensuring, consolidating, and developing social relations and conditions that are in

But this amounts to nothing more than the law of the stronger. Yet every true law is, in fact, the opposite: the law of the weaker—for the strong need no law. Law has always served as a means for the weak to resist the strong, just as freedom of thought and belief is first and foremost the right to think and believe differently. A law that would guarantee citizens the 'right' to constantly applaud and glorify the ruling elite would be a cynical parody of law. The true test of legality in any social order is precisely its treatment of opponents and minorities. The rule of the stronger is a fact, not law. Law begins at the moment and in the place where some limitation of that dominance is introduced—naturally, limitations made in the interest of the weaker, not the stronger. 'Every dictatorship is a suspension of law', says Bloch. This applies equally to the dictatorship of the proletariat. Is this not precisely what Lenin described as 'rule that is unlimited by law and reliant on violence'? In practice, the dictatorship of the proletariat has everywhere devolved into a dictatorship of the secretariat.[48] The claim that law is the will of the ruling class is, therefore, a negation of law itself. The same holds for definitions such as Lenin's 'law is the measure of politics' or Vyshinsky's 'every legal consciousness is a part of political consciousness'. There is no doubt that this negation of law is inseparably linked to the negation of religion, making it a direct consequence of materialist philosophy.

---

line with and beneficial to the ruling class.' A. Vyshinsky, *The Main Tasks of the Science of Soviet Socialist Law* (1938). The author of this definition, as the chief state prosecutor of the USSR during the 'purges' of 1936–1939, had the opportunity to demonstrate in practice where such a view leads.

48 In one of the 'Six Theses on the Next Tasks of Soviet Power' from 1920, Lenin wrote: 'Subordination—without objection—during work to the personal orders of Soviet leaders, dictators elected or appointed by Soviet institutions and vested with dictatorial powers, is still ensured very inadequately.' V.I. Lenin, *Collected Works*, 4th edn (Moscow, 1955), vol. 29, p. 162. And in June 1979, the largest Chinese daily, Renmin Ribao, issued a statement as unexpected as it was bold: 'What was understood as the dictatorship of the proletariat over the past ten or more years was, in fact, a feudal, fascist dictatorship.' Had Mao Zedong not died, it would still be considered 'the authentic rule of the working people.'

For what, other than religion, could provide a basis for limiting the power of the strong? Why, and on what grounds, should a nation tolerate a minority it could easily suppress and from whom it could seize property? What principle—of what kind—did white settlers violate in their destruction and displacement of Indigenous peoples in the Americas? If law is merely the will of the ruling class, then their actions were entirely lawful—they were stronger and historically more progressive, and thus embodied the 'ruling class'. What principles did capitalists violate during what Marx described as the period of 'primitive accumulation' of capital? If the ruling class's will defines the law, then capitalists, in exploiting labour, were not committing injustice but simply exercising their rights. In this case, workers resisting such exploitation would be, paradoxically, acting unlawfully—since they opposed that famed 'will of the ruling class'.

This *reductio ad absurdum* exposes the flaw at the heart of such reasoning: where law exists, it is not the will of the ruling class, but a principle that limits that will. Law is therefore an independent principle.[49]

Examining the nature of this principle presents the same difficulties as examining the nature of life, art, or freedom. True laws in human society are only those that bind not merely through the fear of sanctions, but also through appeal to the conscience of the citizen. Every legal order is either genuinely of this kind or at least presents itself as such. Even where rule or law is, in theory, divorced from all moral components, in practice it tries to cloak itself in moral, human attributes. The dictatorship of the proletariat, in practice, seeks to portray itself as democracy. Law, which is defined as 'the will of the ruling class turned into

49 One striking piece of evidence for this is the fact that even slave-owning Roman law had to declare the principle of human freedom: '*Ab initio omnes homines liberi nascebantur*' (From the beginning all men were born free). Without this, it would not have been law, but rather a 'measure of politics'.

law', ceases to be mere 'will' and seeks to appear as justice, fairness—in other words, law in the higher sense. This 'doubling' is inescapable; it is, in fact, an expression—or an imitation—of the natural, original dualism inherent in every law.[50]

Law ceases to exist if this dualism is destroyed. In one case, it becomes degraded to its subject—interest, force, politics, the Roman *utilitas*; in another, it is sublimated into the realm of abstract justice or moral appeal. In both cases, it ceases to be law.

* * *

It is for this reason that neither Christianity nor materialism can create law. Law cannot be based on a single principle. Christianity sees in law merely an illusory attempt to organise the world—a doomed attempt. Because Christ came to establish love in place of Old Testament justice, and love is not worldly, but a supreme heavenly virtue (Thomas Aquinas, *Summa Theologiae*, II, 1, 91). Christ explicitly rejects the role of judge (Luke 12:13–15), and Hugo Grotius severed the earlier link between natural law and the Sermon on the Mount, citing its, as he put it, 'holier than thou' character. Materialism, by contrast, sees law as an idealistic construct—static, and even reactionary. On one hand, law is interested, social, political, objective, entirely of this world; on the other hand, it is normative and ethical. It seeks to introduce the principle of equity—a principle of moral order—into worldly relations, thus invoking something that is 'not of this world'. Seen this way, law is a bipolar unity—like man, like Islam.

50 All law began as customary law. There was no distinction between custom and morality, which is still reflected in language (for example, in French: *les moeurs*/custom). When a judge ruled according to customary law, they were effectively applying prevailing moral conceptions. This situation later led to endless debates aimed at proving the separation of law from morality. Now, as we can see, the opposite thesis must be proven: the distinction between law and interest. This controversy surrounding law is only possible because law is at once both morality and interest—just as much a 'mathematics of ethics' (Hermann Cohen) as it is a 'measure of politics'. (Lenin)

Thus, law cannot be established through religion or materialism. But it cannot be established against them either.

Without the Christian affirmation of the value of human personality, the intention of equity, inalienable human rights, and everything that Christianity confirmed and established—there is no law. On the other hand, without acknowledging the value and importance of the external world, without interest and force, without everything that Judaism affirmed and sanctioned, law would make no sense. Without the Christian approach, law would not be possible; without the Jewish one, it would not be necessary. The conclusion that every law is Islamic by its nature arises from these two premises. That is why neither Christianity nor Judaism created their own authentic legal systems—only Islam did.

Viewed historically, law is a phenomenon of maturity in the life of a culture. It emerges at the point of balance between religious and socio-political aspirations in human consciousness. It is the moment when religious conceptions remain strong enough to influence perception and behaviour, yet are already significantly limited by the rationalist and utilitarian scruples of an advancing civilised age. Society becomes an independent value, alongside the individual whose worth was affirmed by religion. At this moment, these two are equal values—whose balance (the 'Islamic' balance) makes possible the emergence and full development of law.

This transformation can be observed in the formation of the three most renowned legal systems in history: Roman, Islamic, and European.

The original phase of Roman law, historically known as the period of civil law (the age of the empire and the first three centuries of the republic), was marked by the complete unity of law and religion—*ius* and *fas*. Legal rule (*ius*) had the character of religious norm (*fas*), and vice versa. Later, these two principles would separate organically, but Roman civilisation and its political (state) thought had to be infused with Stoic moral-religious philosophy in order to bring about the advancement of Roman law. The Stoic idealist principle of *lex universalis* merged with the Roman empirical principle of *utilitas*.[51] Neither Roman civilisation nor Stoic philosophy could, on their own, have produced Roman law without the contribution of the other.[52]

In the case of Islam, we encounter a kind of 'personal union' between law and theology. Almost all great 'religious' authorities of Islam wrote legal works.[53] In most cases, it is impossible for a European reader to separate law from theology in these texts. (Islam does not even recognise such a separation.) In a certain sense, law is the natural product of Islam. Alfred V. Kremer writes:

> Arabs are the only nation of the early Middle Ages that achieved significant results in the development and scientific interpretation of legal thought. Their achievements, in their magnificence, stand immediately next to those of the Romans—those legislators of the world.

The development of law in European history begins with the defeat of the supremacy of the Church and continues until the emergence of socialist teachings and socialism on the

51 We certainly owe to the influence of Stoicism those exalted passages where Roman law rises to the true heights of justice. For example: '*iuris praecepta sunt haec: honeste vivere, alterum non laedere, suum cuique tribuere*' ('these are the precepts of law: to live honourably to harm no one, to give each their due').

52 Roman jurists came into contact with Stoic natural law around 150 BC, when Panaetius, one of the most prominent Stoics of the time, stayed in Rome. The most fruitful result of this synthesis is undoubtedly the works of Cicero. For more on the influence of Stoicism on Roman law, see: P. Barth, *Die Stoa*, p. 120 and onwards.

53 For example, the renowned imam Abu Yusuf wrote a treatise on finance (*Kitab al-Kharaj*), while another prominent 'religious' scholar, al-Shaybani, authored a book on the laws of war (*Kitab al-Siyar*).

European stage. This period, spanning a few centuries in which elements of both European culture and civilisation co-exist in parallel, is the age of the great European charters and legal codes. This duality—Islamic in essence—is expressed vividly in the great legal opus of Hugo Grotius, a central figure in European legislative thought. He summarised the teachings of Catholic and Protestant legal writers near the end of the Reformation period and demonstrated how law is simultaneously dependent on and independent of ethics and religion. Thanks to this dualism, a number of writers (such as K. Werner and H. Ahrens) would later attempt to prove that the separation of law and morality was largely the achievement of Grotius, while others (such as Kirchmann) argued the opposite. Yet it is precisely in Grotius's claim that God is the ultimate source of law (*De Iure Belli ac Pacis* (*On the Law of War and Peace*, Book I, 1.10.2) that he unequivocally reaffirms that every law is dependent on religion.

* * *

The independence of law cannot be entirely extinguished, even within the most extreme form of a Marxist state. Despite clear theoretical positions, it has proven impossible to equate law completely with the will of the authorities—there is always an insurmountable gap, whether large or small. Experience has shown that socialism and a developed, independent, and free legal system are fundamentally incompatible.[54] Every legal system requires a degree of separation, distance, and normative detachment. Directness, objectivity, and *action directe* suit socialism. In a socialist system—which transfers the conceptual framework of physics (or biology) to social life—there is no space for law, because law is

54 As late as 1978, thirty years after its establishment, the People's Republic of China still had neither a civil nor a criminal code. The drafting of laws had long been considered a 'forbidden zone' (according to the statement of renowned Chinese jurist Han Ji Tung at a legal consultation in 1978).

the precise opposite of physics, which recognises only what is, not what should be.[55]

The low reputation of courts in the countries of so-called 'people's democracy' is a consequence of an ideological stance towards law, which, despite all pressures, still retains elements of natural law and is not reducible to the will of the ruling class. The court, as a direct executor and enforcer of law, shares the fate of law in general and, as such, becomes 'unfavourable' (the case is the same for social standing of the legal profession, as is easily observed). Every such authority attempts to reduce law to the level of politics and the court to that of a secretariat. However, since this is never fully achieved, the court is circumvented, and in moments of necessity, the regime resorts to direct persecution through police, administrative organs, and concentration camps—thus through extrajudicial and extra-legal means.

The state and its authority represent physical power, whereas the court and the law symbolise moral authority. To acknowledge that the moral authority of the court (of the law) can counterbalance the physical power of the state is, essentially, to admit the supremacy of the idea over matter, of spirit over objects. Judicial independence—even when implying equality or superiority over the state's physical power—is an irrational principle yet affirmed in every culture and, of course, in every religion, but it is incompatible with the system of an atheist state, as it contradicts the very principle upon which that system is founded.[56]

---

55 'Evgeny Pashukanis, the most prominent Soviet legal theorist between the two wars (who disappeared during Stalin's purges), consistently argued that there is no such thing as proletarian law, and that there should no longer be any socialist law.' (J. P., *General Theory of Law and Marxism*, (1929) p. 33) This view should be compared with the opposite, yet 'equally radical' Christian negation of law by Rudolf Sohm: 'Church law stands in contradiction to the very essence of the Church.' (Rudolf Sohm, *Canon Law*).

56 It is worth noting how, in these countries, the principle of judicial permanence—guaranteeing the independence of judges and the rights of

The mere formalism and lack of adherence to their own laws, as well as the excessive production or inflation of subordinate legislation, fall into the same category.[57] This is a consequence of *action directe*, or the aspiration that laws be replaced by political actions or purely political acts, letters, messages, or even speeches by officials, which then become more important than constitutions and laws (recall, for example, the quotations of Mao Zedong). An insufficient authority of representative bodies—appearing more as mere formalities—can be observed in all states of this type, alongside the considerable power granted to executive and law enforcement bodies at the expense of courts and legal practice. Both the attempt by such states to reduce the judiciary to the status of obedient administration and their inability to fully achieve this clearly reveal something essential about the nature of law and the relationship between religion, law, and atheism.

* * *

Almost without exception, people implicitly believe in the existence of the soul when participating in acts of justice and behave accordingly. If someone admits to committing a murder but claims it was unintentional, then what exactly are all parties involved in the judicial process—the prosecutor, defence lawyer, witnesses, experts, and court—actually engaged in? What are they examining, making considerable effort, giving erudite speeches, and meticulously analysing, when the act itself has already been admitted and its external consequences

citizens—has been replaced by the opposite principle: re-election. The re-election system places judges in a position of complete dependence on the authorities. Judges must constantly ensure they remain 'in favour' with those who decide on their reappointment. Needless to say, this situation has severely degraded the judicial profession.

57 For example, in the USSR, during the period from 1937 to 1974, around 370 laws were enacted. In the same period, the executive branch (the Council of Ministers, individual ministries, and similar executive bodies) issued over 700,000 subordinate legal acts.

are both clear and indisputable? All their endeavours concern not the objective external facts, but rather an internal issue: the question of intention—not something that happened externally, but something that occurred internally. Even when evidence presented relates to facts, these facts are relevant only to the extent that they help uncover intention. In reality, we examine facts primarily to reveal what is essential—the state of the soul. Moreover, each participant in this judicial process spontaneously considers matters related to intention, volition, and will as immeasurably more important than the act itself and its external consequences. Thus, all participants, even without being fully aware, implicitly recognise the supremacy of the soul over external reality. A worker who unintentionally causes a mining accident resulting in the deaths of a hundred miners is considered less responsible and receives a lesser punishment than a person who intentionally kills an elderly lady nearing the end of her life for personal gain. Does this seemingly 'illogical' judgement—one that will always be completely understandable to us as long as we remain human—not imply an implicit recognition of the soul's existence, and that we ultimately judge not by what occurred in the external world but rather by what occurred within the perpetrator's soul? Human justice thus aspires and attempts to imitate divine justice. Indeed, human justice comes closer to divine justice precisely by respecting intention, aspiration, and motive.

> There is no blame on you for what you do by mistake, but 'only' for what you do intentionally. (Qur'an, 33:5)

Even minimally respecting intention implies the recognition of God and thus a renunciation of materialism. We can immediately see how this logic, when reversed, inevitably led materialist philosophy towards the negation of personal responsibility, guilt, and justice, and instead affirmed an opposing, objective principle: social protection. This development was entirely logical.

PUNISHMENT AND SOCIAL PROTECTION

The issue we are discussing concerns the justification of sanctions against offenders, and it undoubtedly relates to the classical question of whether human actions are free or determined (either by the offender's constitution, life circumstances, or both). On one side are those who justify the use of sanctions based on the freedom of choice inherent in every individual; on the other side are those who argue that punishment serves no purpose because the perpetrator's behaviour is predetermined. According to this latter view, the offender acts out of necessity, meaning that punishment is as ineffective and unjustified as it would be for a sick person. For these thinkers, there is no place for punishment, only for 'social protection' (*défense sociale*)—measures designed to safeguard society from the actions of individuals who cannot be held morally accountable. Thus, the first group starts from the concept of freedom, while the second group begins with determinism; the former emphasises personality, the latter society.

The dilemma of punishment versus social protection is as old as criminal legislation itself, yet examining it here enables us to revisit some of the questions explored in this book from a fresh angle. The concepts of guilt (*dolus*) and punishment appear as early as the Code of Hammurabi, the oldest known legal code, while R. van der Made has demonstrated that notions of social protection existed among the ancient Greeks.[58]

58 R. van der Made: 'Contribution to the Study of the History of Social Defence', *Revue de Criminologie et de Droit pénal* (1949–1950) p. 944.

Individualists hold that the responsibility for a criminal act lies solely with the offender. Positivists, however, place responsibility upon society and external circumstances—in other words, factors outside the individual. The former perspective does not inherently imply that humans are evil, nor does the latter imply they are inherently good. Rather, the individualist view sees a human as a subject, a free and responsible personality, while the positivist view regards a person as an object among objects, a biological entity subject to the unavoidable laws of nature and thus unable to strive for true freedom. In essence, the first position rests on the belief that humans are inherently capable of being either good or bad, inevitably choosing one or the other. Conversely, the second contains the view that humans, by themselves, are neither good nor bad; instead, circumstances dictate their behaviour, which we subsequently classify as good or evil according to a certain moral code. A positivist does not accept the existence of a free personality as an autonomous bearer of choice and thus responsibility.

However, it would be incorrect to assume that either of these two perspectives has conclusively proven to be harsher or milder in criminal law. As we shall see, the outcome depends on numerous other factors.

Starting from the principle of social protection, it is possible to arrive at different, even opposing conclusions regarding measures taken against perpetrators. One possible conclusion is that cruelty has no justification, as the act results from given circumstances, rendering any punishment senseless. However, it is also possible to conclude that objective danger or considerations of prevention justify the severity of the punishment, potentially leading to very harsh and entirely unjust measures.

The history of criminal law similarly demonstrates that the concept of individual guilt has led both to extremely severe punishments (such as the Inquisition) and to exceptionally humane approaches to punishment. Even in debates concerning the justification of the death penalty, proponents of both perspectives can be found on either side.[59]

The death penalty can be defended and criticised from both standpoints; the difference is that, for individualists, it serves as a sanction against a free personality for an exceptionally severe manifestation of ill will, whereas for advocates of social protection, it represents the 'dismantling' of a corrupt or defective part of the social mechanism. Thus, in the first case, the justification will carry a more humane explanation, whereas in the second, it will be explained in an impersonal, mechanical manner. These explanations clearly reveal their underlying philosophical or metaphysical foundations, evoking the 'prologue in heaven' in the first instance, and Darwinism and evolution in the other. However, one point remains evident: every individualist stance will always incorporate punishment as retribution, while the materialist viewpoint will always adopt measures—perhaps severe and extreme, but always essentially extra-criminal in nature—aiming, as M. Ancel notes, to 'neutralise' the delinquent (note this expression borrowed from physics), either by elimination, isolation, or through methods aimed at treatment or re-education.[60]

Generally speaking, the difference between punishment and protective measures lies in the fact that the former focuses on justice, and the latter on interests; the former addresses personality, while the latter concerns society. The severity of punishment corresponds to the level of guilt, whereas the type of protective measure depends on the objective (social)

59 For example, the Swiss jurist M. Graven, an active representative of the social defence movement, advocates for the reintroduction of the death penalty in Switzerland.

60 In this respect, there is hardly any exception in theory. The idealist Kant (and Hegel) advocates almost literally for 'an eye for an eye'. In contrast, the materialist Holbach completely rejects the principle of retribution in criminal law (Holbach, Système de la nature).

danger posed by the perpetrator. Since both punishment and protective measures usually involve revoking or restricting the rights of the perpetrator, protective measures can entail significant limitations of rights even without the individual bearing any guilt. This can lead to particularly severe and unjust forms when measures are implemented for security reasons or general deterrence, intended to intimidate potential offenders—an approach frequently employed, indeed misused, to suppress political offences. Stalin's purges represent a drastic example of this, with data indicating that almost ten million people were 'purged' from society. It should be noted that a purge is not punishment but rather the removal of elements from society that disturb someone or something. Both 'neutralisation' and 'purge' are mechanical processes and mechanical terms. In contrast, punishment is a moral concept that first appears in religious texts when discussing divine punishment, indicating both terminological and historical connections between religion and the theory of punishment. Idealist philosophy underpins legislation that emphasises punishment, while positivism supports legislation advocating protective measures.

A trial accompanies punishment, just as treatment accompanies social protection measures. Yet, a trial is a drama unfolding around the profound and exalted questions of freedom, responsibility, justice, and injustice. Trials have always been associated with certain ceremonies reminiscent of drama or ritual.[61] Conversely, a protective measure is a matter of expediency, determined by a doctor, psychologist, sociologist, or the authorities—but certainly not by a judge. Principally speaking, setting aside practical inconsistencies, protective measures are an integral part of the broader manipulation of

61 E. Bloch demonstrated that drama has a dual origin: judicial and mystical (E. Bloch, *ibid*, p. 238), while Benjamin showed that its famous three unities—of place, time, and action—also stem from the judicial origins of tragedy (Benjamin, *The Origin of German Tragic Drama* (1928) p. 111).

human individuals in utopias. In utopias, there are no courts or trials, as there is neither freedom nor responsibility—just as there is no ethics or law.

That is why we say: we pronounce judgement and conviction upon a free and responsible individual, whereas we defend ourselves and society from a mere member of society. A member of society carries neither guilt nor responsibility; they can only be harmful or beneficial, not as a matter of choice but simply of facts—and facts in themselves are morally meaningless. Humanism is not necessarily the same as mercy. 'You have compassion toward the lame and blind; why should you not have compassion toward the bad ones? They are bad against their will.' This sentence by Epictetus contains mercy, but it has neither humanism nor religion. Humanism affirms the human as a free being, and therefore as a responsible being. Nothing degrades humans more profoundly than proclaiming their irresponsibility. Humans are responsible; only animals and objects are not. Herein lies the difference between Stoicism (Stoa) and religion. Stoicism places mercy and forgiveness in the foreground, whereas religion emphasises responsibility.[62] Religion is the most consistent proclamation of human responsibility and, accordingly, human value. At its core, *défense sociale* is an inhumane theory—even when it frees people or imposes mild measures—because it declares people irresponsible for their actions. Conversely, the theory of guilt is humane and human, even when it involves harsh punishments. Punishment is a human right of the offender, and its denial is correlated with the denial of other human rights. Hegel consistently maintains that punishment is simply retribution in accordance with the offender's human dignity, and it should not have any other practical goals, such as deterrence or re-education. Responsibility represents the highest expression of human worth and dignity, holding

62 Qur'an, 75:38, 23:16, and others.

moral—that is, otherworldly—significance. Human responsibility on earth, before other humans, exists precisely because his responsibility in an absolute sense exists—responsibility in eternity, before God. Indeed, this eternal responsibility of the free personality for their actions, or more accurately, for their choices, is the condition that enables human responsibility in this world, before other humans. All legislation in the world is merely a pale attempt to realise the Divine court on Earth.

Herein lies the explanation for why materialism will always seek different arguments, such as social utility or harm, rather than the responsibility of the individual. Categories such as responsibility, punishment and trial do not belong within the conceptual framework of materialism.

* * *

The aim of punishment is neither prevention, nor protection, nor compensation, nor deterrence, nor even the improvement of the offender; therefore, it pursues none of these practical worldly goals. Its purpose is the establishment of balance within a moral order that has been disturbed by committing a forbidden action. Punishment represents the negation of an act which itself negates the law. Thus, it is a negation of a negation (Hegel), a *remedium peccati*. Although this definition might sound overly abstract and lifeless, it is inevitable. Regardless of all subsequent developments linking punishment with numerous other considerations—especially those related to prevention and protection—punishment, wherever it exists, invariably retains its original meaning: it remains retribution, a moral response to an immoral act, often practically useless or even damaging. Conversely, a protective measure is always motivated by utility, protecting a greater interest by sacrificing a lesser one, subordinating the individual's interest to that of society. Punishment aims at a moral effect, while protective measures invariably aim at social utility.

The concept of retributive punishment originates from religious notions that crime incurs the wrath of God. Despite all subsequent limitations and adjustments, this idea can never be entirely displaced from the understanding of criminal justice. Some interpretations may invoke an offended moral order instead of God and God's anger, but this represents merely a terminological rather than an essential change, as God is perceived as the creator and guardian of the moral order.

All the points outlined here are, of course, theoretical considerations. Two facts are particularly relevant to the subject discussed in this book: firstly, that alongside the principle of guilt, a theory of social defence inevitably emerged as its inverse counterpart; and secondly, that in practical life, within the law-making process, positive legislation—regardless of the philosophical stance it invokes—never produces 'pure' laws. Each positive law invariably exhibits traces of the theoretically rejected principle. Thus, to the best of our knowledge, no criminal legislation in practice is entirely based on the principle of guilt, nor is there any legislation that consistently implements the concept of social protection. There is only a greater or lesser predominance of one of these two principles.[63]

Even the *Défense sociale* movement itself, which emerged in the nineteenth century initially advocating extreme positions, inevitably evolved over time. One of its prominent proponents, Marc Ancel, writes: 'In the period between the two great wars, a middle-path view (*media via*) finally triumphed in positive legislation, bridging the classical doctrines of guilt-based retribution and social protection.'[64] Ancel further asks: 'Does it necessarily follow, then, that the concept of social

63 The Italian Penal Code may serve as an example of the predominance of the principle of culpability. In contrast, the criminal codes of the Scandinavian countries—and in particular the new Penal Code of Iceland—offer opposing examples.

64 M. Ancel, *The New Social Defence* (Paris, 1954).

protection implies the rejection of any enforced legal procedure, and ultimately, the rejection of punishment in general? Should there be a definitive commitment either to criminal law or social protection? Many committed supporters of social protection, conversely, understand that criminal law and social protection must be unified within a new perspective.'[65] The evolution of the International Union of Criminal Law (*L'Union internationale de droit pénal*) also clearly demonstrates the necessity of such a synthesis. Initially a prominent advocate of social protection since its establishment in 1889, this institution gradually embraced ideas of moral responsibility, ultimately stating in an official document during its twenty-fifth-anniversary celebration in 1914 that 'it now represents both doctrines'. The outcome in legal theory was the emergence of the so-called 'relative theory of punishment', while practical legislation introduced the concept of 'protective punishment' (combining protection and punishment)—a form of 'bipolar unity' within the realm of justice. The 'third way' thus prevailed in practice.

Islam, as a religion, begins from the principle of retribution; however, as an Islamised religion, it also integrates elements of social protection. This development corresponds exactly to the notion of 'obligation towards this world', which transformed prayer into salah, almsgiving into zakat, and a purely spiritual community into the ummah—a community both spiritual and political. Islamic criminal law historically featured a distinct re-education system for minors, closely aligned with modern understandings. Additionally, it employed the principle of free judicial evaluation of evidence and, to some extent, recognised sociological interpretations of offences and offenders.

Marc Ancel further notes:

65 M. Ancel, the same.

Islamic law in the fourteenth century, acknowledging the irresponsibility of children below the age of seven and prescribing exclusively educational measures (without a punitive character) for minors aged between seven and puberty, established a system for adult offenders that could already be regarded as a precursor to modern social protection. With the exception of five major crimes explicitly defined and sanctioned by the Qur'an, a number of offences were left to the discretionary judgement of the court, which was obligated simultaneously to consider the nature of the committed offence, the circumstances under which it was committed, and the personality of the offender.[66]

66 For more on this, see: Said Mustapha el-Said Bey, 'The Notion of Criminal Responsibility' in *Proceedings of the International Week of Muslim Law* (Paris, 1951) and L. Miliot, *Introduction to the Study of Muslim Law* (Paris, 1953).

CHAPTER 10

ON THE IMPOSSIBILITY OF PURE RELIGION AND PURE MATERIALISM

IDEAS AND REALITY

Both religion and utopia become distorted when they enter practical life—when and if they become actual life practices. Their pure and consistent forms exist only within books. In real human practice, religion becomes naturalised; it accepts certain elements of humanity's lower, animalistic nature. Conversely, utopia becomes humanised, acquiring moral characteristics. The deformation of both Christianity and materialism always involves moving closer to human beings, to their genuine, animalistic–human nature. In the first case, it represents a descent from the divine; in the second, an ascent from the animalistic. In both instances, it is essentially a movement towards the humanistic.

Several familiar phenomena from the history of Christianity illustrate different aspects of this inevitable deformation when the religion collides with practical life. These primarily include: the institutionalisation of religion (the establishment of the Church); the recognition of marriage (as opposed to sexual purity); the acceptance of labour (St Augustine); changed attitudes towards property, authority, education, and science (in contrast to the Gospel sentence: 'Blessed are the poor in spirit'); and the embrace of force and violence (such as the Inquisition). In recent times, this also includes Christianity's conciliatory stance towards Marxism, a subject discussed further below.

Similar deviations, albeit in the opposite direction, can be observed in Marxist practice—that is, in materialism. These deviations include the adoption (even if only declaratively) of certain humanist principles proclaimed by the French Revolution (such as the rights of man and citizen); the acceptance of some 'prejudices' from the cultural heritage of past centuries (personal freedom, freedom of thought, the sanctity of correspondence, residence, etc.); the use of moral incentives as a reward for labour (contrary to the principle that humans are exclusively motivated by self-interest); the decisive role of a political party as a subjective and conscious factor; the cult of personality; the presentation of one's own courts and legislation as 'objective', fair, and universally social (contrary to the definition of law as the 'will of the ruling class'); acceptance of marriage, family, private property, and the state (contrary to classic Marxist positions); retaining the principle of guilt in law; the proclamation of heroes; the continued use of terms like 'brotherhood' and 'homeland' ('fraternal assistance', 'fraternal parties'), and the concept of a 'patriotic war' (are brotherhood and homeland not simply bourgeois delusions?); insistence in practice on certain norms of public morality (criticism of pornography, nudity, and sexual licentiousness); appeals to live and work for the glory of the 'socialist homeland'; the adoption of so-called heroic literature; and ideological and theoretical dogmatism (are there 'eternal truths'?), among others.

Regardless of religion essentially being always and exclusively a call to live for the future world, humans have consistently connected their everyday aspirations and hopes with religion—thus, in practice, they have sought Islam. It has been historically established that communal meals called 'agape' significantly contributed to conversions to Christianity during the early period of this religion. There is also evidence suggesting that prayers for the 'forgiveness of sins' were easily misconstrued as requests for the 'forgiveness of debts', prompting one of the Church Fathers, Tertullian, to intervene authoritatively to preserve the authentic meaning of forgiveness of sins. Numerous movements in the Middle Ages simultaneously had religious and social characters, making their precise nature difficult to interpret unambiguously. Moreover, certain modern socialist movements continue to invoke texts from the Holy Scripture. These facts confirm Islam's general view that pure religion and pure politics exist only as abstract ideas; in practical life, only their mixture is present, and in some cases, isolating their distinct components is nearly impossible!

JESUS AND CHRISTIANITY

When we discuss the impossibility of realising pure religion in this world, one essential example cannot be overlooked: the historical failure of Christianity. To properly understand subsequent events, we must differentiate between the history of Christ and the history of Christianity within the phenomenon of Christianity itself. On one side, there is Jesus; on the other, all of Christianity. Over history, this difference has evolved into the distinction between the divine and the human in human consciousness, which it indeed is in a certain sense. It also provided occasion, and subsequently sustained, the dogma of Jesus as the Son of God. Hidden in the Christian myth of the God-man lies the acknowledgment of Christianity's impracticability in real life. 'The last Christian died on the cross', as Nietzsche stated. Some authors argue that the impracticability of Christianity is the hidden idea within Cervantes' famous book, with Don Quixote as a caricature of Christ. Some even termed that book the 'Black Gospel'. Jesus himself objected to his first heir, Peter, stating that he 'savourest not the things that be of God, but those that be of men' (Matthew 16:23, KJV). Yet Peter is 'the rock' upon which the Church was built. With this statement, Jesus marked—ahead of everyone else—the essence of the entire subsequent history of Christianity—of Christianity as a church: its alienation from Christ.

The historical process through which Christianity transformed from Christ's teaching—pure religion—into ideology, Church, and organisation is one of the most dramatic and significant events in human history. After persecutions lasting nearly three centuries—representing history's most persistent wrestling between religion and godlessness—Greco-Roman history began reconciling with this new state of affairs. This reconciliation inevitably signalled its downfall, something which seemingly only Diocletian clearly recognised and predicted. The Roman state and political rule descended the same steep slope that the victorious faith ascended. *The Edict of Toleration* towards Christianity was issued in 311 by Emperor Galerius, and shortly thereafter, in 313, Emperor Constantine issued the edict recognising Christianity officially. By transforming a spiritual community into a solid organisation, a political force out of the Church, Emperor Constantine took the decisive step in the historical deformation of Christianity. Synods confirmed doctrine in the fourth century, and liturgy was enriched with ceremonies and cults, some of which had pagan origins. The cults of saints and the Virgin Mary emerged. Early in the fifth century, Emperor Theodosius II declared Christianity the state religion, followed by an edict against pagans in 435. Thus began the formation of the clergy, and the title of metropolitan emerged.

> Christianity executed a synthesis of two great types of priests known in ancient societies: the Hellenic and the Oriental. The first type was a chosen magistrate and servant of the gods, while the second was initiated into mysteries, a true intermediary.[67]

The New Testament was mostly codified by the end of the second century, and the cross was definitively confirmed as a symbol of faith at the Council of Nicaea in 325. A strict discipline of understanding and interpreting religion and religious texts replaced free, personal interpretation. The bishop assumed spiritual functions and became an absolute authority in religious matters. He was already being paid from the

67 Lucien Henry, *The Origins of Religion.*

church treasury. Membership of the Church was established through the ceremonies of baptism and the Eucharist. The dogmas and teachings were determined by regional bishops' synods, whose meetings were modelled after assemblies. With this, the process of Church formation was largely complete.

All great and true Christians—regardless of the era in which they appeared—have felt that Christ's teaching could not become a science in the true sense of the word, just as no play or painting can become science.[68] For 'personal faith comes from ecstasy; theology comes from mathematics' (Russell). The Church transformed Christianity into a systematised teaching, something akin to mathematics or biology.[69]

The contemporary Catholic theologian Karl Barth writes in his work *Dogmatics*: 'Dogmatics is the science through which the Church explains to itself, at the level of knowledge it has, the content of its preaching. It is a critical discipline etc.' As if the idea of love or universal brotherhood could become a subject of scientific analysis without ceasing to be what it was! This marked the beginning of Christianity's spiritual wandering: the endless debates about dogmas and sacred mysteries that followed shifted the centre of gravity from the moral core to the scholastic aspect of Jesus's teaching. Church organisations, with their erudition, formalism, hierarchy, wealth, and all those tragic fallacies and blunders emerged from Christ's teaching based on theology as science, signifying a process

68 In this regard, we find very clear and explicit lines in a contemporary work by Romano Guardini: 'There is no system of moral values, nor any religious attitude or life programme, that can be separated from the person of Christ and of which one could say: here, this is Christianity. Christianity is He Himself... A doctrinal content is Christian to the extent that it proceeds from His mouth... The person of Jesus Christ, in His historical unity and eternal radiance, is the very category that defines the essence, activity, and teaching of Christianity.' (R. Guardini, *The Essence of Christianity)*

69 B. Russell argues that theology took its model from mathematics just as much in ancient Greece as in the Middle Ages and throughout Europe up to the time of Kant (B. Russell, *A History of Western Philosophy, p. 56).*

of objectification and depersonalisation. That explains why, for instance, the monastic movement—an expression of authentic religious inspiration—arose everywhere outside the church organisation.[70] Christ's teaching is a living spring; the Church is a stagnant lake. The former resembles an artistic painting of wild beauty, while the latter is like a photograph framed in luxurious gold.

The contrast under discussion is deeper than just the difference between vision and reality—its various aspects reach the very essence of the matter. Jesus is the forefather of Christianity, whereas Paul (or Augustine) is the founder of the Church. Christian ethics originates with Jesus, while Christian theology stems from Paul. Even the Church's medieval intellectual oscillation between Plato and Aristotle is a consequence of this fundamental contradiction. Christ's teachings as religion are closer to Plato, whereas Christian theology aligns more with Aristotle. Russell holds that substituting Plato with Aristotle was a mistake, a viewpoint we can readily agree with.[71]

Jodl writes in *History of Ethics*:

> With regard to the atmosphere of practical life, we can differentiate between the teachings of original Christianity—if these can indeed be identified in the Gospels—and the later teachings of the Church (beginning as early as Pauline theology), as well as from the surrounding Jewish or pagan world.[72]

He further notes, 'Christianity as an ethical religion has always been sought and found in the Gospel; Christianity as a mystery religion and path to salvation—in the apostolic writings.' The Church has always appealed to Paul and his letters;

70 St Francis of Assisi, founder of the Franciscan order, was a layman with no theological education. His principal vow—the vow of poverty—was later officially rejected by the Church.

71 B. Russell, *Ibid.*, p. 464.

72 Friedrich Jodl, *History of Ethics in Modern Philosophy, p. 80.*

religion and morality have always appealed to Jesus and the Gospel. The simple yet exalted history of Christ ends with Paul, and the history of the priestly religion—the Church—begins. Unlike the Gospel, Paul affirms ownership, labour, earning a living, class distinctions, marriage, submission to authorities, inequality, and even slavery. On one side stand the Gospel and Christ; on the other side stand theology and the Church. The former represents the idea; the latter, reality.

MARX AND MARXISM

Marxism is largely consistent in theory and necessarily inconsistent in practice. It asserts that the human being is a product of external circumstances, both as a biological and a social entity; that being determines consciousness, rather than the other way around; and that our opinions, beliefs, and psychology merely reflect our social conditions. Historical events are not outcomes of human ideas and conscious actions, but result from objective factors independent of human will, subject to relentless determinism.

Feudalism was not dismantled because people desired or consciously pursued its end, regardless of how strong such desires and efforts might have been. Rather, feudalism disappeared due to changes (developments) in productive forces—material, unconscious, objective factors beyond human power and intent. The evolution of capitalism as a social system occurs entirely independently of the theories confidently put forward by thinkers, economists, lawyers, and ethicists. That evolution is solely a function of the economic base, productive forces, etc.

It would therefore be logical to assume that establishing a socialist order—achieving socialist revolution—does not depend on the influence of political parties, literature, police, or political measures, but primarily, or more precisely, exclusively, on the development of productive forces. A socialist revolution, according to Marxist theory, occurs when technological advancement and the growth of the industrial proletariat surpass existing production relationships to such an extent that they cause imbalance and, thus, inevitable overthrow. Precisely this claim appears in all Marxist textbooks—yet only theoretically.

In real life, just as believers seldom rely solely on divine intervention, atheists rarely trust exclusively in their 'natural course of events'. They leave little to 'objective factors', instead attempting to control people and historical outcomes through conscious actions. They do not wait for ideology to spontaneously arise as a reflection of the 'material conditions of production'. Where a self-emerging ideology does not exist, they import it, creating communist ideology and even political authority in places without a corresponding foundational class—the working class. Those who argue that individuals do not create history nonetheless produce infallible, excessively wise leader-gods out of ordinary, often flawed mortals, and then attribute everything—from battlefield victories to revolutionary advances in linguistic science—to their wisdom. According to the Marxist scheme, one would expect the following development sequence: developed industry → working class → political party. In practice, however, this order often reverses. Among the decisions of communist governments in undeveloped or semi-developed countries, we regularly find directives where the party seeks first to establish industry and thereby create a working class. Thus, the relationship becomes inverted: consciousness shapes being, politics creates history, and the superstructure builds the base. Little remains of Marx's original framework except the political rule of the communist party, which in such conditions usually does not consist of workers, but of socially heterogeneous elements whose common denominator is loyalty to authority.

According to Marx, development occurs gradually and inevitably; it cannot be prevented or forced. Yet Marxists everywhere consistently impose the same prescription for social and economic order, disregarding the reality that existing economic and social developments stand at vastly differing stages. The programme of Communist parties in the USA does not differ significantly from that of Communist parties in Costa Rica or Indonesia. Today, there are over 80 Communist parties worldwide functioning under radically different conditions of economic and social development—from tribal organisations in some African nations to the most developed forms of capitalism in Europe—but all advocate nearly identical economic and socio-political models. If the theory of base and superstructure were accurate, how could one and the same Communist superstructure fit such divergent foundations consistently and everywhere: collective ownership of the means of production, agricultural collectivisation, a single-party political system, ideological and political monopolism, and so forth? How can socialism be grafted onto any kind of socio-economic structure if, indeed, the premises of historical materialism hold true?

The inadequacy of the materialist explanation of historical events can be tested by examining virtually any historical period. There is something of historical irony in the fact that phenomena related to Communist movements and states that appeared on the historical stage in the first half of the twentieth century represent the most evident refutation of historical materialism's postulates. Communist revolutions and their associated authorities do not occur where one would expect them according to historical materialism's theories (particularly the theory of capitalism and socialist revolution). On the contrary, precisely the opposite has taken place. The history of Communist revolutions is a series of anomalies inexplicable from the standpoint of historical materialism. Communist movements succeeded not in places where the so-called objective, material conditions for socialist revolutions had been realised, but rather in those where all necessary subjective conditions were present: a powerful political party or external—hence conscious—intervention.

What emerges is that Marxism as theory had to embrace historical determinism, while Marxism as practice had to abandon it. Both this acceptance and this abandonment are equally symptomatic of the issue at hand. Only someone who understands that this phenomenon was inevitable can correctly interpret it. Engels himself acknowledged that 'astonishing nonsense' sometimes arose from overly consistent applications of the Marxist theory of the conditionality of ideas by the economic aspects of life (in a letter to Conrad Schmidt, 5 July 1890).

He polemicises against Paul Barth's book *Hegel's Philosophy of History and the Hegelians up to Marx and Hartmann* (1890), in which the author claims that Marxism rejects any influence of consciousness on economics. Engels argues for a 'not overly consistent application of the theory of conditionality' and speaks of the so-called 'reverse impact of ideas on the base', only to immediately nullify this by adding, 'but only within the limits of their general dependence on economic conditions.' From the notion of any independent action of consciousness upon being, nothing remains—except the characteristic vacillation and retreat of materialism in the face of clear facts of life. Marxism had to concede many of these facts at the expense of its internal consistency. Positivist thinkers rejected the scientific status of Marxism, claiming it contained numerous conceptual, political, ethical, and even mythical elements. Yet positivism remained literature, while Marxism stepped out to conquer the world. It was able to do so precisely because it never was—nor remained—a pure science.

* * *

The doctrine of alienation, found in the early works of Karl Marx, is essentially idealist in nature. Its origins are best traced to the strong influence of Hegelian philosophy, whose imprint on Marx's soul remained profound. Most likely, both Marx himself and his followers recognised the ambiguous character of the theory of alienation, which may explain why it was seldom referenced later. This likely accounts for the delayed publication of Marx's *Economic and Philosophic Manuscripts*, in which this theory was presented. They were written in 1844 but not published until the 1930s—eighty years after *The Communist Manifesto* and more than sixty years after the first volume of Capital. Another work from this period, the *Theses on Feuerbach*, also bears a similar tone. Both texts, marked by a powerful humanist impulse, belong to the phase of Marx's intellectual development often referred to as his 'inconsistent materialism'.

However, when discussing Marxism, we must refer to the writings of Marx's mature period—above all *Capital* and the Preface to *A Contribution to the Critique of Political Economy*—especially the latter's introduction, in which Marx concisely outlines the materialist conception of history. The incorporation of foreign, non-materialist elements into Marxism continued—inevitably so—as Marxism moved from theoretical construct to lived political practice. It is doubtful that Marx himself would recognise his teachings in many of the contemporary social systems that lay claim to his legacy.

One revealing detail in this regard is that Protestant countries—those which, through the Reformation, freed themselves from Catholic romanticism and mysticism—have remained largely immune to Marxism. By contrast, communist ideas found fertile ground among Roman nations, who have historically been more inclined towards sentiment than rationalism, as well as in economically underdeveloped countries. Protestant societies rejected communism for the same reasons they once rejected Catholicism. Thus we arrive at a paradoxical conclusion: communism has drawn its strength from the same emotional and psychological currents that once nourished religion and mysticism. Where conditions for religion are absent, the same tends to hold true for communism.

* * *

From the standpoint of historical materialism, strictly speaking, we cannot discuss social relationships in terms of justice or injustice—such terms are practical rather than theoretical. According to its logic, there are no 'just' or 'unjust' relations, only those that are sustainable and historically justified, versus those that are unsustainable and historically unjustified. It is worth noting that 'justice' is a moral term, whereas 'sustainability' is a physical or mechanical one. Capitalist relations, as long as they align with the prevailing technical foundation—what Marxists call the 'productive forces'—are thereby sustainable and, by implication, just. They become unjust not when they offend any moral sensibility, but when they fall out of sync with the development of productive forces—that is, according to certain objective factors, completely independent of morality.

The result is a moral inversion: all violence within a system that is still aligned with its technical base is deemed necessary, and therefore neither unjust nor immoral. As Marx states explicitly, 'If the given system of production is necessary, then the exploitation of man by man is necessary too.'

This brilliant and internally consistent definition is ultimately lifeless, as it renders all human action meaningless, so even Marxists do not hold it in high regard. It belongs in textbooks, not in practical life. In practice, Marxists—and even more so politicians and statesmen—invoke the idea of exploitation in a deeply moral and human sense. In public discourse, exploitation ceases to be a mere appropriation of another's labour, a purely economic mechanism within the production process. Instead, it acquires a clearly ethical dimension, even in the works of Marx himself—consider, for instance, the chapter on the working day in *Capital*. Exploitation there is no longer just a technical relationship; it becomes a battle between good and evil. The exploiters are transformed into embodiments of evil, and their victims into personifications of justice and righteousness—a shift reflected even in the evolution from the 'League of the Just' to Marx's 'Communist League', where a moral residue remains etched into the very names.

When giving examples of the exploitation of workers, Marx is brimming with undisguised condemnation—of the kind we find in the Old Testament prophets when they denounce evil and injustice. But the attitude of religious reformers and moral preachers is both understandable and consistent, because from a religious standpoint, evil is not inevitable. The very act of condemnation presupposes that evil is a matter of human choice, of good or bad will; otherwise, such moral judgement would be as meaningless as condemning an earthquake or an epidemic. To condemn necessary exploitation is thus a contradiction in terms. Yet the very fact that we do condemn exploitation—that we respond to it morally, and that even Marx does—reveals that relationships between people cannot be reduced solely to economic terms, as Marx insists. The moral dimension of such relationships is real in its own right.[73]

73 To the wife of his friend Kugelmann, who complained about the difficulty of understanding Capital, Marx recommended beginning the book with Chapter Eight – 'The Working Day'. This section of Marx's main work was published separately in many countries, as it resonated more with people due to its moral rather than historical or purely objective approach. Every person will always feel closer to a moral condemnation of exploitation than to a philosophy that explains that exploitation through historical necessity or reduces it to a mere economic-technical aspect of production. It is not possible for a person to be 'disconnected' from a moral perspective on things. In principle, every drama is incomparably more complex than any mathematical abstraction. Yet every person will more easily 'understand' a drama than a law of physics or chemistry. The same is true of 'The Working Day'.

One of the central contradictions of Marx's teaching lies in his condemnation of exploitation. In doing so, Marx is sincere but not consistent. The most renowned materialist thinker was, in the final analysis, not a consistent materialist—and the heart of the issue lies in the fact that he could never have been that to begin with.[74] We might even ask how pure Lenin's own materialism or atheism truly was, if, as he himself admitted, his favourite writer was Tolstoy. It appears that the enduring vitality of Marxism stems partly from these very inconsistencies, from the presence of moral and idealist elements that Marx was never fully able to cast off. For while Marxism sought to present itself as a science, in truth it more closely resembled a form of messianism—Old Testament in its origin—an appeal, a hope, a cry for historical justice, and, in a deeper sense, a vision of humanity. Despite Marx's intentions, the capitalist and the worker do not appear merely as functional roles within a production process; they emerge as moral figures, archetypes of oppressor and oppressed. And in this moral classification, the European spirit once again relives the original Jewish dichotomy between the just and the unjust.

It is particularly noteworthy that the condemnation of so-called *economism*—the attempt to build an economy grounded solely on economic laws, that is, on interest—emerged within socialism itself. In opposition to economism, socialism began to demand the self-denial of the present generation for the benefit of future ones. The admission of moral principles into the practice of Marxism—despite the unambiguous stance of its founding theorists—is, in effect, an admission of the impossibility of applying consistent materialism in real life. It is well known that even the Second International began

74 Russell observes something similar: 'Marx declared himself an atheist but retained a cosmic optimism which can only be justified by theism.' (B. Russell, *A History of Western Philosophy*, p. 754)

to deviate from Marxist rejection of morality and to reaffirm the principle of justice, despite the popular slogan that 'the end justifies the means'.

Later developments brought appeals for sacrifice and self-denial in the name of the collective good, particularly that of the Party. A claim (attributed to Liu Shaoqi) that 'every man is above all most important to himself' was harshly criticised in China during the so-called Cultural Revolution. Similarly, the practice of promoting so-called moral, rather than material, incentives for labour in the USSR and China stands as an inexplicable paradox within communist systems, ostensibly founded upon materialist philosophy. The reality becomes clear: even when we desire to be consistent atheists and materialists with all our heart, we cannot fully succeed.

MARRIAGE

We have chosen this ancient institution—one as old as humanity itself—because it illustrates, with remarkable clarity, the conflict between pure ideas and lived reality, or in other words, between pure ideas and Islam.

Pure religion demands chastity; materialism, in principle, permits complete sexual freedom. Yet, when both doctrines descend from the heights of theory into the complexity of practical life, facing numerous difficulties along the way, each ultimately evolves towards the institution of marriage as a middle ground.

There is no true foundation for the institution of marriage in the original Christian teaching. Christ advocated complete chastity:

> Ye have heard that it was said by them of old time, Thou shalt not commit adultery: But I say unto you, That whosoever looketh on a woman to lust after her hath committed adultery with her already in his heart. (Matthew 5:27–28)

Tolstoy writes that these words can mean nothing other than that a human being should strive for complete chastity in accordance with Christ's teaching. He concludes: 'Those who believe that the marital ceremony absolves one from the duty of sexual abstinence in pursuit of higher purity are gravely mistaken.' And Saint Paul writes in one of his epistles: 'He that is unmarried careth for the things that belong to the Lord, how he may please the Lord. But he that is married careth for the things that are of the world, how he may please his wife.' (1 Corinthians 7:32–33)

Generally speaking, marriage is viewed not as an ideal but as a necessary evil—an inevitable degradation of perfection: 'It is good for a man not to touch a woman. Nevertheless, to avoid fornication, let every man have his own wife, and let every woman have her own husband.' (1 Corinthians 7:1–2)

A weakening of the original Christian principle can already be felt in Paul's final messages—a compromise marking early Christianity's turn towards the realities of life and human nature. From a Christian perspective, marriage is not a principle but a practical concession: 'to avoid fornication', as Paul himself puts it.

At the other extreme, we find a similar rejection of marriage—though arising from entirely opposite reasons:

> Individual marriage emerges as the subjugation of one sex by the other.... The first class-based antagonism in history coincides with the development of the antagonism between husband and wife within individual marriage.... The transfer of the means of production to collective ownership causes the individual family to cease being the economic unit of society. The private household becomes a branch of the social economy... Society assumes equal responsibility for all children, regardless of whether they are born in or out of wedlock. This removes the primary social, moral, and economic concern that currently prevents a girl from giving herself to the man she loves without hesitation. Will this not suffice to gradually bring about sexual freedom, and with it a more liberal public opinion on questions of virginity and female dishonour?[75]

There is a clear link between the Christian worldview and the demand for sexual abstinence.[76] Some materialist-oriented

75 F. Engels, *The Origin of the Family, Private Property and the State*

76 This demand took on more extreme forms in certain cases. Within Christianity, there was always a strong and persistent tendency towards castration. Origen performed self-castration as a means of bodily purification. Members of the Christian sect of Valerians in Arabia practised castration and

thinkers in the West interpret this as a correlation between sexual repression and regressive social systems. The theories of Wilhelm Reich, Trotsky, and the so-called Frankfurt School fall into this category. Herbert Marcuse, for example, argues that capitalism represses sexual freedom as a means of redirecting and exploiting sexual energy in other domains.

Celibacy—the vow of chastity—is not founded directly on divine command nor on the original tradition of the Church (it was introduced only in 1139 by a decree of the Second Council of the Lateran). Yet, despite this, celibacy is a logical consequence of Christianity, just as sexual freedom is the natural demand of materialism. Attempts were made during the most recent Vatican Council to initiate a debate on the abolition of celibacy, but the discussion was swiftly curtailed. Of course, it remains true that neither of these principles can ever be fully realised in practice, nor can the other be entirely repressed. Celibacy has remained the practice of a small, chosen minority, while in the USSR, not long after the revolution and following very negative experiences with absolute sexual 'freedom', there was a notable return to the institution of marriage.

Thus, the institution of marriage finds no solid grounding in either a strictly religious or strictly materialist worldview. It is not 'tailored' to Christianity or to communism. Yet, confronted with real human nature and driven by the desire to turn doctrine into practice, both teachings gravitate towards the institution of marriage—albeit from entirely opposite starting points. Christianity approaches from the demand for complete sexual chastity; communism from the premise of unlimited sexual freedom. Over time, Christianity arrives at the notion of marriage as a sacrament, while materialism

---

even imposed it on travellers passing through their lands. Castration was also known in some other religions. It was only at the end of the nineteeth century that the Church officially prohibited castration.

conceptualises it as a contract—sometimes even a formal, ceremonial agreement (as illustrated by the evolution of Soviet marital law). The chasm between Catholic and civil marriage remains unresolved, largely due to the unsolvable issue of divorce. A holy matrimonial bond, if breakable, becomes an ordinary contract; if absolutely unbreakable, it ceases to be a contract and becomes a fetish—something every form of positivism must reject.

Islamic marriage bridges these two types. From a European perspective, it appears simultaneously religious and civil. Some define it as a contract, others as a ceremonial religious act—with equal justification for both views. It is conducted before a 'priest' and a state officer, but in fact, they are one and the same person. It is both a 'registration' and a religious ceremony—simultaneously and inseparably so. Islamic marriage is dissolvable—because it is a contract—but divorce lies at the very edge of what is permitted: 'The most detestable of all permissible acts', said the Prophet Muhammad (pbuh). This reflects a distinctly religious–moral stance. In essence, marriage is a typical Islamic institution. Like much in Islam, it represents a solution aiming to reconcile spiritual aspiration with physical need—to preserve chastity without denying love, to establish a sexual life of an animal that can become fully human, but never an angel. This goal is Islamic at its core.

Marriage belongs to the same family of ideas as justice: concepts of a rougher, more grounded composition that preserve more good and more chastity in this world than their Christian counterparts—namely, the lofty ideals of sexual purity and universal love. Why this is so remains one of the deeper mysteries of human existence. Tolstoy observes this phenomenon, though he fails to draw the correct conclusion from it:

> Since there is no basis at all in true Christian teaching for the institution of marriage, that is why people of our Christian

world, who feel that the institution has no basis in Christian teaching, and do not see Christ's ideal—sexual purity—because it is obscured by today's dominant teachings, do not know how to behave themselves regarding marriage. This gives rise to a phenomenon that may appear strange at first glance: that among nations whose religious teachings are, by their essence, of far lesser value than Christianity, but which have clear external orientation, their family principles and spousal fidelity are incomparably more stable than in so-called Christian nations. In these other traditions, there may be formal companionships, polygamy, or polyandry, all within defined limits—but not the kind of sexual wantonness that dominates under the banner of monogamy in the Christian world.[77]

77 Leo Tolstoy, *The Road to Life*

TWO KINDS OF SUPERSTITION

If our observations are correct, there exist two kinds of 'superstition': the first occurs when science attempts to explain the inner world of humans; the second, when religion attempts to explain natural phenomena.

In interpreting the spiritual realm, science objectifies it—transforming the soul into the psyche, and God into a root cause. Conversely, religion continually personifies nature, turning it into something unnatural. These are fallacies of the same kind but in reverse—mirror errors, each in opposition to the other.

Primitive religions—with their magicians, taboos, and belief in the miraculous powers of spells or objects—border on superstition, often indistinguishable from it. Yet even these religions, in their own way, reflect humanity's inner discord—our fundamental duality. They arise from two essential preoccupations of early humans and early societies. The first is spiritual: a growing awareness of the self as something distinct from the nature into which one is born or 'cast into'. The second is physical: the drive for survival in a hostile, dangerous world. Primitive religions are the product of these two powerful but contradictory impulses. Religious awareness, under the pressure of worldly needs (survival instincts), turns outward rather than inward. The goal becomes natural and worldly—successful hunting, fertility, good harvests, protection from disease or disaster—but the method remains inadequate and religious: spells, rituals, dances, chants, symbols, and idols. Primitive religion is thus misdirected religious awareness. Instead of turning inward—toward the human—it turns outward, toward nature. And because it cannot effect real change in the natural realm, it leaves the critical mind with an impression of human helplessness, even delusion—which, in some sense, it is.

A religion that seeks to replace reason, science, or human action is inevitably in conflict with the intellect. This collision is unavoidable if religion sets out to substitute dogma for scientific truth, mysticism for free thought, or ritual for personal and social engagement. Conversely, true religion can coexist with science—as evidenced by the religious sensibilities of many great astronomers, mathematicians, and physicists. In fact, science can support religion by broadening our understanding of the universe and helping clear away the weeds of superstition that naturally tend to gather around religious belief. But when science and religion become entirely detached, each becomes lopsided: religion tends towards backwardness, and science drifts toward atheism.

Similarly, science has its own forms of superstition. These scientific superstitions arise when science steps beyond the boundaries of nature—the realm where it properly belongs. While it proves infallible in the inorganic world (physics, mechanics, astronomy), science often appears tentative and awkward when it ventures into the realm of life—biology, psychology, for example—and it proves wholly inadequate in articulating a coherent philosophy of life. By applying its methods of analysis and quantification to the domain of human experience, science has often ended up denying some of the most essential phenomena of life and spirituality, reducing them to their external manifestations. The sociology of religion has missed the essence of religion; biology has missed the essence of life; psychology has missed the soul; and history has overlooked its human interiority.[78] When science is tasked with explaining the world and the events within it, it inevitably reconstructs a vision that is completely mechanical in nature.

So-called dialectical and historical materialism offer particularly distinct examples of the scientific method's limitations when applied to life and history. Thus, we encounter dogmatic assertions such as: 'religion is the opium of the masses'; 'law is the will of the ruling class'; 'the abolition of slavery was an economic necessity for emerging capitalism'; Kant and Goethe were 'philistines who defended the capitalist system'; or that the philosophy of the absurd is merely an expression of the inner crisis and despair of a decaying capitalist order. One Marxist critic went so far as to explain Sartre's existentialism—its preoccupations with limits, anguish, and death—as merely a reflection of the crisis of capitalism, a socioeconom ic malaise of a particular mode of production.[79] In the same vein, it was once officially 'established' that socialist realism was the only correct method in art—just as, centuries earlier, a church council 'established' that the Earth is the centre of the universe.

Even Honoré de Balzac, the keen observer of human character, contributed to these kinds of fallacies. In the lesser-known Foreword to his celebrated *La Comédie humaine* book series, he attempted to apply scientific and positivist methods to explain human personality and failed remarkably. For the truths

78 The development of psychology as a science is highly indicative in this regard. Behaviourism, which represents the final conclusion of this development, proclaims the 'expulsion of the soul from biology', or the establishment of a 'psychology without a soul'. A logical consequence of this is the view of the human being as existing 'beyond freedom and dignity'. It is precisely under this title that a recent book by a psychologist of this school was published (B. F. Skinner, *Beyond Freedom and Dignity* (New York, 1971)).

79 Lucien Goldmann in a survey conducted by the journal Art on questions of existentialism.

about humanity he captured so vividly in his novels bear little resemblance to the rigid intellectual constructs he presents in his theoretical introduction.

When science attempts to explain a work of art, it reduces it to a psychological phenomenon. The artist becomes a clinical subject. Psychoanalyst Wilhelm Stekel claimed that his research brought him to the irrefutable conclusion that there is no difference between a poet and a neurotic. Psychoanalysis, often seen as the most promising scientific lens through which to examine artistic creation, has yielded paradoxical conclusions—chief among them, the supposed compatibility between creativity and neurosis.[80]

If we approach it from a purely rationalist perspective, we find no grounds to object to artificial cities, nor any compelling argument against barracks in favour of authentic architecture. 'If we build honestly, a cathedral cannot be different from a factory', declares Mies van der Rohe, the ideologist of functionalism—drawing a conclusion as logically consistent as it is absurd.

In biology, science has led us to the realisation that the human is not a human but an animal, that the animal is not an animal but a thing, and that life, in the final instance, is mere mechanics—that is, not life at all. A similar reduction occurred in ethics: reason concluded that morality is nothing more than an enlightened form of selfishness—in other words, that morality is the negation of morality. Psychoanalysis equated creativity with illness. And so on. The cumulative result of scientific activity in the realm of the human—the supranatural—has been a series of negations. Intelligence first denied God, and then, following a descending gradation, it denied the human, then life itself, and finally arrived at the determination

80 See the highly interesting book by Dr Vladeta Jerotić, *Illness and Creation* (Belgrade, 1976) for more on this subject.

that everything is nothing more than mechanism, a play and interaction of molecular forces. Intelligence, in the end, could discover nothing beyond itself in the world—and that, precisely, is mechanism and causality.

CHAPTER 11

THE THIRD PATH OUTSIDE ISLAM

THE DUALISM OF THE ANGLO-SAXON WORLD

Europe formed its foundational notions in the harsh school of the Middle Ages. Like the impressions left by childhood, these could never be erased from the European spirit—they became its very way of thinking. Whether religious or not, Europe will always think in Christian categories: soul or body, the Kingdom of Heaven or the Kingdom of Earth. It will either reject science bitterly and irreconcilably, or it will reject religion with the same vehemence. No religious denomination in Europe will ever carry a social programme. Both European religiosity and its atheism have always been radical and exclusive.

Yet, one part of the Western world, owing to its geography and history, remained outside the direct influence of medieval Christianity, even outside the deep-rooted complexes of this powerful epoch. That part of the world sought—and found—a middle path, one that outwardly quite resembles the Islamic middle path. We are speaking, of course, of England, and to a certain extent, the Anglo-Saxon world as a whole.[81]

England stands as a distinct chapter in European history that must be studied separately. Without England, Europe has only two historical periods: the age of the Church and the age of the State. The middle, Islamic age in European history

81 Further on, we shall see how diluted forms of this phenomenon can be found in most countries of reformed Christianity.

exists only in the form of the English age.[82] Democracy, this fusion of secular and metaphysical principles, is an English invention in Europe. The history of England is the history of European democracy. Nietzsche, a man who embodied the European spirit as few others did, captured this difference between the English and European minds brilliantly in his famous sentence: 'Who will save Europe from England—and England from democracy!'

From the perspective of the philosophy of history, the emergence of England—and of the Anglo-American spirit more broadly—within the history of the West corresponds to the emergence of Islam within the history of the East. This is the underlying meaning of Spengler's parallel: Muhammad (pbuh) - Cromwell (from *The Decline of the West*), figures he saw as 'contemporaries' within his world-historical vision. The history of the unified English Church and state—and the global English state—begins with Cromwell. The history of the unique Islamic faith and state—and the global Islamic community—begins with Muhammad (pbuh). Both were resolute, puritanical believers and founders of universal empires. This is something natural to both the Islamic and Anglo-Saxon spirit—just as it is foreign to the continental European one. Louis the Pious brought about the collapse of the Frankish state, while in Islam, every political and social renaissance begins with a religious revival. As soon as the European state grew in power, it demanded supremacy—just as the Church had done centuries earlier. It was the second Canossa in Europe (the first being in 1077, when Henry IV submitted to Pope Gregory VII). The Inquisition, which ravaged much of Europe, never reached England. England is

82 Christianity was compelled to split the history of the Western world into two entirely separate and opposing periods: the Middle Ages and the modern era, which stand in contrast as religion to science, and Church to State. This historical framework does not apply to England—or at least not in the same sense as it does on the Continent.

unfamiliar with both Canossa and the Inquisition—just as Islam is. The English Reformation simultaneously abolished two extremes: papal and imperial dominance—as if guided by an innate logic. England was revolutionary for fifteenth- and sixteenth-century Europe. Today, it is conservative. Yet unlike in continental Europe, conservatism in England carries a positive connotation. It signifies the desire to preserve the authentic English spirit—a spirit rooted in the middle path, in the broadest sense of the word.

Even the foreword to the official English translation of the Bible begins with the words: 'The wisdom of the Anglican Church, ever since the first framing of her public liturgy, hath been to keep the mean between the two extremes.' It seems this vow has become second nature to the English.

This dualism inherent to the English mode of thinking becomes clearer when we recall that it was Roger Bacon who laid the foundations for all subsequent intellectual progress in England. From the outset, he structured English thought on two distinct bases: inner experience, through which one attains mystical illumination or religious insight, and empirical observation, through which one arrives at true science (*scientia experimentalis*). Although the religious dimension—much like in Islam—was accentuated, Bacon remained a committed dualist. He never attempted to collapse the methods of scientific and religious inquiry into one another, but instead preserved them in a state of balance. The majority of English people consider Bacon to be the best and most genuine expression of the English spirit and sentiment, and much of later English philosophy is seen as a mere continuation of Baconian principles. His immense influence on the development and trajectory of English science and philosophy can only be fully understood in light of this, at first glance, paradoxical approach. Yet, one particularly significant fact remains insufficiently known or acknowledged: the father of

English philosophy and science was, in fact, a student of the Arabs. Islamic thinkers left a profound impact on Bacon—most notably Ibn Sina, whom Bacon regarded as the greatest philosopher after Aristotle.[83] This influence may not only help us understand the nature of Bacon's thought but also illuminate the roots of the dualism that has come to define English intellectual tradition.[84]

Little has changed in this regard, and England has remained true to this spirit. The personality of another great Englishman from more recent times, Bernard Shaw, provides further confirmation of these claims. Shaw was both poet and politician, an advocate of socialism and a champion of anarchist individualism. Someone once described him as 'the inimitable unity of contradictions'—an apt characterisation of a man who was at once a satirist and a mystic, a relentless critic of society and an irrepressible idealist.

On the European continent, the empiricist is almost invariably an atheist. In England, however, the chief ideologue of empiricism, John Locke, placed the idea of God at the centre of his ethical theory and defended the necessity of otherworldly sanction—reward and punishment—with priestly fervour.

> If human hope is confined solely to this life, if this is the only realm in which joy can be pursued, then it is neither strange nor unreasonable to seek happiness by avoiding all that is

83 See B. Russell, *A History of Western Philosophy*, pp. 452–453. A similar claim is made by the author of the most comprehensive history of logic, Karl Prantl: 'Roger Bacon derived all the results attributed to him in the field of natural sciences from the Arabs.' (K. P., *History of Logic*, Vol. III, (Leipzig, 1972) p. 121)

84 When attempting to explain this phenomenon, it is interesting to consider Russell's interpretation. According to him, the English aversion to generalising theories stems from their negative experience of the Civil War: 'The conflict between King and Parliament in the Civil War instilled in the English, once and for all, a love of compromise and moderation, and a fear of pushing any theory to its logical conclusions—a fear which still holds them today.' (B. Russell, op. cit., p. 578)

> unpleasant and chasing all that brings pleasure. If there is nothing beyond the grave, then the conclusion naturally follows: let us eat and drink, rejoice in mirth, for tomorrow we die.[85]

This renowned empiricist even laid out, in detail, his arguments for the existence of God,[86] while Hobbes—himself a positivist and materialist—sought to reconcile his conception of natural law with the Bible: '*Quod lex naturalis est lex divina*' (That the natural law is divine law).[87]

This is a distinctly English manner of thinking. Later European philosophers would declare, almost unanimously and with sound logic, that 'Lockean position is unsustainable'. Yet the fact remains: it was this very position—this paradoxical philosophy of Locke, Bacon, and Hobbes—that served as the foundation for the intellectual and social dynamism of England.

The continental contrast between the natural and the moral, rooted in Christian thinking, gave way in England to a gradual convergence of the two. In some cases, such as with Shaftesbury, they were brought into full harmony. Shaftesbury's morality is defined as a balance between selfish and altruistic feelings—one that can be upset not only by an excess of selfishness, but also by an overemphasis on selflessness. This is reminiscent of Aristotle's doctrine of 'rational ethical self-love', and even of certain messages in the Qur'an. The so-called English 'Commonsense' philosophy belongs to this same tradition—a philosophy of sound judgement and moderation, as does John Stuart Mill's celebrated formula for reconciling individual freedom with the wellbeing of society.

---

85 J. Locke, *An Essay Concerning Human Understanding*, Book II, Chapter 28, §10 and onwards.

86 Ibid., Chapter X: 'Our Knowledge of the Existence of God'.

87 Hobbes, *De Cive*, Chapter IV.

The aim of the renowned Cambridge school can be summarised most succinctly as the 'rationalisation of theology'. Writing about one of its key figures, R. Cudworth, F. Jodl notes:

> The intimate connection between philosophy and religion, speculation and faith, is characteristic of the entire Cambridge school. It therefore becomes understandable that the same individual who, as a philosopher, so sharply emphasised the purely rational essence of morality—grounded in itself—should, as a preacher, so powerfully stress the necessity of religious elevation. It is a philosophy that provides sufficient means for the satisfaction of religious needs, and a religion that harmonises with reason and is permeated by the warmth of a revitalising feeling. This is the shared outlook of the Cambridge thinkers.[88]

The English spirit surpassed itself in the development of the so-called theory of utility-based morality—an ethically significant direction of the eighteenth century. This 'square circle' is a typical product of the eclectic English mind and is often referred to in literature as the 'English morality of utility'. Particularly noteworthy is the fact that this theory later took on a theological form in England—an orientation known as 'theological utilitarianism'. Figures such as Butler, with his assertion that 'conscience and self-love, if we understand our happiness rightly, point in the same direction'; Hartley, with his 'peaceful coexistence of materialist psychology alongside belief in God and the immortality of the soul' (Jodl); as well as Warburton, Paley, and—in a certain sense—Richard Price, all belong within this category.

Paley's exposition on the alignment of Divine will with the good of all creatures—grounded in the observation of nature—is a distinctly Islamic method and reminiscent of several verses in the Qur'an (see Paley, *Natural Theology)*. Among

88 F. Jodl, *History of Ethics*, p. 145.

this group of thinkers advocating a 'middle path', the name of Adam Smith stands out in particular. Smith authored two works whose contents may appear contradictory, yet are in fact closely aligned: *The Theory of Moral Sentiments* and *An Inquiry into the Nature and Causes of the Wealth of Nations*—both among the most influential texts of the eighteenth century. The former, which laid the foundations of his ethics, began with the principle of sympathy; the latter, concerned with political economy, adopted self-interest as its guiding idea—seemingly in opposition. However, as a professor at the University of Glasgow, Smith taught ethics, economics, and politics as components of a single, unified course in practical philosophy. More than that: Smith explicitly emphasised the connection between ethics and the science of national prosperity, both in these works and in his other writings. In *The Theory of Moral Sentiments*, he writes:

> Just as egoism is a fact, so too are ethical feelings. They were accounted for within the general economy of the Divine plan. Man is a unity; in his economic life, he cannot be anything other than what he already is.

Totomianc offers a number of quite reasonable observations regarding the perceived contradiction within certain parts of Smith's opus—an impression that Europeans have always held in regard to the Qur'an and Islam. His, and likewise Hume's, antipathy towards clericalism, priestly religion, and Church organisation inevitably calls to mind similar phenomena in Islam.

Spencer's *Education* could have been written by a Muslim without hesitation, and his teaching that morality is essentially a harmonisation between the individual and society (*Principles of Ethics*), along with the idea that development proceeds in such a way that individualisation becomes ever more refined while mutual dependence simultaneously deepens—whether true or not—is characteristically English.

While the irreconcilable divide between spiritualist and positivist schools continued to dominate in Catholic France, English ethics began to be shaped by an understanding that equated the principles of welfare with those of conscience. The reflections of J.S. Mill on economics, his emphasis on reconciling individual and collective principles, as well as his acknowledgement of the moral dimension of wealth, carry a distinctly zakat-like, Qur'anic tone. It is also worth noting the emergence of English neo-idealism in the second half of the nineteenth century (J. Martin, F.H. Bradley, P.H. Green, and others), following a period of dominant empiricism—clearly consistent with the aforementioned English pattern.[89]

I cannot avoid quoting a longer passage about English political life, written by R. H. S. Crossman, a contemporary English writer of socialist orientation. Having pointed out that every simplified interpretation of English political life is almost certainly incorrect and misleading, Crossman continues:

> The Victorian employer based his politics on religious foundations, contrary to the utilitarian theoretician. He despised oligarchy not only because it protected the big landowners but also because it manifestly violated moral principles... Viewing the new industrialism as a vast potential tool for the common good, he felt that the development of his business was a divine calling... That theological staging of the capitalist economy gave it an irresistible force in English life... The intellectual energy of the Victorian age was not directed at criticism of utilitarian economics but toward theological speculation... Gladstone genuinely believed that becoming a politician was just as noble a vocation as becoming a priest. The splendid moral stability and self-confidence of the nineteenth century can only be understood if that

89 That 'middle-ground' solutions do not yield 'middling' results is demonstrated precisely by England. This country gave the world Shakespeare, the poet 'who knew everything about humanity', and Newton, who defined the fundamental law governing our universe.

religious conviction is taken seriously. All the fervour of gospel zeal was channelled into the improvement of good deeds, and the harshness of capitalist economics was softened by a new philanthropic philosophy which held that Christian love and generosity alone could transform capitalism into the Kingdom of Heaven. The abolition of slavery, the revival of missionary work, the stigmatisation of child labour, the expansion of public education, and a multitude of other movements did not originate from political conviction but from Christian consciousness of community... The great majority of the reformist movements of the nineteenth century stemmed from that very source, and it was only after they rekindled the public imagination that they were adopted into the programmes of political parties. It was mostly a matter of timing and opportunity as to which of the two parties would carry them out... Only in the light of that religious conviction can one form a true image of English political ideals.

And further:

British democracy stood in close connection with the struggle for religious freedom... In this way, the religious motive, in its primitive Christian form, could be placed in the service of democracy, and the triumph of liberalism brought about a religious restoration in Victorian England. Such a development was only possible in America as well... But for German and Italian liberals, progress, nation, and democracy became the object of a secular cult... A loyal Catholic felt that an unbridgeable gap separated faith in Christ from faith in progress, while a loyal liberal believed that clerical domination over the mind was incompatible with democracy and freedom.[90]

English socialism is specific as well. On the Continent, socialism is closely tied to materialist or atheist philosophy, but

90 R. H. S. Crossman, *The Government and the Governed*

'one can hear as many Bible quotes from Labour platforms in England as from the church pulpits in that country', writes an astonished reporter for a French newspaper.

Likewise, Bertrand Russell unmistakably expresses an authentically English understanding when he says that 'the problem of one social order that would be permanently satisfactory could be solved only by combining the firmness of the Roman Empire with the idealism of Augustine's *Divine State*', or when he reflects on whether ideas shape the world or vice versa: 'As for me, I believe that the truth lies between these two extremes. There is a reciprocal effect between ideas and practical life, just as there is in all things.'[91]

It is not difficult to recognise the spiritual sources of American pragmatism in these and similar views. With its dualism, its acceptance of both religion and science—'if they prove their practical worth'—and its postulation of life practice as the measure of truth, pragmatism is a typical Anglo-Saxon philosophy and, at the same time, thoroughly non-European. The essence of this school of thought was presented by William James in his main work *Pragmatism*. It is necessary to cite at least a few characteristic passages from this extraordinary book:

> Most of us desire good things from both sides of the line. Facts are good, of course—give us a lot of facts; principles are good—give us a wealth of principles. The world is undoubtedly only one, if observed in one way, but it is likewise multitudinous if observed in a different way. It is at the same time one and a multitude, so let us adopt then a sort of pluralist monism. Everything is of course necessarily determined, and yet our will is free: some kind of determinism of free will would be the most accurate philosophy. The evil of the parts is undeniable, but a whole cannot be evil: this is

91 B. Russell, *A History of Western Philosophy*, p. 473.

how practical pessimism can be joined with metaphysical optimism.[92]

James excellently captures here the natural human leaning towards dualism—towards a sort of natural Islam. He subtitled his book Pragmatism as 'A new name for some old ways of thinking'. He continues:

> And then, what sort of philosophies are offered to you in your trouble? You find empiricist philosophy, which is not religious enough, and religious philosophy, which is not empirical enough for what you want of it.[93]

And further:

> Your perplexity is therefore this: you find that the two systems you seek are hopelessly separated. You find empiricism, but with it non-humanism and non-religiousness; or you find rationalist philosophy, which might call itself religious, but which abstains from every specific contact with real facts and joys and sorrows.[94]

Bertrand Russell offered a very acceptable formula for understanding pragmatism, identifying the two fundamental philosophical dilemmas of the founder of this school of thought: 'The philosophical interest of William James was twofold: scientific and religious. Studying medicine, from a scientific side, gave his thoughts a certain materialist direction, which was then, however, restrained by his religious sentiment.'[95] Let us recall how English thought (here meaning American as well) began with the same dual premises in the work of Roger Bacon seven centuries earlier. During that time, Europe completed the entire arc—from Thomas Aquinas on one end to Lenin on the other.

---

92 William James, *Pragmatism, p. 16.*

93 *Ibid., p. 17.*

94 *Ibid., p. 19.*

95 *B. Russell, op. cit., p. 774.*

We do not know what kind of impression pragmatism truly left on the European soul, but we can be certain that it provoked a certain kind of repulsion. To a European, pragmatism appears illogical, heterogeneous, inconsistent—epithets often ascribed to Islam as well. Yet, pragmatism is the first great philosophical system that America produced, and one that Europe was *a priori* incapable of producing. It is certain that pragmatist philosophy was either a stimulus for—or an expression of—or most likely both—the extraordinary vitality and practical dynamism of the American individual.

This parallelism between the English and Islamic spirit can be traced through a series of symptomatic facts that warrant separate analysis. The English Revolution of 1688 was not overly radical ('the most temperate and successful of all revolutions', as Bertrand Russell puts it), and many events in English political history did not push matters to their extremes or into pure ideological forms, but rather halted at a balanced midpoint. The rebellion against monarchy in England, for instance, did not lead to its abolishment, and elements of aristocracy continued to coexist with democratic institutions.

In the English language, the word 'minister' also denotes a priest. A similar dualism of terminology exists in Islamic discourse. Unlike most European countries, England recognised a significant form of tax for the benefit of the poor, akin to zakat. A similar spirit naturally tends to yield similar expressions in practical life.

It can be expected, in the future as well, that while Europe accepts all the consequences of scientific development—including its potentially inhuman dimensions—England and America will once again pause at the middle, pragmatic point. For in Europe, religion is religion and science is science, consistent with the Christian approach to the matter, while in England, it is practice—that is, life itself—that remains the supreme arbiter.

HISTORICAL COMPROMISE AND SOCIAL DEMOCRACY

Tendencies toward a middle path can be observed in other parts of the world. However, unlike in England—where they are found in theory, that is, in the domain of sentiment and worldview—in Europe they appear only at the level of practical implementation and emerge not as a matter of conviction, but rather out of practical necessity. The phenomenon itself manifests differently in Catholic and Protestant countries. In countries that have been more heavily influenced by Catholicism, ideological polarisation is more pronounced, and attempts to find a middle ground are fraught, dramatic, and often yield uncertain results. In a certain sense, these countries are either incapable of—or have been incapacitated from—pursuing a third path. Italy, France, Spain, and Portugal have been, or still are, examples of extremely polarised societies. Public opinion is divided irreconcilably between Christian (right-wing) and Marxist (left-wing) parties and movements. The political centre is either drastically limited or entirely obliterated. Here, the two most renowned dogmatisms—Catholic and Communist—stand opposed, exhausted from a confrontation that, by its very nature, cannot yield a victor. A typical example of such a scenario was Spain on the eve of its civil war. In the 1936 elections, leftist parties won 51.9 per cent of the vote, right-wing parties 43.24 per cent, while the centre received only 4.86 per cent.[96] Present-day Italy is approaching a similar level of polarisation, nearing the Spanish 50:50 divide. France displays a comparable political landscape.

The inner disintegration of these two dogmatisms can be traced through a series of symptoms. One such symptom is the emergence of dialogues between Marxists and Catholics, which began tentatively in the mid-1960s.[97] These dialogues are indicative of the state of mind in Europe and reflect the evolving dynamics on the ideological frontlines of the long-standing conflict between Marxism and religion—a confrontation that has persisted for over a century, without interruption and without compromise. They signal a weariness and a growing recognition of the futility of attempting to organise human life around a single, absolute principle. For their part, Marxists were compelled to retreat from their classical assertion that religion is 'the opium of the people', while Catholics had to acknowledge that the Marxist pursuit of restructuring social relationships aimed toward a more just social order.

At one such dialogue between Marxists and Catholics, organised by The Society of Saint Paul, a report was presented whose title spoke volumes: *Christian Philanthropy and Marxist Humanism*. At a meeting held in Salzburg, the renowned Marxist writer Roger Garaudy declared:

> With the arrival of Christianity, for the first time in our history there was an appeal for a community without borders, for a totality that encompasses all other totalities… There is a glorification of the idea of love within it—a love by which

96 As we write this (1977), Spain is preparing for its first free elections. Some predict that, for the first time in its history, the Spanish people will opt for the centre. If that happens, both right- and left-wing dogmatists alike should learn a lesson from Spain's example.

97 As far as I know, the first such dialogue took place in Salzburg in 1965, initiated by liberal Catholic theologians from West Germany. This practice was later continued.

> a man realises and fulfils himself only with the help of another man, and in another man—and this idea represents the highest image that man could form of himself and the meaning of life.

The leader of the Italian Communist Party, Palmiro Togliatti, also underscored the necessity for Marxism to revise its position on religion in his famous final document *(Il memoriale di Yalta)*, urging Marxists to recognise this need as soon as possible. Correspondingly, new understandings began to emerge within the Catholic Church, especially as reflected in papal encyclicals such as *Pacem in Terris* and *Populorum Progressio*. These included: recognition of the primacy of social goods over private ownership; affirmation of the right of public authorities to intervene in the economic sphere; support for agrarian reform and nationalisation in the public interest; and endorsement of workers' participation in the management of enterprises, among others.[98]

The Twenty-First Council of the Catholic Church (the Second Vatican Council) rejected the proposal by traditionalists to officially condemn Marxism. Judging by the speeches of numerous authoritative figures, this council was marked by an implicit acknowledgment of the untenability of Christianity's extreme spiritualist stance. Cardinal de Chardin stated: 'I believe that the world will conform to the hopes of Christianity only if Christianity adjusts itself to the hopes of the world. Only then will it divinise them.' Is this not, in essence, an *Islamisation* of Christianity?

Such tendencies are often complex and intertwined, as evidenced by some recent developments in France. The Permanent Council of the French Episcopate issued a notable

98 Pope John Paul II recently (during his visit to the USA in 1979) stated that 'the systematic threat to human rights is connected with the distribution of material goods'. Only one who truly understands the nature of Christianity can appreciate the turn that this statement signifies.

declaration in 1977 titled *Marxism, Humanity, and Christian Faith.* In it, the French bishops acknowledged 'the failure of the social policies of liberalism', concluding that 'Marxism contains within itself a portion of truth that we do not ignore'. A year earlier, the leader of the French Communist Party, Georges Marchais, made a striking declaration in his now-famous *Lyon Appeal*: 'Our goal is for Communists and Christians to affirm one another and to stand together in their respective authenticity, shoulder to shoulder in the effort to build a more humane society.'

This phenomenon can be traced with dramatic clarity in the case of Italy. After years of irreconcilable confrontation, the Italian Communist Party chose what might have seemed an unexpected path, but in fact, it was perhaps the only logical solution: it called for a so-called 'historic compromise'.

If our interpretation is correct, this call was not a tactical manoeuvre aimed at short-term gain. Rather, it was a sincere proposal, born out of the realisation that no other way forward existed. The proposal was directed towards Christians—indeed, it could not have been directed towards anyone else. Once all other contenders had fallen away and arguments had been exhausted, only two enduring forces remained on the turbulent stage. We may say without hesitation that they are two indestructible forces. On the surface, it appears as a confrontation between Christian democracy and communism. But at a deeper level, it is the confrontation between religion and materialism.

Italy represents an experiment for the future of a part of the world.[99]

---

99 In the statute of the Italian Communist Party, we find a previously unthinkable provision that party members may be 'all those who accept the Party's programme, regardless of their religious and philosophical beliefs' (Article 2 of the ICP Statute). Although the altered stance on religion by the Italian Communist Party is not unique, the majority of such parties still advocate a

The so-called 'Eurocommunism' reflects the same tendency characteristic of polarised societies—namely, the countries of European Catholicism such as Italy, France and Spain. Although a relatively recent phenomenon, it is already clear that it signifies Communism minus the dictatorship of the proletariat, plus democracy. It marks a shift from the far left, once fortified by the barrier of dogma, towards the centre.[100] Under the pressure of reality, Communism is abandoning its dogmatic stance and adopting the ideals of freedom and pluralism—essentially idealistic concepts. This development gives Eurocommunism its distinct character. The key difference between the idea of Eurocommunism and the historical compromise lies in this: the former concerns a corrected, modified version of Communism, while the latter concerns the meeting of Communism and Christianity as two equal forces.[101]

The search for a middle path in other, mostly Protestant (non-Catholic) countries is reflected in the increasing influence of centrist or centre-leaning parties within their political landscapes. This part of Europe rejects both purely Christian and purely Communist governments and consistently demonstrates a tendency towards middle-ground solutions. In practice, this sentiment is expressed through a growing orientation towards social democracy. Protestant countries

---

form of pronounced, even combative atheism. This is particularly the case in backward, unenlightened environments. Nonetheless, this deviation is evident and will inevitably continue.

100 The same significance applies to the abandonment of the so-called 'Cultural Revolution' in China, shortly after the death of Mao Zedong. This, the most persistent and far-reaching attempt so far to establish a utopia, evidently ended in failure. 'Standing on one leg'—in essence an ultra-left stance—was something China could barely sustain for ten years. An inevitable return to a more natural state followed. If we adopt the usual right-left terminology, then China is currently moving from the left towards the centre.

101 A number of Communist parties in Europe have removed the term 'dictatorship of the proletariat' from their party documents.

have found in social democracy the solution that traditionally Catholic societies are seeking through historical compromise. This movement—which in Europe represents a compromise between freedom and social intervention, between Christian traditions and Marxist influences—has made steady progress throughout the post-war period, a trend that undoubtedly carries deeper significance and is symptomatic of a wider global development.[102] A comparison of election results immediately following the war with those held twenty-five or thirty years later reveals a marked rise in social democratic support in nearly all countries with free elections. This increase amounts to 22 per cent in Sweden, 36 per cent in Denmark, 54 per cent in the Netherlands, 27 per cent in Norway, 38 per cent in Malta, and over 100 per cent in West Germany, among others. In England, the increase is just 5 per cent, but this is due to the fact that the process began much earlier there, and the country reached a point of balance well before the rest of Europe. Social democracy has proven to be a stable compound—a form of social and political equilibrium in Europe.

The two most stable countries within the generally unstable region of Latin and South America are Mexico and Venezuela—nations that lie very close to the ideals of social democracy. In Japan as well, political development is not moving towards polarisation, but rather towards the consolidation of the centre.[103] The term 'third way' is appearing with increasing frequency in political discourse in both Mexico and

102 The more ideologically zealous part of the world, of course, does not see things in this way. For example, the Moscow journal Komunist (July 1978 issue) claims that development along a 'third path' is objectively impossible. According to this journal, there is no alternative in the form of a 'third world'. In reality, there are only two antagonistic socio-political systems. The polarisation process is not weakening but intensifying, so sooner or later all countries will side either with the capitalist or the socialist system.

103 The results of the December 1976 elections, as well as the split within Japan's Socialist Party (with Saburō Eda and many of his supporters leaving the party), clearly favour the political centre.

Japan. A social democratic gathering held in Caracas in 1976 was deemed historic, not only for the significance of its resolutions, but even more so for the sense that it might represent the first step towards the formulation of a new doctrine. The nature of this emerging doctrine can be inferred from the statement made by Mexican official Gonzalez Souza: 'Capitalism, communism, and social democracy are now the three major options in the world, and Mexico must choose among them.'

The internal tensions within socialist countries are, for the most part, not concerned with socialism as an economic system. These tensions do not reflect a desire to return to private capitalist enterprise. Rather, all serious forms of resistance revolve around the issue of human rights. People across the globe appear to yearn for a form of Christianity that incorporates a social programme—or a kind of socialism without atheism and dictatorship; in other words, 'socialism in human form'.[104]

For example, in China, following the death of Mao Zedong, the ban on Beethoven and Shakespeare is gradually and cautiously being lifted—just as, earlier in the USSR, the prohibition on Dostoevsky, Chagall and Kafka was removed, albeit reluctantly and unconvincingly. The demand for freedom is growing increasingly insistent across the Eastern European bloc. Although the pace may be slow, the direction is clear. The tendency is unmistakable.

Conversely, crises in capitalist countries are accompanied by increasing demands for greater social intervention, which at times entails a certain limitation of freedoms. Practical realities are pulling American corporations in the direction of socialisation, just as they once pushed Soviet economic

104 This is what Maurice Diverger called the inexorable process of 'liberalisation in the East and socialisation in the West' (M. D., *Introduction à la politique* (Gallimard, Paris, 1970) p. 367). In truth, the Western way of life is not sufficiently social, whereas the Eastern way of life is not sufficiently free.

enterprises away from rigid centralism towards greater autonomy. Professor M. L. Weidenbaum has referred to contemporary American corporations as 'half-nationalised', alluding to their extensive dependence on the state.

At a meeting of prominent political and public figures from the USA, Europe and Japan, held in Kyoto in 1975 (the so-called Trilateral Commission), the issue of 'excessive democracy' in developed capitalist countries was raised. In the resulting report, *The Crisis of Democracy*, the authors argued for 'moderation in democracy', even suggesting the need for certain adjustments regarding the unchecked freedom of the press. The report also supported economic planning and called for 'more efficient management'. A prominent American newspaper commented on the report by stating that, although it was not a fully developed framework for public policy, it signalled the emergence of a new ideological climate.

Thus, the developmental tendencies of modern societies are not proceeding in the same direction, but they are converging. Over time, these tendencies tend to settle toward a middle ground—one that closely resembles the Islamic position.

However, no matter how symptomatic these tendencies may be, they are neither Islam nor do they naturally lead to it, because they appear forced, inconsistent and incomplete. Islam is a conscious rejection of any one-sided religious or social demand; it is a conscious embrace of a dual principle—a bipolar foundation. Yet the oscillations, concessions and inevitable compromises described above represent the triumph of human nature and lived reality over rigid and exclusive ideologies—and in that sense, they constitute an indirect victory for the Islamic conception of life.

ADDENDUM

SUBMISSION

Nature is governed by determinism; human beings are governed by destiny. Accepting this destiny is the highest and final message of Islam.

But does what we call destiny truly exist, and if so, in what form? Let us reflect on our own lives and ask ourselves: what remains of the dreams of our youth or of our most cherished plans? Did we not enter this world without our consent, finding ourselves endowed—without choice—with a particular character, with a greater or lesser degree of intelligence, with an appearance that might be appealing or off-putting, with a stature that might be diminutive or imposing? We were born into the home of a king or a pauper, in a turbulent or tranquil era, during the reign of a tyrant or a just ruler—into political, geographic and social circumstances over which we had no say.

How narrow is the scope of what we call our will, and how vast and unfathomable is what we call our destiny!

Man is cast into the world, subject to countless forces beyond his control. Even the most remote phenomena can shape his fate just as much as the nearest ones. During the Allied invasion of Europe in 1944, there was a widespread disruption in radio communications—an interference that could have critically affected the entire operation. It was later discovered that the cause was a massive explosion in the Andromeda galaxy, millions of light years away. Some types of catastrophic earthquakes on our planet are the result of solar surface disturbances.

As our knowledge of the universe expands, so does our awareness that we will never be the absolute masters of our fate. Even with the most advanced scientific achievements, the ratio between what we can control and what remains forever beyond our reach will remain infinitesimal. Human beings and the world are not in proportion. The movement of the cosmos does not revolve around man or the span of human life. Hence, the perpetual insecurity of man—a condition that can manifest psychologically as pessimism, rebellion, despair or, alternatively, as submission to destiny and the will of God.

Islam, as an endeavour to organise the world through education and law, represents a narrower plan of resolution; submission, however, is the broader and more comprehensive one.

Perfect justice for the individual can never be fully realised within the conditions of existence. We may follow all Islamic commandments, which are ultimately meant to ensure happiness 'in both worlds'; we may adhere to every other set of norms—medical, social, and moral—yet, due to the terrifying entanglement of destinies, conscious will and uncontrollable coincidence, we may still suffer spiritually and physically.

What solace is there for a mother who has lost her only son? What consolation exists for the man who is left crippled by an unpredictable accident?

> Let us witness our human position. We are always in some kind of situation... I can act to change the situation. But there are situations that are essentially unchangeable, even when their appearance shifts and their victorious force hides

> under veils: I have to die, I have to suffer, I have to struggle, I am subject to circumstances, I constantly stumble in guilt. These basic situations of our existence are called 'borderline situations'. [105]

> Man has to fix everything that can be fixed in the real world: after that, children will still keep dying unfairly, even in a perfect society. Even in the greatest effort, man can only task himself with reducing the pain in the world arithmetically. But injustice and suffering will remain, and no matter how limited they become, they will never cease to be an outrage.[106]

Submission or rebellion—these are two opposing responses to the same dilemma.

There is something of every form of human wisdom in submission—except one: shallow optimism. It is the tale of human destiny, and as such, it inevitably carries a note of pessimism, for 'every destiny is tragic and dramatic, if one reaches its bottom' (Ortega y Gasset).

Submission to destiny is a striking response to the profound human theme of unavoidable suffering. It is the recognition of life as it truly is, and a conscious resolve to endure and bear it all. In this regard, Islam stands in stark contrast to the shallow optimism of European philosophy and its naïve narrative of 'the best of all possible worlds'. Submission is a soft glow beyond the veil of pessimism.

Yet, although it emerges from a sense of powerlessness and insecurity, submission itself becomes a new source of strength and assurance. Faith in God and His providence brings a sense of security that no other power can replace or compensate. Emerson once noted that all heroic nations believed in destiny.

---

105 Karl Jaspers, *Introduction to Philosophy*

106 Albert Camus, *L'Homme révolté, The Rebel*

For submission does not imply passivity, as many mistakenly assume. It is not a matter of 'yielding to destiny' for our relationship with destiny holds a fundamentally moral dimension. Submission is an inward stance of the soul toward the totality of the world and the consequences of one's own actions.

To submit to Divine will is to be independent of the will of men. Surrender to God precludes submission to human domination. It redefines the relationship between human and God—and therefore redefines the relationship between human and human.

Therefore, to accept destiny is to feel free in the fullest sense.

But it is a freedom earned through the fulfilment of one's destiny—through agreement with it. What makes our striving and struggle truly human and reasonable, what lends them their air of balance and tranquillity, is the conviction that the final outcome lies beyond our control.

Our duty is to strive and act—the result belongs to God.

To truly understand one's life in this world means to begin investing effort without the ambition to grasp or conquer everything, but with the readiness to accept the time and place into which we are born—our destiny, which is the will of God.

Submission is the only human and dignified path out of the irresolvability and seeming meaninglessness of life—a path that avoids rebellion, despair, nihilism and suicide. It is a heroic feeling—not of a hero, but of an ordinary person enduring the inevitable burdens of life, the tragic serenity of a shahid (martyr) who has fulfilled his duty and accepts his fate.

Islam did not derive its name from its laws, its commands and prohibitions, or even the physical and spiritual effort it requires—but from something deeper, something that encompasses and transcends all of that: from a moment of profound realisation, from a strength of soul measured against the march of time, from the willingness to endure everything that human existence may demand—from the truth of submission.

Submission—thy name is Islam!